GRUBER'S
SAT 2400

Advanced Strategies for the Perfect Score

Gary R. Gruber, PhD

SOURCEBOOKS, INC.®
NAPERVILLE, ILLINOIS

D1361486

Published by Sourcebooks, Inc.
P.O. Box 4410, Naperville, Illinois 60567–4410
(630) 961–3900
Fax: (630) 961–2168
www.sourcebooks.com

Cataloging-in-Publication data is on file with the publisher.

Printed and bound in the United States of America.
SB 10 9 8 7 6 5 4 3 2 1

Recent and Forthcoming Study Aids from Dr. Gary Gruber Include

Gruber's Essential Guide to Test Taking: Grades 3–5
Gruber's Essential Guide to Test Taking: Grades 6–9
Gruber's Complete SAT Guide 2009 (12th Edition)
Gruber's Complete SAT Math Workbook
Gruber's Complete SAT Reading Workbook
Gruber's Complete SAT Writing Workbook

www.sourcebooks.com
www.drgarygruber.com

DEDICATION

To the memory of my parents Edward and Martha, who gave me the interest, encouragement, and support for my lifelong mission of helping students realize their potential, achieve the highest level, and excel in their careers.

To my treasured wife Raquel, who continues that support and encouragement.

To my son Ian, who has great insight into SAT preparation and is a terrific SAT teacher and collaborator.

CONTENTS

The SAT Writing Test   143

The Hardest Actual SAT Questions and Their Top Strategic Solutions   191

The Shortest SAT Test—16 Questions to Approximate Your SAT Score and the Exact Strategies You Need to Improve Your Score   199

SAT Practice Test   206

ACKNOWLEDGMENTS

To Todd Stocke for starting the ball rolling with Sourcebooks and me, to Dominique Raccah for her enormous vision, insight, and continued support in creating the SAT series, to Peter Lynch for the numerous and very helpful dialogues and for the development of the series and other books, to Heather Moore for her innovation and highly creative promotional efforts, to Erin Nevius for her outstanding help and expertise in production, to Melanie Thompson for her creativity in the school arena, to Tom Galvin for his sales expertise and follow-through, and to all others at Sourcebooks who were instrumental in making the SAT series and my other test preparation books successful.

IMPORTANT NOTE ABOUT THIS BOOK AND ITS AUTHOR

This book was written by Dr. Gary Gruber, the leading authority on the SAT, who knows more than anyone else in the test-prep market exactly what is being tested for in the SAT. In fact, the procedures to answer the SAT questions rely more heavily on the Gruber Critical Thinking Strategies than ever before, and this is the only book that has the exact thinking strategies you need to use to maximize your SAT score. Gruber's SAT books are used more than any other books by the nation's school districts and are proven to get the highest documented school district SAT scores.

Dr. Gruber has published more than 30 books with major publishers on test-taking and critical thinking methods, with over 7 million copies sold. He has also authored over 1,000 articles on his work in scholarly journals and nationally syndicated newspapers, has appeared on numerous television and radio shows, and has been interviewed in hundreds of magazines and newspapers. He has developed major programs for school districts and for city and state educational agencies for improving and restructuring curriculum, increasing learning ability and test scores, increasing motivation and developing a "passion" for learning and problem solving, and decreasing the student dropout rate. For example, PBS (Public Broadcasting Service) chose Dr. Gruber to train the nation's teachers on how to prepare students for the SAT through a national satellite teleconference and videotape. His results have been lauded throughout the country by people from all walks of life.

Dr. Gruber is recognized nationally as the leading expert on standardized tests. It is said that no one in the nation is better at assessing the thinking patterns of "how" a person answers questions and providing the mechanism to improve the faulty thinking approaches. SAT score improvements by students using Dr. Gruber's techniques have been the highest in the nation.

Gruber's unique methods have been and are being used by PBS, by the nation's learning centers, by international encyclopedias, by school districts throughout the country, in homes and workplaces across the nation, and by a host of other entities.

His goal and mission is to get people's potential realized and the nation "impassioned" with learning and problem solving so that they don't merely try to get a "fast" uncritical answer, but actually enjoy and look forward to solving the problem and learning.

Because of his enthusiasm, ability, and creativity in solving problems, the *Washington Post* and many other papers have called Dr. Gruber "America's Super Genius."

For more information on Gruber courses and additional Gruber products, visit www.drgarygruber.com.

Important: Many books do not reflect the current SAT questions or the proper methods for solving those questions. Don't practice with questions that misrepresent the actual questions on the SAT. For example, the math questions created by the test makers are oriented to allow someone to solve many problems without a calculator as fast as with one, and some faster without a calculator. This book reflects the SAT more accurately than any other commercial book, and the strategies contained in it are exactly those needed to be used on the SAT. It is said that only Dr. Gruber has the expertise and ability to reflect the exam far more closely than any competitor! Don't trust your future with less than the best material.

A PERSONAL NOTE
FROM THE AUTHOR

SAT 2400—Thinking Your Way to a Perfect SAT Score

The way to get a perfect or close-to-perfect score on the SAT is to develop a natural approach to answering questions—"natural" in that you can look at any problem, extract what's unusual about it, and use that to launch a solution without ever getting panicky. If you already have the basic skills, such as knowing your math rules, having a good working vocabulary, and tending to score in top 50 percent on standardized tests, with the critical thinking skills and specific strategies in this book you can definitely aim for a perfect SAT score.

What I'll get you to do is to think of the test as a challenge and a game, so that you'll actually enjoy taking it. You'll look at the hardest questions and say, "I see what they're trying to test—and I know exactly what strategy and method to use." I just hope you don't do what I did on tests: I got so involved, I started grading the test itself. "This is a good question, but you could have made it harder and more interesting if you…"

My methods and strategies will teach you to really think on your feet. Here's an example: I was lecturing to teachers at a math conference once (there must have been around 500 people present), and I noticed that a lot of the attendees, worn out from the conference, were practically asleep. I decided to shock them, so that I'd fire them up. I said, "I am going to show you that any problem can be solved by my strategies. If it can be done by a genius in a minute, I can solve it in a minute. If I can't, you can all leave."

Someone in the audience from College Board (the people who write the actual SAT tests) stood up and said, "OK; let's see if you can solve this question—it was field tested for the SAT but is not yet on the test, and it can only be solved by the brightest people in a minute."

This was the problem:

> A blend of coffee is made by mixing Columbian coffee at $8 a pound with espresso coffee at $3 a pound. If the blend is worth $5 a pound, how many pounds of the Columbian coffee are needed to make 50 pounds of the blend?

My first reaction was just to rush into an answer like a normal student, but then I thought, I had better use my critical thinking skills and practice what I preach. I looked for something in the question that would give me a clue, something to launch another step in the problem without worrying or fixating on solving for an answer. I translated, "how many pounds of the Columbian coffee are needed to make 50 pounds of the blend," into, "If C is Columbian coffee and E is espresso, then $C + E = 50$ pounds." Basic math skills dictate that to solve an equation such as this one, I needed another equation in C and E.

I did get the other equation from what was given, and solved the problem for the astonished group of teachers. But the important thing is that, if I hadn't gotten the first equation using my critical thinking skills, I wouldn't have known how to solve the problem.

Thinking on your feet is a crucial skill whether you are being challenged with math or verbal problems. I was once on a major radio talk show when the host said to me, "Dr. Gruber, you have developed a list of 50 prefixes and roots that reveal the meaning of more than 150,000 words. Can you tell me how you would figure out the meaning of the word "consider" using your methods?"

"Consider" is a tough word to figure out by prefix and root, but not impossible. "Con" means "with," and I knew that astronomers use something called "sidereal time" to measure the position of the earth in its rotation around its axis. So I took a chance and said that the "sid" part in the word denotes having to do with time, making it: "to think about in time."

You can figure out the meanings of many words using prefixes, roots, and simple associations like that one. I was on the phone with a student once who asked me what the word "inextricable" meant. I didn't want to embarrass myself and tell her that I didn't know what it meant, so I did some quick mental reasoning. "In" means "not," and "able" means "to." At first I thought "extric" might mean "extra," but "not to extra" does not make a word. So I tried another association— "extric" to "extract." That made sense: "not to extract," or "inseparable." I was honest with my student and told her I figured out the word through thinking skills, so that next time, she would do the same thing if she didn't remember the word's meaning.

Through this book, you'll be developing mastery with these approaches through specific strategies and practice. Armed with the right thinking skills, you'll be able to correctly answer every question on the SAT.

—**Gary R. Gruber**

FORMAT OF THE SAT

Total time for "counted" (not experimental) CRITICAL READING: 70 minutes—67 questions

Total time for "counted" (not experimental) MATH: 70 minutes—54 questions

Total time for "counted" (not experimental) WRITING (Multiple-Choice): 35 minutes—49 questions

Total time for WRITING (Essay): 25 minutes—1 or 2 prompts

Total time for experimental, pre-test items: 25 minutes—number of questions varies

Note: The following represents a form of an SAT. The SAT has many different forms, so the order of the sections may vary and the experimental section* may not be the third section as we have here. However, the first section will always be the *Essay* and the last section will be a 10-minute Multiple-Choice *Writing* section.

10 Sections of the SAT*	Number of Questions	Number of Minutes
Section 1: WRITING (Essay)	1	25
Section 2: MATH	20	25
Regular Math	20	
		5 minute break
Section 3: EXPERIMENTAL*	varies	25
Could be Writing, Critical Reading, or Math		
Section 4: CRITICAL READING	24	25
Sentence Completions	8	
1 short passage (60–125 wds)	2	
1 short passage (60–125 wds)	2	
1 passage (650–850 wds)	11–13	
OR		
Double reading passage (350–450 wds each)	11–13	
		1 minute break

10 Sections of the SAT*	Number of Questions	Number of Minutes
Section 5: WRITING (Multiple Choice)	**35**	**25**
Improving Sentences	11	
Identifying Errors	18	
Improving Paragraphs	6	
Section 6: MATH	**18**	**25**
Regular Math	8	
Student-Produced ("Grid-Type")	10	
		5 minute break
Section 7: CRITICAL READING	**24**	**25**
Sentence Completions	5	
1 paired short passage (about 130 wds each)	4	
1 passage (400–550 wds)	5–7	
1 passage (550–700 wds)	8–10	
Section 8: MATH	**16**	**20**
Regular Math	16	
Section 9: CRITICAL READING	**19**	**20**
Sentence Completions	6	
Double reading passage (350–450 wds each)	13	
OR		
1 passage (650–850 wds)	13	
Section 10: WRITING (Multiple Choice)	**14**	**10**
Improving Sentences	14	
	TOTAL MINUTES = 225 (3¾ hours)	

*The order of the sections on the actual test varies since the SAT has several different forms.

There will be passages on Humanities, Social Sciences, Natural Sciences, and Narrative (fiction or non-fiction). Total number of counted reading questions will be 48.

Note: One of the sections is experimental. An experimental section does not count in your SAT score. You cannot tell which of the sections of the test is experimental.

INTRODUCTION

Important Facts About the SAT

What Is on the SAT?

It will include a student-written essay and a multiple-choice writing section testing a student's ability to identify sentence errors, improve sentences, and improve paragraphs. Although grammar and usage will be tested, students will not be asked to define or use grammatical terms, and spelling and capitalization will not be tested. This essay section will be the first part of the test. The Math section will include arithmetic, geometry, algebra I, and some advanced math covering topics in Algebra II, statistics, probability, and data analysis. The test will measure reasoning ability and problem-solving skills. The other parts of the test will contain some long and shorter reading passages, a long paired passage, a short paired passage, and sentence completion questions.

How Will the Test Be Scored?

There will be a range of three scores each from 200–800 for the Writing, Math, and Critical Reading sections.

How Long Will the Test Be?

The total time of the test will be 3 hours and 45 minutes.

What Verbal Background Must I Have?

The reading and vocabulary level is at the 10th- to 12th-grade level, but strategies presented in this book will help you even if you are at a lower grade level.

What Math Background Must I Have?

The Math part will test first- and second-year algebra (Algebra I and II) and geometry. However, if you use common sense and rely on just a handful of geometrical formulas and learn the strategies and thinking skills presented in this book, you don't need to take a full course in geometry or memorize all the theorems. If you have not taken algebra, you should still be able to answer many of the math questions using the strategies presented in this book.

Is Guessing Still Advisable?

Although there is a small penalty for wrong answers ($\frac{1}{4}$ point for 5-choice questions), in the long run, you *break even* if you guess *or* leave the answer blank. For a full explanation of why, see p. 4, General Strategy 5. So it really will not affect your score in the long run if you guess or leave answers out. And, if you can eliminate an incorrect choice, it is imperative that you do not leave the answer blank.

Can I Use a Calculator on the Math Portion of the Test?

Students can use a four-function, scientific, or graphing calculator. While it is possible to solve every question without the use of a calculator, it is recommended that you use a calculator if you don't immediately see a faster way to solve the problem without a calculator.

Should I Take an Administered Actual SAT for Practice?

Yes, but only if you will learn from your mistakes by seeing what strategies you should have used on your exam. Taking the SAT merely for its own sake is a waste of time and may in fact reinforce bad methods and habits. Note that the SAT is released to students on their *Question and Answer*

Service three times a year, usually in the January, May, and October administrations. It is wise to take exams on these dates if you wish to see your mistakes and correct them.

A Table of What's on the SAT

Math

Time	70 min. (Two 25 min. sections, one 20 min. section)
Content	Multiple-Choice Items Student-Produced Responses Measuring: Number and Operations Algebra I, II, and Functions Geometry, Statistics, Probability, and Data Analysis
Score	M 200–800

Critical Reading

Time	70 min. (Two 25 min. sections, one 20 min. section)
Content	Sentence Completion Critical Reading: Short and Long Reading Passages with one Double Long Passage and one Double Short Passage
Score	CR 200–800

Writing

Time	60 min. (25 min. essay, 35 min. multiple-choice in two sections)
Content	Multiple-Choice: Identifying Errors, Improving Sentences and Paragraphs, and Student-Written Essay: Effectively Communicate a Viewpoint, Defining and Supporting a Position

Score   W 200–800
               Essay Subscore: 2–12
               Multiple-Choice Subscore: 20–80

Note: There is an experimental section that does not count toward your SAT score. This section can contain any of the SAT item types (writing [multiple-choice], critical reading, or math) and can appear in any part of the test. Do not try to outguess the test maker by trying to figure out which of the sections are experimental on the actual test (believe me, you won't be able to)—treat every section as if it counts toward your SAT score.

A Table of What's on the PSAT

Math	
Time	50 min. (Two 25 min. sections)
Content	Multiple-Choice Items Student-Produced Responses Measuring: Number and Operations Algebra I and Functions Geometry and Measurement, Statistics, Probability, and Data Analysis
Score	20–80
Critical Reading	
Time	50 min. (Two 25 min. sections)
Content	Sentence Completion Critical Reading: Short and Long Reading Passages, with one Double Long Passage and one Double Short Passage
Score	20–80
Writing	
Time	30 min. (One section)
Content	Multiple-Choice: Identifying Errors Improving Sentences and Paragraphs Measuring: Grammar, Usage, Word Choice
Score	20–80

Can I Get Back the SAT with My Answers and the Correct Ones after I Take It? How Can I Make Use of This Service?

The SAT is disclosed (sent back to the student on request with an $18 payment) three of the seven times it is given through the year. You can also order a copy of your answer sheet for an additional $25 fee. Very few people take advantage of this fact or use the disclosed SAT to see what mistakes they've made and what strategies they could have used on the questions.

Check in your SAT information bulletin or log on to www.collegeboard.com for the dates this Question and Answer Service is available.

Should I Use Scrap Paper to Write on and to Do Calculations?

Always use your test booklet (not your answer sheet) to draw on. Many of my strategies expect you to label diagrams, draw and extend lines, circle important words and sentences, etc., so feel free to write anything in your booklet. The booklets aren't graded—just the answer sheets (see General Strategies 8 and 9, page 6).

Should I Be Familiar with the Directions to the Various Items on the SAT before Taking the SAT?

Make sure you are completely familiar with the directions to each of the item types on the SAT—the directions for answering the Sentence Completions, the Reading, the Writing, the Regular Math, and especially the Grid-Type (see General Strategy 1, page 1).

What Should a Student Bring to the Exam on the Test Date?

You should bring a few sharpened #2 pencils with erasers, and also your ID.

Bring a calculator to the test, but be aware that every math question on the SAT can be solved without a calculator; in many questions, it's actually easier not to use one.

Acceptable calculators: Graphing calculators, scientific calculators, and four-function calculators (the last is not recommended) are all permitted during testing. If you have a calculator with characters that are one inch or higher, or if your calculator has a raised display that might be visible to other test takers, you will be seated at the discretion of the test supervisor.

Unacceptable calculators: Laptops or portable/handheld computers; calculators that have a QWERTY keyboard, make noise, use an electrical outlet, or have a paper tape; electronic writing pads or stylus-driven devices; pocket organizers; and cell phone calculators will not be allowed during the test.

How Should a Student Pace Himself/Herself on the Exam? How Much Time Should One Spend on Each Question?

Calculate the time allowed for the particular section. For example, 25 minutes. Divide by the number of questions. For example, 20. That gives you an average of spending $1\frac{1}{4}$ minutes per question in this example. However, the first set of questions within an item type in a section are easier, so spend less than a minute on the first set of questions and perhaps more than a minute on the last set. With the reading passages you should give yourself only about 30 seconds a question and spend the extra time on the reading passages. Also, more difficult reading questions may take more time.

How Is the Exam Scored? Are Some Questions Worth More Points?

Each question is worth the same number of points. After getting a raw score—the number of questions right minus a penalty for wrong answers—this is equated to a "scaled" score from 200 to 800 in each of the Critical Reading, Math, and Writing sections. A scaled score of 500 in each part is considered "average."

It's Three Days Until the SAT; What Can a Student Do to Prepare?

Make sure you are completely familiar with the structure of the test (page xv), the basic math skills needed (pages 77–113), and the basic verbal skills, such as prefixes and roots (pages 16). Refresh your understanding of the strategies used to answer the questions.

What Is the Most Challenging Type of Question on the Exam and How Does One Attack It?

Many questions, especially at the end of a section, on the test can be challenging. You should always attack challenging questions by using a specific strategy or strategies and common sense.

What Should a Student Do to Prepare on Friday Night? Cram? Watch TV? Relax?

On Friday night, I would just refresh my knowledge of the structure of the test, some strategies, and refresh some basic skills (verbal or math). You want to do this to keep the thinking going so that it is continual right up to the exam. Don't overdo it, just enough so that it's somewhat continuous—this will also relieve some anxiety, so that you won't feel you are forgetting things before the exam.

The Test Is Given in One Booklet. Can a Student Skip between Sections?

No—you cannot skip between the sections. You have to work on the section until the time is called. If you get caught skipping sections or going back to earlier sections, then you risk being asked to leave the exam.

Should a Student Answer All Easy Questions First and Save Difficult Ones for Last?

The easy questions usually appear at the beginning of the section, the middle difficulty ones in the middle, and the hard ones toward the end. So I would answer the questions as they are presented to you, and if you find you are spending more than 30 seconds on a question and not getting anywhere, go to the next question. You may, however, find that the more difficult questions toward the end are actually easy for you because you have learned the strategies in this book.

What Is the Recommended Course of Study for Those Retaking the Exam?

Try to get a copy of the exam that you took if it was a disclosed one—the disclosed ones, which you have to send a payment for, are usually given in October, January, and May. Try to learn from your mistakes by seeing which strategies you could have used to get questions right. Certainly learn the specific strategies for taking your next exam.

What Are the Most Crucial Strategies for Students?

All specific Verbal (Critical Reading) and Math Strategies are crucial, including the general test-taking strategies (described on pages 1–6), guessing, writing and drawing in your test booklet, and being familiar with question-type directions. The key Reading Strategy is to know the four general types of questions that are asked in reading—main idea, inference, specific details, and tone or mood. In math, it's the translations strategy—verbal to math, drawing of lines, etc. Also make sure you know the math basic skills cold (see page 77 for these rules—*make sure you know them*).

I Know There Is an Experimental Section on the Exam That Is Not Scored. How Do I Know Which Section It Is?

The SAT people have now made it so difficult to tell which is the experimental section, I would not take a chance second-guessing them and leaving it out. It will look like any of the other sections. It is true that if you have, for example, two of the same sections, such as two sections that both deal with grid questions, one of them is experimental—but you won't know which one it is. Also, if you have two sections where there is a long double reading passage, one of those sections is experimental, but again you won't know which one it is.

Can I Take the Test More Than Once, and If So, How Will the Scores Be Reported to the Schools of My Choice? Will All Scores Be Reported to the Schools, and How Will They Be Used?

Check with the schools you are applying to to see how they use the reported scores, e.g., whether they average them, whether they take the highest. Ask the schools whether they see unreported scores; if they do, find out how the individual school deals with single and multiple unreported scores.

How Do Other Exams Compare with the SAT? Can I Use the Strategies and Examples in This Book for Them?

Most other exams are modeled after the SAT, and so the strategies used here are definitely useful when taking them. For example, the GRE (Graduate Records Examination, for entrance into graduate school) has questions that use the identical strategies used on the SAT. The questions are just worded at a slightly higher level. The ACT (American College Testing Program), another college entrance exam, reflects more than ever strategies that are used on the SAT.

How Does the Gruber Preparation Method Differ from Other Programs and SAT Books?

Many other SAT programs try to use "quick fix" methods or subscribe to memorization. So-called "quick fix" methods can be detrimental to effective preparation because the SAT people constantly change questions to prevent "gimmick" approaches. Rote memorization methods do not enable you to answer a variety of questions that appear in the SAT exam. In more than thirty years of experience writing preparation books for the SAT, Dr. Gruber has developed and honed the Critical Thinking Skills and Strategies that are based on all standardized tests' construction. So, while his method immediately improves your performance on the SAT, it also provides you with the confidence to tackle problems in all areas of study for the rest of your life. He remarkably enables you to be able to, without panic, look at a problem or question, extract something curious or useful from the problem, and lead you to the next step and finally to a solution, without rushing into a wrong answer or getting lured into a wrong choice. It has been said that test taking through his methodology becomes enjoyable rather than a pain.

The Inside Track on How SAT Questions Are Developed and How They Vary from Test to Test

When an SAT question is developed, it is based on a set of criteria and guidelines. Knowing how these guidelines work should demystify the test-making process and convince you why the strategies in this book are so critical to getting a high score.

Inherent in the SAT questions are Critical Thinking Skills, which present strategies that enable you to solve a question by the quickest method with the least amount of panic and brain-racking and describe an elegance and excitement in problem solving. Adhering to and using the strategies (which the test makers use to develop the questions) will let you "sail" through the SAT. This is summed up in the following statement:

> *Show me the solution to a problem, and I'll solve that problem. Show me a Gruber strategy for solving the problem, and I'll solve hundreds of problems.*
>
> —Gary Gruber

Here's a sample of a set of guidelines presented for making up an SAT-type question in the Math area:

The test maker is to make up a hard math problem in the regular math multiple-choice area, which involves

(A) algebra
(B) two or more equations
(C) two or more ways to solve: one way being standard substitution, the other faster way using the **strategy** of merely *adding* or *subtracting* equations.*

Previous examples given to test maker for reference:

1. If $x + y = 3$, $y + z = 4$ and $z + x = 5$, find the value of $x + y + z$.

    (A) 4
    (B) 5
    (C) 6
    (D) 7
    (E) 8

Solution: *Add* equations and get $2x + 2y + 2z = 12$; divide both sides of the equation by 2 and we get $x + y + z = 6$. (Answer C)

2. If $2x + y = 8$ and $x + 2y = 4$, find the value of $x - y$.

    (A) 3 $x - y = 4$
    (B) 4
    (C) 5
    (D) 6
    (E) 7

Note: See Math Strategy #14 on p. 100.

Solution: *Subtract* equations and get $x - y = 4$.
(Answer B)

Here's an example from a recent SAT.

3. If $y - x = 5$ and $2y + z = 11$, find the value of $x + y + z$.

(A) 3
(B) 6

$$y + z + x = 6$$

(C) 8
(D) 16
(E) 55

Solution: *Subtract* equation $y - x = 5$ from $2y + z = 11$.
We get $2y - y + z - (-x) = 11 - 5$.
So, $y + z + x = 6$. (Choice B)

What Are Critical Thinking Skills?

Critical Thinking Skills, a buzz phrase now in the nation, are generic skills for the creative and most effective way of solving a problem or evaluating a situation. The most effective way of solving a problem is to extract some piece of information or observe something curious from the problem then use one or more of the specific strategies or Critical Thinking Skills (together with basic skills or information you already know) to get to the next step in the problem. This next step will catapult you toward a solution with further use of the specific strategies or thinking skills.

> 1. EXTRACT OR OBSERVE SOMETHING CURIOUS
> 2. USE SPECIFIC STRATEGIES TOGETHER WITH
>   BASIC SKILLS

These specific strategies will enable you to "process" think rather than just be concerned with the end result, the latter which usually gets you into a fast, rushed, and wrong answer. The Gruber strategies have been shown to make one more comfortable with problem solving and make the process enjoyable. The skills will last a lifetime, and you will develop a passion for problem solving. These Critical Thinking Skills show that conventional "drill and practice" is a waste of time unless the practice is based on these generic thinking skills.

Here's a simple example of how these Critical Thinking Skills can be used in a math problem:

> Which is greater, $7\frac{1}{7} \times 8\frac{1}{8} \times 6\frac{1}{6}$ or $8\frac{1}{8} \times 6\frac{1}{6} \times 7$?

Long and tedious way: Multiply $7\frac{1}{7} \times 8\frac{1}{8} \times 6\frac{1}{6}$ and compare it with $8\frac{1}{8} \times 6\frac{1}{6} \times 7$.

Error in doing the problem the "long way": You don't have to *calculate*; you just have to *compare,* so you need a *strategy* for *comparing* two quantities.

Critical Thinking Way: 1. *Observe:* There is a common $8\frac{1}{8}$ and $6\frac{1}{6}$

2. *Use Strategy:* Since both $8\frac{1}{8}$ and $6\frac{1}{6}$ are just weighting factors, like the same quantities on both sides of a balance scale, just *cancel* them from both multiplied quantities above.

3. You are then left comparing $7\frac{1}{7}$ with 7, so the first quantity, $7\frac{1}{7}$, is greater. Thus $7\frac{1}{7} \times 8\frac{1}{8} \times 6\frac{1}{6}$ is greater than $8\frac{1}{8} \times 6\frac{1}{6} \times 7$.

Here's a simple example of how Critical Thinking Skills can be used for a Verbal problem:

If you see a word such as DELUDE in a sentence or in a reading passage, you can assume that the word DELUDE is negative and probably means "taking away from something" or "distracting," since the prefix DE means "away from" and thus has a negative connotation. Although you may not get the exact meaning of the word (in this case the meaning is to "deceive" or "mislead"), you can see how the word may be used in the context of the sentence it appears in, and thus get the flavor or feeling of the sentence, paragraph, or sentence completion. I have researched and developed more than 50 prefixes and roots (present in this book) that can let you make use of this context strategy.

Notice that the Critical Thinking approach gives you a fail-safe and exact way to the solution without superficially trying to solve the problem or merely guessing at it. This book contains all the Critical Thinking Strategies you need to know for the SAT test.

Dr. Gruber has researched hundreds of SAT tests (thousands of SAT questions) and documented the Critical Thinking Strategies (all found in this book) coursing through every test. These strategies can be used for any Math, Verbal, or Logical Reasoning problem.

In short, you can learn how to solve a specific problem and thus find how to answer that specific problem, or you can learn a powerful strategy that will enable you to answer hundreds of problems.

Multi-Level Approaches to the Solution of Problems

How a student answers a question is more important than the answer given by the student. For example, the student may have randomly guessed, the student may have used a rote and unimaginative method for solution, or the student may have used a very creative method. It seems that one should judge the student by the "way" he or she answers the question and not just by the answer to the question.

Example:

Question: Without using a calculator, which is greater:
355×356 or 354×357?

Case 1: **Rote Memory Approach** (a completely mechanical approach not realizing the fact that there may be a faster method that takes into account patterns or connections of the numbers in the question): The student multiplies 355×356, gets 126,380, and then multiplies 354×357 and gets 126,378.

Case 2: **Observer's Rote Approach** (an approach which makes use of a mathematical strategy that can be memorized and tried for various problems): The student does the following:

Divide both quantities by 354:

He or she then gets $355 \times 356/354$ compared with $354 \times 357/354$.

He or she then divides these quantities by 356 and then gets $355/354$ compared with $357/356$.

Now he or she realizes that $355/354 = 1$ and $1/354$; $357/356 = 1$ and $1/356$.

He or she then reasons that since the left side 1 and $1/354$ is greater than the right side, 1 and $1/356$, the left side of the original quantities, 355×356, is greater than the right side of the original quantities 354×357.

Case 3: **The Pattern Seeker's Method** (most mathematically creative method—an approach in which the student looks for a pattern or sequence in the numbers and then is astute enough to represent the pattern or sequence in more general algebraic language to see the pattern or sequence more clearly):

Look for a pattern. Represent 355×356 and 354×357 by symbols.

Let $x = 354$.

Then $355 = x + 1$, $356 = x + 2$, $357 = x + 3$.

So $355 \times 356 = (x + 1)(x + 2)$ and $354 \times 357 = x(x + 3)$.

Multiplying the factors we get

$355 \times 356 = (x \text{ times } x) + 3x + 2$ and $354 \times 357 = (x \text{ times } x) + 3x$.

The difference: $355 \times 356 - 354 \times 357 = (x \text{ times } x) + 3x + 2$ minus

$(x \text{ times } x)$ minus $3x$, which is just 2.

So 355×356 is greater than 354×357 by 2.

Note: You could have also represented 355 by x. Then $356 = x + 1$; $354 = x - 1$; $357 = x + 2$. We would then get $355 \times 356 = (x)(x + 1)$ and $354 \times 357 = (x - 1)(x + 2)$. Then we would use the method above to compare the quantities.

—OR—

You could have written 354 as a and 357 as b. Then $355 = a + 1$ and $356 = b - 1$. So $355 \times 356 = (a + 1)(b - 1)$ and $354 \times 357 = ab$. Let's see what $(355 \times 356) - (354 \times 357)$ is. This is the same as $(a + 1)(b - 1) - ab$, which is $(ab + b - a - 1) - ab$, which is in turn $b - a - 1$. Since $b - a - 1 = 357 - 354 - 1 = 2$, the quantity $355 \times 356 - 354 \times 357 = 2$, so 355×356 is greater than 354×357 by 2.

Case 4: **The Astute Observer's Approach** (simplest approach—an approach which attempts to figure out a connection between the numbers and uses that connection to figure out the solution):

   $355 \times 356 = (354 + 1) \times 356 = (354 \times 356) + 356$ and

   $354 \times 357 = 354 \times (356 + 1) = (354 \times 356) + 354$

   One can see that the difference is just 2.

Case 5: **The Observer's Common Relation Approach** (this is the approach that people use when they want to connect two items to a third to see how the two items are related): 355×356 is greater than 354×356 by 356.

   354×357 is greater than 354×356 by 354.

So this means that 355×356 is greater than 354×357.

Case 6: **Scientific, Creative, and Observational Generalization Method** (a highly creative method and the most scientific method, as it spots a critical and curious aspect of the sums being equal and provides for a generalization to other problems of that nature): Represent $354 = a$, $357 = b$, $355 = c$, and $356 = d$

We have now that (1) $a + b = c + d$

(2) $|b - a| = |d - c|$

We want to prove: $ab < dc$

Proof:

Square inequality (2): $(b - a)^2 > (d - c)^2$

Therefore: (3) $b^2 - 2ab + a^2 > d^2 - 2dc + c^2$

Multiply (3) by (-1) and this reverses the inequality sign:

$-(b^2 - 2ab + a^2) < -(d^2 - 2dc + c^2)$

or

(4) $-b^2 + 2ab - a^2 < -d^2 + 2dc - c^2$

Now square (1): $(a + b) = (c + d)$ and we get:

(5) $a^2 + 2ab + b^2 = c^2 + 2dc + d^2$

Add inequality (4) to equality (5) and we get:

$4ab < 4dc$

Divide by 4 and we get:

$ab < dc$

The generalization is that for any positive numbers a, b, c, d when
$|b - a| > |d - c|$ and

$a + b = c + d$, then $ab < dc$.

This also generalizes in a geometrical setting where for two rectangles whose perimeters are the same ($2a + 2b = 2c + 2d$), the rectangle whose absolute difference in sides $|d - c|$ is <u>least</u> has the <u>greatest</u> area.

Case 7: **Geometric and Visual Approach*:** (this is the approach used by visual people or people that have a curious geometric bent and possess "out-of-the-box" insights):

Where $a = 354$, $b = 357$, $c = 355$, and $d = 356$, we have two rectangles where the first one's length is d and width is c, and the second one's length is b (dotted line) and width is a.

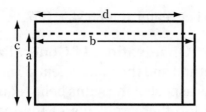

Now the area of the first rectangle (dc) is equal to the area of the second (ab) minus the area of the rectangular slab which is $(b - d)a$ plus the area of the rectangular slab $(c - a)d$. So we get: $cd = ab - (b - d)a + (c - a)d$. Since $b - d = c - a$, we get $cd = ab - (c - a)a + (c - a)d = ab + (d - a)(c - a)$.

Since $d > a$ and $c > a$, $cd > ab$. So $355 \times 356 > 354 \times 357$.

This method of solution was developed by and sent to the author from Dr. Eric Cornell, a Nobel Laureate in Physics.

- -

Note: Many people have thought that by multiplying units, digits from one quantity and comparing that with the multiplication of the units, digits from the other quantity that they'd get the answer. For example, they would multiply $5 \times 6 = 30$ from 355×356 then multiply $4 \times 7 = 28$ from 354×357 and then say that 355×356 is greater than 354×357 because $5 \times 6 > 4 \times 7$. They would be lucky. That works if the sum of units, digits of the first quantity is the same as or greater than the sum of units, digits of the second quantity. However, if we want to compare something like $354 \times 356 = 126{,}024$ with $352 \times 359 = 126{,}368$, that initial method would not work.

GENERAL TEST-TAKING STRATEGIES

Before studying the specific strategies for the Math and Verbal questions, you will find it useful to review the following General Strategies for taking the SAT test.

Know the Directions to the Question Types Before You Take the Actual Test

All SAT tests are standardized. As an example, all the sentence completion questions have the same directions from test to test. You can take advantage of this fact by memorizing the sets of directions and familiarizing yourself with their types of questions before you take your actual SAT. Never spend time reading directions during the test or doing sample questions that don't count.

Here's an example of a set of SAT directions, together with an accompanying example for the Sentence Completion type of questions.

For each question in this section, select the best answer from among the choices given and fill in the corresponding oval on the answer sheet.

Directions:

Each sentence below has one or two blanks, each blank indicating that some thing has been omitted. Beneath the sentence are five words or sets of words labeled A through E. Choose the word or set of words that, when inserted in the sentence, <u>best</u> fits the meaning of the sentence as a whole.

Example:

Medieval kingdoms did not become constitutional republics overnight; on the contrary, the change was—.

    (A) unpopular
    (B) unexpected
    (C) advantageous
    (D) sufficient
    (E) gradual

If on your actual test you spend time reading these directions and/or answering the sample question, you will waste valuable time.

Don't Rush into Getting an Answer without Thinking

A lot of test-takers panic when they take a test like the SAT. The result is that they rush into choosing answers. It's OK to work quickly, but you have to think carefully, too. If your answer seems to come too easily, beware! When you rush into getting an answer and have not thought the problem out critically, it will probably be the wrong answer.

Here's an example of what to watch out for:

> Below is a picture of a digital clock. The clock shows that the time is 6:06. Consider all the times on the clock where the hour digit is the same as the minute digit, as in the clock shown below. Another such "double" time would be 8:08 or 9:09. What is the *smallest* time period between any two such doubles?
>
> **6:06**
>
> (A) 61 minutes
> (B) 11 minutes
> (C) 60 minutes
> (D) 101 minutes
> (E) 49 minutes

Did you subtract 8:08 from 7:07 and get 1 hour and 1 minute (61 minutes)? If you did, you probably chose Choice A. Think—do you really believe that the test-maker would give you such an easy question? The fact that you figured it out so easily should make you think twice. The thing you have to realize is that there is another possibility: 12:12 to 1:01 gives 49 minutes and so Choice E is correct.

Look out for Traps

Especially, beware of the Choice A answer. It's often a "lure" for test-takers who aren't thinking critically and carefully. Here's an example of how you may be lured into an incorrect answer.

If $x + y = 6$ and $xy = 5$, what is $x^2 + y^2$?
- (A) 36
- (B) 25
- (C) 31
- (D) 11
- (E) 26

Did you think that $(x + y)^2 = x^2 + y^2$ and choose the answer $6x = 36$ (Choice A)? What you really have to know is how to obtain the quantity $x^2 + y^2$ from $x + y$ and from xy. The answer is Choice E. I'll show you how to get that answer *without* having to solve for x and y later.

One way to avoid the "Choice A lure" is to look at Choice E first and work backwards. Of course, you should be aware that Choice A answers do occur, especially if there is no "lure" choice. But if you get the answer easily and it's a Choice A answer, think again. You may have fallen for the "Choice A lure."

If Two Choices Look Equally Good, Guess and Go On

If you have narrowed all the choices down to a choice between two answers but cannot decide between them, *just pick one of the two at random*. Don't waste time! Go on to the next question. This way you will not psychologically exhaust yourself trying to pick the correct answer. Research shows that it is actually psychologically better for you to get the previous question wrong than always to wonder whether you should go back and change the answer.

It's OK to Guess

On the SAT you lose a percentage of points if you guess and get the wrong answer. But the penalty for guessing is much smaller than you may think. Here's why:

Suppose you're taking a test with five-choice questions. If you guess at five of the questions, you would probably get one right and four wrong. That is, from a probability standpoint, you have a one-in-five chance of getting each five-choice question right if you randomly guess at the answers. Since $\frac{1}{4}$ point is taken off for each wrong five-choice question, you've gotten $1 - (\frac{1}{4} \times 4) = 0$ points, because you've gotten 1 question right and four wrong. Thus you break even. So the moral is, whether you randomly guess at questions you're not sure of at all or whether you leave those question answers blank, it doesn't make a difference in the long run!

It May Be Wiser *Not* to Leave an Answer Blank

If you don't mark every line on your answer grid, you run the risk of mismarking future answers. And if you *do* mark every line, you have at least a *chance* of getting the answer right!

STRATEGY 7

If You Have to Try All the Choices, Start with Choice E

Here's an example:

If x is an integer, which number is sometimes even?

    (A) $2x + 1$
    (B) $2x - 1$
    (C) $4x - 1$
    (D) $(2x + 1)$
    (E) $(x + 1)^2$

Many students would try different numbers for x and substitute those numbers in each of the choices. That's OK. But the student would start with Choice A first! Take my advice and start with Choice E first, then try Choice D, etc. Let's try a simple number for x like $x = 1$. You can see that substituting $x = 1$ in Choice E, you get $(1 + 1)^2 = 2^2 = 4$. The number 4 is even, so Choice E is correct. No need to work on the other choices!

So, for questions where one usually has to test out all the choices and eliminate the incorrect ones, the test-maker usually has an answer Choice E or Choice D. This is because the test-maker wants to test to see if the student is able to eliminate all or most of the incorrect choices before arriving at the correct one. And since most students usually start with Choice A, then try Choice B, etc., the test-maker puts the correct choice at the end of the choices.

A word of warning: This strategy works only in the special circumstances when a question cannot be answered without looking at all the choices. For example, you would not use it to find the answer to a question like this:

If $x = 5$, what is $x^2 + 3$?

    (A) 8
    (B) 13
    (C) 28
    (D) 30
    (E) 45

In this question, you do not need to look at the choices at all to get the correct answer. You would first calculate that $x^2 + 3 = 28$, and only then go to the choices to find which one is the same as your answer. So the strategy does not apply.

A second warning: The strategy of starting with Choice E is not designed to give you the correct answer by itself. It is designed to help you find the correct answer faster when you start working through the choices.

Write as Much in Your Test Booklet as You Want

Many students are afraid to mark up their test booklets. But only the answer grids are graded! Underline, figure, write notes—make any marks you want. In fact, some of the strategies in this book demand that you extend or draw lines in geometry questions or label diagrams, or circle incorrect answers, etc. That's why when I see computer programs that show only the questions on a screen and prevent the student from marking a diagram or circling an answer, I realize that such programs prevent the student from using many powerful strategies. *So write all you want on your test booklet—use your test paper as you would scrap paper.*

Use a Coding System to Tell You Which Questions to Return To

If you have extra time after completing a test section, and you have used a coding system, you'll know exactly which questions need more attention.

When you are sure that you have answered a question correctly, mark your question paper with ✔. For questions you are not sure of but for which you have eliminated some of the choices, use **?**. For questions that you're not sure of at all or for which you have not been able to eliminate any choices, use **??**. This will give you a bird's-eye view of what questions you should return to, if you have time left after completing a particular test section.

CRITICAL READING STRATEGIES

Vocabulary Strategies

STRATEGY 1

Familiarize Yourself with SAT Vocabulary Words

Although there is no specific vocabulary test, your knowledge of words and their meanings will be a critical factor in determining how you do on the verbal parts of the test.

We have made a computerized analysis of frequently occurring words on 47 complete recent SAT exams. (1,175 questions were examined.) Following is a list of 132 SAT words appearing *more than once* on these 47 actual SAT tests.

Definitions have not been included here because we want you to *refer to a dictionary* to learn the meanings of these words.

Note that after each word is a numeral that indicates the number of times that the word has appeared on the 47 SAT exams.

Also note that certain pairs of words have a left-side bracket. The bracket indicates that the words are very closely allied in meaning, so that if you learn the meaning of one of the two words in the pair, you will easily arrive at the meaning of the other word of the pair.

Vocabulary Building

A List of Vocabulary Words Appearing More Than Once on Actual SAT Exams

Learn the meanings of these words, since they have a tendency to be repeated in the vocabulary questions of the SAT.

abolish 2	acquiesce 2 *assent*	ameliorate 2	[bane 1 *cause of trouble/ruin*	[capitulate 1 *surrender/yield*
abridge 2	affirmation 2	amity 2	[baneful 1	[capitulation 1
abstemious *not self-indulgent*	amass 2	anchor 2	bizarre 2	capricious 4 *impulsive/unpredictable*
[accent 1	[ambivalence 1 *mixed*	antediluvian 2 *before the flood, antiquated*	blunder 2	clemency 2 *mildness/mercy*
[accented 1	[ambivalent 1 *feelings toward something*	ascendancy 2	bungle 2 *mismanage/botch*	[coalesce 2 *combine*
accolade 2 *praise*	ambulatory 2	atrophy 2	burgeon 2 *begin to grow rapidly*	[coalescence 1

cohere 1
coherent 1

compress 1
compression 1

confide 1
confidential 1

confound 2

congeal 2

contaminant 1
contaminate 2

converge 2

convivial 2

copious 2

corroborate 2
give support to/confirm

corrugated 2

corrupt 1
corruption 1

cursory 2
hasty/hurried

daunt 3
dauntless 1

debilitate 2

deplete 2

discrepancy 3

disentangle 2

disputatious 1
dispute 2

distend 1
distention 1

drawback 2

efface 3

effervesce 1
effervescent 1

enhance 2

enigmatic 2

ephemeral 3

equilibrium 3

euphonious 1
euphony 1

evacuate 2

evanescent 2

expedite 1
expeditious 1

expendable 1
expenditures 1

exclude 2

facilitate 2

fallow 2

fertile 2

flourish 3
flower 1

fraudulent 3

fruitful 1
fruitless 1

garner 2

guile 2

hackneyed 2

hefty 2

hideous 2

hilarity 2

humane 2

hypocrisy 1
hypocritical 1

innocuous 2

irascible 2

jettison 2

kindle 2

leniency 1
lenient 1

levity 1
levitate 1

listless 2

maladroit 2

mitigate 2

mobile 2

munificent 2

munificence 1

myriad 2

nefarious 2

obscure 1
obscurity 1

opaque 1
opacity 1

parsimony 2

paucity 2

penury 2

peripheral 2
periphery 2

placate 2

precise 1
precision 1

premature 2

premeditated 2

prevalent 2

proclivity 2

prodigal 1
prodigious 2

profuse 1
profusion 2

pulverize 1
pulverized 1

rant 2

recalcitrant 2

recant 2

replete 2

rescind 2

reserve 2

ruffle 2

rupture 2

saccharine 2

salubrious 2

somber 4

specify 1
specificity 1

spurn 2

squander 2

stymie 2

subtle 2

summary 2

summon 3

sumptuous 2

surreptitious 1
surreptitiously 1

tantamount 2

tenacious 1
tenacity 1

transience 1
transient 1

turbulence 3

venturesome 3

viable 2

vibrancy 1
vibrant 1

vilification 2

virulence 1
virulent 1

whet 2

zany 2

The 291 Most Important SAT Words and Their Opposites

This is a list of popular SAT words and their opposites. These words fit into specific categories, and it may be a little easier to memorize the meaning of these important words if you know what category they fit into.

POSITIVE	NEGATIVE	POSITIVE	NEGATIVE
TO PRAISE	TO BELITTLE	PLEASANT	UNPLEASANT
acclaim	admonish	affable	callous
applaud	assail	amiable	cantankerous
commend	berate	agreeable	captious
eulogize	calumniate	captivating	churlish
exalt	castigate	congenial	contentious
extol	censure	cordial	gruff
flatter	chastise	courteous	irascible
hail	chide	decorous	ireful
laud	decry	engaging	obstinate
panegyrize	denigrate	gracious	ornery
resound	denounce	obliging	peevish
tout	disparage	sportive	perverse
	excoriate	unblemished	petulant
	execrate	undefiled	querulous
	flay		testy
	lambaste		vexing
	malign		wayward
	reprimand		
	reproach		
	scold		
	upbraid		
	vilify		

POSITIVE	NEGATIVE	POSITIVE	NEGATIVE
TO CALM OR MAKE BETTER	**TO MAKE WORSE OR RUFFLE**	**ABUNDANT OR RICH**	**SCARCE OR POOR**
abate	alienate	affluent	dearth
accede	antagonize	bounteous	deficit
accommodate	contradict	copious	destitute
allay	dispute	luxuriant	exiguous
ameliorate	fend off	multifarious	impecunious
appease	embitter	multitudinous	impoverished
assuage	estrange	myriad	indigent
comply	incense	opulent	insolvent
concede	infuriate	penurious	meager
conciliate	nettle	plenteous	paltry
gratify	oppugn	plentiful	paucity
mitigate	oppose	plethoric	penurious
mollify	rebuff	profuse	scanty
pacify	repel	prosperous	scarcity
palliate	repulse	superabundant	sparse
placate	snub	teeming	
propitiate		wealthy	
quell			
satiate			

YIELDING	NOT YIELDING	CAREFUL	CARELESS
accommodating	adamant	chary	culpable
amenable	determinate	circumspect	felonious
compliant	immutable	conscientious	indifferent
deferential	indomitable	discreet	insouciant
docile	inflexible	exacting	lackadaisical
flexible	intractable	fastidious	lax
inclined	intransigent	gingerly	negligent
hospitable	recalcitrant	heedful	perfunctory
malleable	relentless	judicious	rash
obliging	resolute	meticulous	remiss
pliant	steadfast	provident	reprehensible
submissive	tenacious	prudent	temararious
subservient		punctilious	
tractable		scrupulous	
		scrutiny	
		wary	

POSITIVE	NEGATIVE	POSITIVE	NEGATIVE
GENEROUS	**CHEAP**	**COURAGEOUS**	**TIMID**
altruistic	frugal	audacious	diffident
beneficent	miserly	dauntless	indisposed
benevolent	niggardly	gallant	laconic
charitable	paltry	intrepid	reserved
effusive	parsimonious	stalwart	reticent
hospitable	penurious	undaunted	subdued
humanitarian	provident	valiant	timorous
magnanimous	skinflint	valorous	
munificent	spartan		
philanthropic	tight-fisted		
thrifty			

POSITIVE	NEGATIVE	POSITIVE	NEGATIVE
LIVELY	**BLEAK**	**HAUGHTY**	**HUMBLE**
brisk	dejected	affected	demure
dynamic	forlorn	arrogant	diffident
ebullient	lackluster	aristocratic	indisposed
exhilaration	lugubrious	audacious	introverted
exuberant	melancholy	authoritarian	laconic
inspiring	muted	autocratic	plebian
provocative	prostrate	condescending	reluctant
scintillating	somber	disdainful	restrained
stimulating	tenebrous	egotistical	reticent
titillating		flippant	subdued
		flagrant	subservient
		imperious	taciturn
		impertinent	timid
		impudent	timorous
		insolent	unassuming
		ostentatious	unostentatious
		pompous	unpretentious
		proud	
		supercilious	
		vainglorious	

Note:

In many cases you can put a prefix such as *dis-, im-,* or *un-* in front of the word and change its meaning to an opposite.

Examples:

courteous/discourteous, pecunious/impecunious, ostentatious/unostentatious

Use Prefixes and Word Roots to Figure out Word Meanings

Is there a shortcut to learning vocabulary? Well, there certainly is a more efficient way to learn the meaning of words than by memorizing a word list. The SAT chooses words from a list of over 30,000.

Just 20 prefixes and 14 roots can help you to get the meaning of over 100,000 words. Here are those roots and prefixes and many more, which can give you the meaning of more than 120,000 words:

ROOT	MEANING	EXAMPLE
act, ag	do, act	activity, agent
apert	open	aperture
bas	low	basement
cap, capt	take, seize	capable, capture
ced, cess	give in, go	concede, recession
cred	believe	credible
curr, curs	run	current, precursor
dict	speak	dictionary, predict
due, duct	lead	induce, conduct
equ	equal	equality, equanimity
fac, fact	make, do	facile, artifact
fer	bear, carry	offer, confer
graph	write	monograph, graphite
log	word, study of	dialog, biology
mitt, miss	send	permit, admission
par	equal	parity, disparate
plic	fold	complicated
pon	put, place	component
scrib, script	write	transcribe, subscription
sequ, secu	follow	sequel, consecutive
spec, spect	see	specimen, aspect
sto, stat, sisto	stand, cause to stand	statue, insist
tact	touch	contact, tactile
ten	hold	retentive, tenacious
tend, tent, tens	stretch	extend, tension
un, uni	one	unilateral, unanimous
ven, vent	come	convenient, advent
ver	true	verify

PREFIX	MEANING	EXAMPLE
a, ab, abs	away, from	absent, abstinent
ad, a, ac, af, ag, an, ar, at, as	to, toward	adhere, annex, accede, adapt
bi, bis	two	biped, bicycle
circum	around	circumference, circumlocution
com, con	together, with	combination, connect
de	opposite, from	detract, demerit
dis, dif, di	apart	disperse, difference
epi	upon, on top of	epilogue
equi	equal	equality, equitable
ex, ef, e	out, from	eject, exhale, exit
in (en)	in, into	inject, endure
mal, male	bad, ill	malpractice, malevolent
mis	wrong	misplace, misunderstand
mono	alone, one, single	monotone, monopoly
non	not	nonsense
ob	in front, against	obviate, obvious
omni	everywhere, all	omnipresent, omnipotent
per	through	perceive, pervade
poly	many	polygon
post	after	posterior, postpone
pre	before	precursory, preface
pro	forward	proceed, promote
re	again	recall, recede
se	apart	secede
sub	under	subliminal, subway
super	greater, beyond	supernatural, superstition
trans	across	transpire, transcontinental
un, uni	one	unilateral, unity
un (pronounced *uhn*)	not	unethical

You will find that this list will be of considerable help in getting at the meaning of words. For example, take the word DISPARITY. If you remember what the list tells you—that PAR means **equal** and DIS means **apart**—you can reason that DISPARITY means **dissimilarity** or **difference.**

Now try using the information in the list to choose the meanings of some typical SAT vocabulary words.

1. PRECURSORY
   (A) antecedent
   (B) flamboyant
   (C) cautious
   (D) simple
   (E) cheap

2. TENACIOUS
   (A) smooth
   (B) careful
   (C) steadfast
   (D) argumentative
   (E) polite

3. CIRCUMVENT
   (A) to go round about
   (B) alleviate
   (C) to prey on one's emotions
   (D) scintillate
   (E) perceive correctly

4. MALEDICTION
   (A) sloppiness
   (B) curse
   (C) health
   (D) religiousness
   (E) proof

Knowing the prefix or root or both of the given word, you should be able to zero in on the correct synonym without mulling over the incorrect choices. In 1, you should know that PRE means **before** and CURS means **to run.** Therefore, PRECURSORY must mean **to run before;** so a word with a similar meaning would be ANTECEDENT, Choice A. In 2, TEN means **to hold,** so TENACIOUS means **persistent,** and its synonym would be STEADFAST, Choice C. In 3, CIRCUM means **around.** And, VENT means **come,** so CIRCUMVENT must mean to **come around.** The answer, then, would be to go round about, Choice A. In 4, MAL means **ill** or **bad.** DICT means **speak.** So, MALEDICTION must mean something that **speaks ill** of someone. The answer would be **curse,** Choice B.

Notice how this method of knowing prefixes and roots helps you to zero in on the right choice. On the other hand, if you do not know how to get the meaning of a word by its prefix or root and you are not familiar with the word, you might as well guess immediately and then go on to the next question. Remember, do not try to psych out the test-maker or waste time mulling over a word! And remember, if you're not sure which of two or three choices is correct, just choose one of them at random and move on. You can always go back to the question later if you have time. The time you spend mulling over choices will take valuable time away from you, time that you may be able to use to get many more questions right. Also, mulling over a question puts you at a psychological disadvantage. Wondering whether you made the right choice in the preceding question

keeps you from looking freshly at upcoming questions and can psychologically exhaust you for the rest of the exam.

Look for Related Words or Words with a Similar Feel

Many times you can figure out the meaning of a vocabulary word just
by being able to associate the word with a related word or a word (or
words) with a similar "feel." Try to figure out the meaning of the word
FIREBRAND:

FIREBRAND

  (A) an intellect
  (B) one who is charitable
  (C) one who makes trouble
  (D) a philanthropist
  (E) one who is peaceful

Here you should get the feeling from FIRE
in FIREBRAND that FIREBRAND is a very
harsh or violent-sounding word. Therefore,
you are looking for some word that imparts
a *harsh* or *troublesome* feeling. Choice C fits
the bill!

Here's another example:

LEVITY

  (A) insightfulness
  (B) merriment
  (C) viciousness
  (D) smoothness
  (E) curiosity

Think of what LEVITY could mean. What
other words might contain the root LEV?
Elevate means to raise up. *Levitate* means
much the same thing. So LEV probably has
something to do with raising up. How does
this help? None of the choices means "raising up." But in using this strategy, you are
not looking for literal meanings. The *feel* of
the root LEV is lightness, airiness. The feel
closest to this is happiness or lighthearted-
ness. So Choice B, **merriment**, is your best
choice.

Hot Prefixes and Roots

Here is a list of the most important prefixes and roots that impart a certain meaning or feeling. They can be instant clues to the meanings of more than 110,000 words.

PREFIXES THAT MEAN *TO*, *WITH*, *BETWEEN*, OR *AMONG*

PREFIX	MEANING	EXAMPLES
ad, ac, af, an, ap, ap, as, at	to, toward	adapt—to fit into adhere—to stick to attract—to draw near
com, con, co, col	with, together	combine—to bring together contact—to touch together collect—to bring together co-worker—one who works together with another worker
in, il, ir, im	into	inject—to put into impose—to force into illustrate—to put into example irritate—to put into discomfort
inter	between, among	international—among nations interact—to act among the people
pro	forward, going ahead	proceed—to go forward promote—to move forward

PREFIXES THAT MEAN *BAD*

PREFIX	MEANING	EXAMPLES
mal	wrong, bad	malady—illness malevolent—bad malfunction—bad functioning
mis	wrong, badly	mistreat—to treat badly mistake—to get wrong

PREFIXES THAT MEAN *AWAY FROM*, *NOT*, OR *AGAINST*

PREFIX	MEANING	EXAMPLES
ab	away from	absent—not to be present, away abscond—to run away
de, dis	away from, down, the opposite of, apart, not	depart—to go away from decline—to turn down dislike—not to like dishonest—not honest distant—apart
ex, e, ef	out, from	exit—to go out eject—to throw out efface—to rub out, erase
in, il, ir, im	not	inactive—not active impossible—not possible ill-mannered—not mannered irreversible—not reversible
non	not	nonsense—no sense nonstop—having no stops
un	not	unhelpful—not helpful uninterested—not interested
anti	against	anti-freeze—a substance used to prevent freezing anti-social—refers to someone who's not social
ob	against, in front of	obstacle—something that stands in the way of obstinate—inflexible

PREFIXES THAT DENOTE DISTANCE

PREFIX	MEANING	EXAMPLES
circum	around	circumscribe—to write or inscribe in a circle circumspect—to watch around or be very careful
equ, equi	equal, the same	equalize—to make equal equitable—fair, equal
post	after	postpone—to do after postmortem—after death
pre	before	preview—a viewing that goes before another viewing prehistorical—before written history
trans	across	transcontinental—across the continent transit—act of going across
re	back, again	retell—to tell again recall—to call back, to remember
sub	under	subordinate—under something else subconcious—under the conscious
super	over, above	superimpose—to put something over something else superstar—a star greater than other stars
un, uni	one	unity—oneness unanimous—sharing one view unidirectional—having one direction

ROOTS

ROOT	MEANING	EXAMPLES
cap, capt, cept, ceive	to take, to hold	captive—one who is held receive—to take capable—to be able to take hold of things concept—an idea or thought held in mind
cred	to believe	credible—believable credit—belief, trust
curr, curs, cours	to run	current—now in progress, running cursor—a moveable indicator recourse—to run for aid
dic, dict	to say	indicate—to say by demonstrating diction—verbal saying
duc, duct	to lead	induce—to lead to action aqueduct—a pipe or waterway that leads water somewhere
fac, fic, fect, fy	to make, to do	facile—easy to do fiction—something that has been made up satisfy—to make happy affect—to make a change in
jec, ject	to throw	project—to put forward trajectory—a path of an object that has been thrown
mit, mis	to send	admit—to send in missile—something that gets sent through the air

pon, pos	to place	transpose—to place across
		compose—to put into place many parts deposit—to place in something
scrib, script	to write	describe—to write or tell about scripture—a written tablet
spec, spic	to look	specimen—an example to look at inspect—to look over
ten, tain	to hold	maintain—to hold up or keep retentive—holding
ven, vent	to come	advent—a coming convene—to come together

Sentence Completion Strategies

The questions in the Sentence Completion section begin with a sentence that has one or two words missing. You have to find the missing word or words. Here's a very simple example:

You may think Bill is tall, but his brother is even _____.

    (A) younger
    (B) taller
    (C) older
    (D) wiser
    (E) happier

The best word to fill in the blank is Choice B, **taller.**

Watch for Key Words in the Sentence

As you can see from the preceding example, the sentence is constructed with enough clues for you to find the missing words. You have to watch for key words *that link the sentence together.* Or watch for key words that give you the *tone of the sentence.* The important *linkage* words are words like **but, while, if, and, because, although, since, by contrast to, nevertheless,** etc. Key words like **powerful, only, long range** describe the extent to which something is happening, and are also important.

Try to Complete the Sentence Before You Look at the Choices

You will often find that the quickest, easiest way of finding the missing word or words is to try and complete the sentence by yourself, without looking at the choices at all. Then, after you have come up with your own word or words to complete the sentence, you can look among the choices. Chances are good that you will find your word or another one with a meaning close to it. For example:

Although the senator was admired personally, his ideas and policies were not _____.

    (A) initiated
    (B) well founded
    (C) supported
    (D) contrived
    (E) interesting

The key word *although* gives it away. It contrasts one part of the sentence with the other. The word *although* tells us that in one case the senator was liked, but in another case something negative is happening to his ideas and policies. So, even without looking at the choices, we can see that the senator's ideas were not well *accepted, supported,* etc. We can see then that Choice C fits the bill without analyzing the other choices. Note that in this example, you could have tried to fit all the choices (A), (B), etc., into the sentence, but in a case like this it is easier and more efficient to complete the sentence by yourself, supported by understanding the gist of the sentence and how the word *although* contrasts the two parts of the sentence.

Just in case some of you wonder why Choice B is not correct: As the senator was *admired,* something has to be *done to* the senator. Choices like *accepted, supported,* etc. are *active;* something is *done to* the senator. And so, Choice C fits the bill. But a choice like *well founded* describes the senator's ideas, and *not something done actively to the senator,* as acceptance or support.

Let's try a sentence completion question involving *two* missing words.

Science is forever trying to understand the_____aspects of the universe; one day humankind will possibly understand the_____structure of nature.

(A) important . . . simulated
(B) grandiose . . . simple
(C) philosophical . . . poetic
(D) direct . . . complete
(E) fundamental . . . basic

Here there must be a link between the two parts. We should realize that the adjective modifying the word *aspects* must be related to the adjective modifying the word *structure*. Very likely the words will mean the same thing. So you can see that Choice E, *fundamental . . . basic*, fits the bill.

These two-word missing sentence completions are somewhat more difficult than the one-word missing sentence completions, but if you can figure out the linkage of the parts in the sentence and how the missing words supply the linkage, you will make the question fairly easy.

Note that in the above example, you could have tried substituting all the choices in the sentence. You would then see that Choice A does not make too much sense, then you would see that Choice B is almost contradictory with words like *grandiose* and *simple*. You could use this method substituting the rest of the choice sets. But note that if you really understood the gist of the sentence and that you were looking for words of similar meaning, you could almost zero in on Choice E as being the correct one. And, although you can always substitute all the choices to test them for correctness, the best way to answer these sentence completion questions is to try to zero in on the correct choice without having to substitute the rest of the incorrect choices. Be cautious—in *some* cases you may not be astute enough to find a clever linkage in the sentence, and in that case it would be better for you to substitute in all the choices. In that case, I would *start with Choice E and work backwards,* substituting Choice D next, then Choice C, etc., in that order. Many times, when the test-taker has to substitute all the choices, the test-maker will make sure that the correct answer is either Choice D or E, the correct answer being at the far end of the choices. This insures that if the test-taker makes a mistake in the first few choices and gets one of the first choices as an answer, he/she will be justifiably penalized for the wrong answer.

STRATEGY 3

Look for Negative-Positive Contrasts

Sometimes it is possible to zero in immediately on the correct choice by noting that one part of the sentence has a positive (or negative) feeling whereas the other part of the sentence has a negative (or positive) feeling. So for one blank you would choose a positive (or negative) word and for the other blank you would choose a word that has an opposite feeling (a negative or positive word). Here's a typical SAT example:

When Mr. Simmons _____ a thought, he discounts it cleverly, but when anything appeals to him, he is able to be _____ enough.

    (A) discovers . . . fearful
    (B) thinks of . . . irresponsible
    (C) analyzes . . . distrustful
    (D) is uncomfortable with . . . responsive
    (E) is afraid of . . . hostile

The key words are *discounts* and *but*. The word *but* contrasts an opposite feeling to the one brought out in the first part of the sentence. The word *discounts* has a *negative* feeling, so the word in the first blank probably has a negative feeling. Because the word *but* in the second part of the sentence contrasts with the first part, and because of the positive nature of the word *appeals,* the second blank requires a positive-sounding word. Note that of all the choices, the only choice that describes a *negative word for the first blank and a positive word for the second blank* is Choice D. And so, Choice D is correct. Here's another example illustrating the above point:

She is so far from achieving a true _____ of human relations that she has_____ almost completely unto herself.

    (A) perspective . . . developed
    (B) understanding . . . withdrawn
    (C) animosity . . . retreated
    (D) void . . . managed
    (E) value . . . transformed

In the first part of the sentence, the words *true* and *human relations* suggest a *positive* feeling, and the words *so far from* and *that* indicate a *negative* feeling in the second part of the sentence. Also the words *almost completely unto herself* suggest a negative feeling. Thus the first blank must be *positive* and the second blank must be *negative*. The only choice that fits the bill is Choice B. Note that in Choice A the word *developed* has positive or neutral connotations, and in Choice E the word *transformed* is neutral. Thus Choices A and E are incorrect.

Work "Backward" from the Part of the Sentence without the Blank

You will often be able to zero in on the missing word in a sentence by carefully considering the part of the sentence *without* the blank. For example:

Insight is so _____ in problem-solving that we seem to take it for granted.

  (A) extraordinary
  (B) theoretical
  (C) partial
  (D) important
  (E) common

The part of the sentence without the blank is *we seem to take it for granted,* and there are no "negative" linking key words like *but* or *although.* What is something that we would take for granted? Something ordinary, everyday, expected. Choice E, *common,* fits the bill perfectly.

A negative key linking word in this sentence would signal you to look for the *opposite* of the part of the sentence without the blank. For example, suppose the sentence had been this one:

Although common sense is actually _____, we nevertheless take it for granted.

Here the key words *although* and *nevertheless* tell you to look for the opposite of something you would *take for granted.* The best word would be something like *rare, unusual,* or *uncommon.*

Remember—when you work backward from the part of the sentence without the blank, be sure to check for key linking words that show you how it relates to the part with the blank.

Don't Panic If You See Difficult Words in the Choices—Sometimes the Easier Words Have the Answer

Sometimes you may understand the meaning of every word in the sentence, but not in the choices. Should you give up? Should you guess? Here's an example:

Let us not _____ the man for his action; he could not have been aware of the _____ of his crime.

    (A) criticize . . . animosity
    (B) excommunicate . . . nature
    (C) promulgate . . . timeliness
    (D) condemn . . . gravity
    (E) belittle . . . legality

Here you may not know what the words *promulgate, excommunicate,* or *animosity* mean. And you may not want to spend time looking at the other two choice sets. In that case you would be wise to guess and go on to the next question on the test. However, you may try to quickly see the gist of the sentence. Note that the sentence implies that we are not going to do *something* as the person was not aware of the extent of the crime. Doesn't it look like Choice D is correct? If you didn't know the meaning of gravity, just think of gravity on earth. Gravity makes things heavy, so you'd be on safe ground assuming that the word *gravity* meant something that is heavy. Now the sentence makes sense if we say, "Let us not *condemn* the man for his action; he could not have been aware of the *gravity* of his crime."

Reading Comprehension Strategies

The Reading Comprehension sections of the SAT contain passages of about 400 to 900 words in length. After each passage there is a set of 4 to13 questions. (Longer passage have about 12 to 13 questions, shorter passages have 4 to 9 questions.) One section will contain a "double passage" with some questions relating to both passages.

Become Familiar with the Main Categories of Reading Questions

It will be very useful for you to become familiar with the principal types of questions that are asked after each reading selection. By becoming familiar with these types, you will get a feeling for what you should concentrate on in your reading of the passage, and you will in addition be prepared for many of the actual questions that follow the passage. The principal types are—

1. Questions based on the passage as a whole.
2. Questions based on one or more specific sections of the passage.
3. Questions based on particular words, phrases, or sentences.

The lists below contain the typical recurring question types found in each main category, as derived from analysis of actual SATs. Each listed question type is followed by one or more examples of the kind of wording that the SAT uses in its actual questions.

Questions Based on the Passage as a Whole

QUESTION TYPE

1. MAIN POINT—
   What is the passage trying to tell you?

2. PRIMARY PURPOSE OF AUTHOR—
   What does the author want to tell you?

3. MOOD OR ATTITUDE OF AUTHOR—
   What is the tone or attitude of the author?

EXAMPLES OF SAT WORDING

The passage is mainly concerned with . . .

The author's primary purpose in the passage is to . . .

On the basis of the passage, the author's attitude toward Mrs. Alden can most accurately be termed as one of . . .

QUESTION TYPE	EXAMPLES OF SAT WORDING
4. ASSUMPTIONS MADE BY AUTHOR— What assumptions are made by the author but not directly stated in the passage?	Which of the following is an assumption made by the author?
5. APPLICATIONS OF MAIN IDEAS— How can you extend the main ideas of the passage?	The author provides information that would answer all of the following questions EXCEPT . . . According to the author, the effort of taking a nationwide vote on the proposed program would be . . .
6. IMPLICATIONS OF PASSAGE OR OF THE AUTHOR— What does the author or the passage imply?	The author implies that a work of art is properly judged on the basis of its . . .
7. SUMMARY OF PASSAGE— In a few words how would you describe the passage? What title would you give the passage?	Which of the following titles best summarizes the content of the passage? Which of the following would be the most appropriate title for the passage?
8. CONTENT OF THE PASSAGE— What is the passage really about?	Which of the following describes the content of the passage?
9. INFERENCES— What can you infer from the passage as a whole?	It can be inferred from the passage that the . . .
10. STATEMENTS THAT THE AUTHOR WOULD BE IN AGREEMENT WITH— What could you say that the author would agree with, knowing the way he/she wrote the passage?	With which of the following statements regarding ragtime would the author probably agree?

Questions Based on One or More Specific Sections of the Passage

QUESTION TYPE	EXAMPLES OF SAT WORDING
1. INFERENCES— What can you infer from specific sections in the passage?	It can be inferred that the ancients' atomic theory was primarily based on . . .
2. APPLICATIONS— How can you apply information in specific sections of the passage to other areas?	The author provides information that answers which of the following questions? **EXAMPLES OF SAT WORDING**

QUESTION TYPE	EXAMPLES OF SAT WORDING
3. WHAT PRECEDES PASSAGE OR COMES AFTER PASSAGE— What do you think was written right before the passage or right after the passage?	It can be inferred that in the paragraphs immediately preceding the passage, the author discussed . . .
4. STATED IDEAS— Can you find in the passage a specific reference to a stated idea?	According to the passage, blacks were denied entrance into antislavery societies because . . .
5. IMPLICATIONS— What is implied by a section in the passage?	The author implies that many Americans' devotion to the ideal of brotherhood of man is . . . In describing American attitudes about the land (lines 7–8), the author implies that . . .
6. TONE OR MOOD— What is the tone or mood of a section in the passage?	At the conclusion of the passage, the author's tone is one of . . .

Questions Based on Particular Words, Phrases, or Sentences

QUESTION TYPE	EXAMPLES OF SAT WORDING
1. REASON FOR USE— Why are certain words or phrases or sentences mentioned or used in the passage?	The author mentions Newton's *Principia* in order to . . .
2. MEANING OF A WORD OR PHRASE— What is the meaning of a certain word, phrase, or sentence in the passage?	The enemy referred to in the last sentence is probably . . . According to the author, the words in the Declaration of Independence, "all men are created equal," were meant to represent . . . By "this skepticism" (line 35), the author means . . .

STRATEGY 2

Read the Passage and Anticipate the Questions That Might Be Asked About It

The key approach for doing well on answering reading comprehension questions is getting involved and interested in the passage before you read the questions. While you read the passage, try to figure out the motive of the person that wrote the passage. Why is he or she saying what is in the passage? Do you agree or disagree with what is being said? Are you angry at what is being stated? You will find that if you get interested and involved in reading the passage, you will be able to anticipate many of the test questions.

And this brings me to a question many test-takers ask: "Should I look at the questions before reading the passage?" The answer I usually give students is that you can use one of two methods: You can look at the questions (not the choices!) first. But if you do, you may spend time that you could have used reading the passage. On the other hand, if you can get involved with the passage, you will, in fact, anticipate many of the questions that follow the passage. And in that case, there would be no point in wasting any time in looking at the questions first. In your practice you may want to try it both ways and see which way proves best for you.

To get an idea of what I mean, look over the following passage. When you are done, I'll show you how you might read it so as to get involved with the passage and with the author's intent.

We should also know that "greed" has little to do with the environmental crisis. The two main causes are population pressures, especially the pressures of large metropolitan populations, and the desire—a highly commendable one—to bring a decent living at the lowest possible cost to the largest possible number of people.

The environmental crisis is the result of success—success in cutting down the mortality of infants (which has given us the population explosion), success in raising farm output sufficiently to prevent mass famine (which has given us contamination by pesticides and chemical fertilizers), success in getting the people out of the tenements of the 19th-century cities and into the greenery and privacy of the single-family home in the suburbs (which has given us urban sprawl and traffic jams). The environmental crisis, in other words, is largely the result of doing too much of the right sort of thing.

To overcome the problems that success always creates, one must build on it. But where to start? Cleaning up the environment requires determined, sustained effort with clear targets and deadlines. It requires, above all, concentration of effort. Up to now we have tried to do a little bit of everything—and tried to do it in the headlines—when what we ought to do first is draw up a list of priorities.

Now I'll go over the passage with you, showing you what might go through your mind as you read. This will let you see how to get involved with the passage, and how this involvement facilitates answering the questions that follow the passage. In many cases, you'll actually be able to anticipate the questions. Of course, when you are preparing for the SAT, you'll have to develop this skill so that you do it rapidly and almost automatically.

Let's look at the first sentence:

We should also know that "greed" has little to do with the environmental crisis.

Immediately you should say to yourself, "So something else must be involved with the environmental crisis," Read on:

The two main causes are population pressures, especially the pressures of large metropolitan populations, and the desire—a highly commendable one—to bring a decent living at the lowest possible cost to the largest possible number of people.

Now you can say to yourself, "Oh, so population pressures and the desire to help out the people in the community caused the environmental crisis." You should also get a feeling that the author is not really against these causes of the environmental crisis, and that he or she believes that the crisis is in part a side effect of worthwhile efforts and enterprises. Read on:

The environmental crisis is the result of success—success in cutting down the mortality of infants (which has given us the population explosion), success in raising farm output sufficiently to prevent mass famine (which has given us contamination by pesticides and chemical fertilizers), success in getting the people out of the tenements of the 19th-century city and into the greenery and privacy of the single-family home in the suburbs (which has given us urban sprawl and traffic jams).

Now you should say to yourself, "It seems that for every positive thing that the author mentions, there is a negative occurrence which leads to the environmental crisis."

Now read the last sentence of this paragraph:

The environmental crisis, in other words, is largely the result of doing too much of the right sort of thing.

Now you can say to yourself, "Gee, we wanted to do the right thing, but we created something bad. It looks like you can't have your cake and eat it, too!"

Now you should anticipate that in the next and final paragraph, the author will discuss what may be done to reduce the bad effects which come from the good. Look at the first sentence of the third paragraph:

To overcome the problems that success always creates, one must build on it.

Now you can say to yourself, "Well, how?" In fact, in the next sentence the author asks the very question you just asked: *But where to start?* Read on to find out the author's answer:

Cleaning up the environment requires determined, sustained effort with clear targets and deadlines. It requires, above all, concentration of effort.

So now you can say to yourself, "Oh, so that's what we need—definite goals, deadlines for reaching those goals, and genuine effort to achieve the goals."

The author then discusses what you may have already thought about:

Up to now we have tried to do a little bit of everything—

What the author is saying (and you should realize this) is that up to now, we haven't concentrated on one particular problem at a time. We used "buckshots instead of bullets."

Read on:

—and tried to do it in the headlines—when what we ought to do first is to draw up a list of priorities.

So you can now see that, in the author's opinion, making a list of priorities and working on them one at a time, with a target in mind, may get us out of the environmental crisis and still preserve our quality of life.

STRATEGY 3

Highlight Important Details as you Read

As you read, underline or highlight main ideas and key words. Draw arrows or put exclamation points next to ideas that look important. Underlining will help to reinforce your memory of the passage, and if you need to look back you'll find important information more quickly. Here's an example:

The <u>two main causes</u> are <u>population pressures</u>, especially the pressures of large metropolitan populations, and the <u>desire</u>— a highly commendable one—to <u>bring a</u> <u>decent living at the lowest possible cost to the largest possible number of people.</u>

This section tests comprehension, not memory. It's OK to check the passage. If you've read carefully and highlighted important points, a quick glance back can help you choose the right answer. A few words of caution, though—don't highlight everything. Stick to the main points only. And don't depend on being able to look back for each answer. You'll waste valuable time.

Making the Best Use of Your Time

Before we start to answer the questions, let me just tell you the best and most effective way of answering passage questions. You should read the question and proceed to look at the choices in the order of Choice A, Choice B, etc. If a choice (such as Choice A) doesn't give you the definite feeling that it is correct, don't try to analyze it further. Go on to Choice B. Again, if that choice (Choice B) doesn't make you feel that it's the right one, and you really have to think carefully about the choice, go on to Choice C. The first choice that gives you a definite feeling of being correct (let's say it's Choice C) is the one you should mark on your answer sheet. Don't bother going on to the rest of the choices. In other words, stop at the choice that you feel is obviously the right one.

Suppose you have gone through all the five choices, and you don't know which one is correct, or you don't see any one that stands out as obviously being correct. Then quickly guess, and go on to the next question. You can go back after you have answered the other questions relating to the passage. But remember, when you go back to the questions you weren't sure of, don't spend too much time on them. Try to forge ahead on the test.

Let's proceed to answer the questions now. Look at the first question:

1. This passage assumes the desirability of

   (A) using atomic energy to conserve fuel
   (B) living in comfortable family lifestyles
   (C) settling disputes peacefully
   (D) combating cancer and heart disease with energetic research
   (E) having greater government involvement in people's daily lives

Look at Choice A. That doesn't seem correct. Now look at Choice B. Do you remember that the author claimed that the environmental crisis is the result of the successful attempt to get people out of their tenements into a better environment? We can only feel that the author *assumes* this desirability of *living in comfortable family lifestyles* (Choice B) since the author uses the word *success* in describing the transition from living in tenements to living in single-family homes. Therefore Choice B is correct. You don't need to analyze or even consider the other choices, since we have zeroed in on Choice B.

Let's look at Question 2:

2. According to this passage, one early step in any effort to improve the environment would be to

   (A) return to the exclusive use of natural fertilizers
   (B) put a high tax on profiteering industries
   (C) ban the use of automobiles in the cities
   (D) study successful efforts in other countries
   (E) set up a timetable for corrective actions

Again, let's go through the choices in the order Choice A, Choice B, etc. until we come up with the right choice. Choices A, B, C, and D seem unlikely to be correct, but we may want to go back to Choices C and D. Now look at Choice E. We remember that the author said that we should get "clear targets and deadlines" to improve the environment. That looks pretty much as if Choice E is correct.

Let's look at Question 3:

3. The passage indicates that the conditions that led to overcrowded roads also brought about

(A) more attractive living conditions for many people
(B) a healthier younger generation
(C) greater occupational opportunities
(D) the population explosion
(E) greater concentration of population pressures

Here we would want to go back to the part where overcrowded roads was discussed in the passage. This is where (2nd paragraph) the author says that "urban sprawl and traffic jams" are one result of success in getting people out of tenements to single-family homes. So you can see that Choice A is correct. Again, no need to consider other choices, since you should be fairly comfortable with Choice A.

Let's look at Question 4:

4. It could logically be assumed that the author of this passage would support legislation to

(A) ban the use of all pesticides
(B) prevent the use of automobiles in the cities
(C) build additional conventional power plants immediately
(D) organize an agency to coordinate efforts to cope with environmental problems
(E) restrict the press coverage of protest led by environmental groups

This is the type of question which asks you to understand what the author would feel about something else, when you already know something about the author's sentiments on one particular subject.

Choices A, B, and C do not seem correct. But look at Choice D. The author said that the way to get out of the energy crisis is to set targets and deadlines in order to cope with specific problems. The author would therefore probably organize an agency to do this. Choice D is correct.

"Double Passage" Reading Questions

On the SAT there are paired passages with one set of questions relating to both. The questions are based on the content of the passages and on the relationship between them. Answer the questions on the basis of what is *stated* or *implied* in the passages and in any introductory material that may be provided.

In the following example, two passages describe different time periods. Passage A discusses the medieval time period, Passage B describes the present and speculates on the future.

PASSAGE A

Line   To the world when it was half a thousand years younger, the outlines of all things seemed more clearly marked than to us. The contrast between
5   suffering and joy, between adversity and happiness, appeared more striking. All experience had yet to the minds of men the directness and absoluteness of the pleasure
10   and pain of child-life. Every event, every action, was still embodied in expressive and solemn forms, which

raised them to the dignity of a ritual. Misfortunes and poverty were more afflicting than at present; it was more difficult to guard against them, and to find solace. Illness and health presented a more striking contrast; the cold and darkness of winter were more real evils. Honors and riches were relished with greater avidity and contrasted more vividly with surrounding misery. We, at the present day, can hardly understand the keenness with which a fur coat, a good fire on the hearth, a soft bed, a glass of wine, were formerly enjoyed. Then, again, all things in life were of a proud or cruel publicity. Lepers sounded their rattles and went about in processions, beggars exhibited their deformity and their misery in churches. Every order and estate, every rank and profession, was distinguished by its costume. The great lords never moved about without a glorious display of arms and liveries, exciting fear and envy. Executions and other public acts of justice, hawking, marriages and funerals, were all announced by cries and processions, songs and music. The lover wore the colors of his lady; companions the emblem of their brotherhood; parties and servants the badges of their lords. Between town and country, too, the contrast was very marked. A medieval town did not lose itself in extensive suburbs of factories and villas; girded by its walls, it stood forth as a compact whole, bristling with innumerable turrets. However tall and threatening the houses of noblemen or merchants might be, in the aspect of the town, the lofty mass of the churches always remained dominant.

The contrast between silence and sound, darkness and light, like that between summer and winter, was more strongly marked than it is in our lives. The modern town hardly knows silence or darkness in their purity, nor the effect of a solitary light or a single distant cry. All things presenting themselves to the mind in violent contrasts and impressive forms, lent a tone of excitement and passion to everyday life and tended to produce that perpetual oscillation between despair and distracted joy, between cruelty and pious tenderness which characterize life in the Middle Ages.

PASSAGE B

Line In 1575—over 400 years ago—the French scholar Louis Le Roy published a learned book in which he voiced despair over the upheavals caused by the social and technological innovations of his time, what we now call the Renaissance. "All is pellmell, confounded, nothing goes as it should." We, also, feel that our times are out of joint; we even have reason to believe that our descendants will be worse off than we are. The earth will soon be over-crowded and its resources exhausted. Pollution will ruin the environment, upset the climate, damage human health. The gap in living standards between the rich and the poor will widen and lead the angry, hungry people of the world to acts of desperation including the use of nuclear weapons as blackmail. Such are the inevitable consequences of population and technological growth *if* present trends continue. But what a big *if* this is! The future

is never a projection of the past. Animals probably have no chance to
100 escape from the tyranny of biological evolution, but human beings are blessed with the freedom of social evolution. For us, trend is not destiny. The escape from existing trends is
105 now facilitated by the fact that societies anticipate future dangers and take preventive steps against expected upheavals. Despite the widespread belief that the world has become too
110 complex for comprehension by the human brain, modern societies have often responded effectively to critical situations.

The decrease in birth rates, the
115 partial banning of pesticides, the rethinking of technologies for the production and use of energy are but a few examples illustrating a sudden reversal of trends caused not by political
125 upsets or scientific breakthroughs, but by public awareness of consequences. Even more striking are the situations in which social attitudes concerning future difficulties undergo rapid
130 changes before the problems have come to pass—witness the heated controversies about the ethics of behavior control and of genetic engineering even though there is as yet
135 no proof that effective methods can be developed to manipulate behavior and genes on a population scale.

One of the characteristics of our times is thus the rapidity with which
140 steps can be taken to change the orientation of certain trends and even to reverse them. Such changes usually emerge from grassroots movements rather than from official directives.

1. Conditions like those described in Passage A would most likely have occurred about
   (A) 55 A.D.
   (B) 755 A.D.
   (C) 1055 A.D.
   (D) 1455 A.D.
   (E) 1755 A.D.

2. The phrase "with greater avidity" in line 21 is best interpreted to mean with greater
   (A) desire
   (B) sadness
   (C) terror
   (D) silence
   (E) disappointment

3. In Passage A, all of the following are stated or implied about towns in the Middle Ages *except*
   (A) Towns had no suburbs.
   (B) Towns were always quite noisy.
   (C) Towns served as places of defense.
   (D) Towns always had large churches.
   (E) Merchants lived in the towns.

4. The author's main purpose in Passage A is to
   (A) describe the miseries of the period
   (B) show how life was centered on the town
   (C) emphasize the violent course of life at the time
   (D) point out how the upper classes mistreated the lower classes
   (E) indicate how religious people were in those days

5. According to Passage A, people at that time, as compared with people today, were
   (A) worse off
   (B) better off

(C) less intelligent
(D) more subdued
(E) more sensitive to certain events

6. In the first paragraph of Passage B, the mood expressed is one of

(A) blatant despair
(B) guarded optimism
(C) poignant nostalgia
(D) muted pessimism
(E) unbridled idealism

7. According to Passage B, if present trends continue, which one of the following situations will *not* occur?

(A) New sources of energy from vast coal deposits will be substituted for the soon-to-be-exhausted resources of oil and natural gas.
(B) The rich will become richer and the poor will become poorer.
(C) An overpopulated earth will be unable to sustain its inhabitants.
(D) Nuclear weapons will play a more prominent role in dealings among people.
(E) The ravages of pollution will render the earth and its atmosphere a menace to mankind.

8. Which of the following is the best illustration of the meaning of "trend is not destiny" in line 103?

(A) Urban agglomerations are in a state of crisis.
(B) Human beings are blessed with the freedom of social evolution.
(C) The world has become too complex for comprehension by the human brain.
(D) Critical processes can overshoot and cause catastrophes.

(E) The earth will soon be overcrowded and its resources exhausted.

9. According to Passage B, evidences of the insight of the public into the dangers which surround us can be found in all of the following *except*

(A) an increase in the military budget by the president
(B) a declining birth rate
(C) picketing against expansion of nuclear plants
(D) opposition to the use of pesticides
(E) public meetings to complain about dumping chemicals

10. The author's attitude in Passage B is one of

(A) willing resignation
(B) definite optimism
(C) thinly veiled cynicism
(D) carefree abandon
(E) angry impatience

11. If there is a continuity in history, which of the following situations in Passage A is thought in Passage B to lead to violence in the future?

(A) the overcrowding of the population
(B) the executions in public
(C) the contrast between the social classes
(D) the contrast between illness and health
(E) the contrast between religion and politics

12. One can conclude from reading both passages that the difference between the people in Passage A and the people in Passage B is that

(A) the people in Passage B act on their awareness in contrast to the people in Passage A.

(B) the people in Passage B are more intense and colorful than the people in Passage A.

(C) there was no controversy between sociology and science in the society in Passage B in contrast to what was mentioned in Passage A.

(D) the people in Passage A are far more religious.

(E) Sociological changes were faster and more abrupt with the people of Passage A.

13. From a reading of both passages, one may conclude that

(A) people in both passages are equally subservient to authority.

(B) the future is a mirror of the past.

(C) the topic of biological evolution is of great importance to the scientists of both periods.

(D) the evolution of science has created great differences in the social classes.

(E) the people in Passage A are more involved in everyday living, whereas the people in Passage B are usually seeking change.

Explanatory Answers

1. (D) Choice D is correct. Line 1 ("To the world when it was half a thousand years younger . . .") indicates that the author is describing the world roughly 500 hundred years ago. Choice D—1455 A.D.—is therefore the closest date. Although Choice C is also in the Middle Ages, it is almost a thousand years ago.

So it is an incorrect choice. Choices A, B, and E are obviously incorrect choices.

2. (A) Choice A is correct. We can see that "with greater avidity" is an adverbial phrase telling the reader how "honors and riches" were enjoyed and desired. See lines 23–27: "We, at the present day . . . formerly enjoyed." The reader thus learns that even simple pleasures such as a glass of wine were more keenly enjoyed then. Choices B, C, D, and E are incorrect because the passage does *not* state or imply that "with greater avidity" means with greater sadness *or* terror *or* silence *or* disappointment.

3. (B) Choice B is not true—therefore it is the correct choice. See lines 57–61. "The contrast between silence and sound . . . than it is in our lives." The next sentence states that the modern town hardly knows silence. These two sentences together imply that the typical town of the Middle Ages did have periods of silence. Choice A is true—therefore an incorrect choice. See lines 47–49: "A medieval town . . . in extensive suburbs of factories and villas."
Choice C is true—therefore an incorrect choice. See lines 50–52: ". . . it (a medieval town) stood forth . . . with innumerable turrets."
Choice D is true—therefore an incorrect choice. See lines 55–56: ". . . the lofty mass of the churches always remained dominant."
Choice E is true—therefore an incorrect choice. See lines 52–54: "However tall . . . in the aspect of the town."

4. (C) Choice C is correct. Throughout Passage A, the author is indicating the strong, rough, uncontrolled forces that pervaded the period. See, for example, the following references. Lines 14–15: "Misfortunes and poverty were more afflicting than at present." Lines 28–29: "Then, again, all things in life . . . cruel publicity." Lines 38–42: "Executions . . . songs and music." Therefore, Choice C is correct. Choice A is incorrect because the passage speaks of joys as well as miseries. See lines 23–27: "We, at the present day . . . formerly enjoyed." Choice B is incorrect for this reason: Although the author contrasts town and country, he gives no indication as to which was dominant in that society. Therefore, Choice B is incorrect. Choice D is incorrect. The author contrasts how it felt to be rich or poor but he does not indicate that the rich mistreated the poor. Choice E is incorrect because the pious nature of the people in the Middle Ages is only one of the many elements discussed in the passage.

5. Choice E is correct. See lines 7–10: "All experience . . . pain of child-life." Throughout the passage, this theme is illustrated with specific examples. Choices A and B are incorrect because they are one-sided. In the passage, many conditions that may make the Middle Ages seem worse than today are matched with conditions that may make the Middle Ages seem better than today. Choice C is incorrect because nowhere in the passage is intelligence mentioned or implied. Choice D is incorrect because the third paragraph indicates that, far from being subdued, people went about their lives with a great deal of show and pageantry.

6. Choice A is incorrect because the author stops short of outright despair in the last sentence of the first paragraph by tempering the outbursts of the Renaissance scholar with the milder "our times are out of joint." Choices B and E are incorrect because there is no positive feeling expressed in the first paragraph. Choice C is incorrect because there is no feeling of attraction toward an earlier age. Choice D is correct because the negative feeling is not quite full-bodied.

7. (A) There is no mention of energy sources at any point in the selection. Therefore this answer is correct. Choices B, C, D, and E are mentioned in paragraph 2.

8. (B) The positive outlook of the words, "trend is not destiny" is best exemplified by Choice B which implies that man can improve his situation. The other statements are negative or pessimistic pronouncements.

9. (A) The author cites Choices B, C, D, and E in paragraph 5 as examples of renewed public awareness. The reference to the president's increase in the military budget does not indicate evidence of the public's insight regarding a danger.

10. (B) Choices A and C are incorrect because the author is consistently expressing optimism in man's ability to learn from past mistakes. Choice B is the correct answer. Accordingly, Choice D contradicts the realistic tone of the essay. Choice E is not at all characteristic of the writer's attitude.

11. (C) Choice C is correct. See lines 23–27 and lines 88–93. Note that the author in Passage B states that *if* present trends continue, the gap in living standards between the rich and the poor will lead to acts of desperation, including the use of nuclear weapons.

12. (A) Choice A is correct. See lines 114–126. Note, choice B is incorrect: See lines 64–72 and the descriptions in the rest of Passage A. Choice C is incorrect: See lines 131–134. Choice E is incorrect: See lines 138–144.

13. (E) Choice E is correct. See lines 114–144 and lines 64–73 and throughout Passage A. Choice A is incorrect: See lines 142–144. Choice B is incorrect; Passage B says "The future is never a projection of the past (lines 97–98). Choices C and D are incorrect: biological evolution and the evolution of science are not discussed as factors.

STRATEGY 4

Practice Your Reading Skills on Everyday Reading Material

You do not have much opportunity to practice SAT math skills in everyday life. But you have every opportunity in the world to sharpen your reading comprehension skills.

Read selections from any of the following sources:

- Newspaper stories
- Newspaper editorials
- Newspaper political columns
- News magazines (particularly columns and essays)
- Science fact magazines
- Encyclopedia articles
- Nonfiction books
- General interest magazines like *Reader's Digest*

When you read any selection, read it in units of three to six paragraphs—units about the length of an actual SAT selection. As you read it, keep in mind the question types listed in the first strategy of this section. When you are done, go to the list of question types and use them as a guide to make up your own questions for the selection, as if you were a test-maker for the SAT. Then answer your own questions. The practice this will give you will help enormously when you take the SAT. And it will make you a better reader as well.

Practice Exercises

This section contains questions modeled after specific items that appeared in the critical reading sections of recent SATs. It will give you the opportunity to practice the strategies you have learned for answering questions.

Before each question you will see the number of the strategy in this book that will be useful in solving it. However, when you do these practice exercises, try not to look back at the strategies first. See if you can answer the questions without looking back. Look back only if you find you don't know how to approach a question. It's a good idea to put off doing these practice exercises until you are reasonably sure that you have mastered the strategies.

If you get an answer wrong, the discussions after the answers will help you analyze your mistake. Remember, each question in this section is based on an actual SAT question. If you get one of these questions wrong, you might get any similar SAT question wrong too. If you can find where you made your mistake, you'll be able to avoid similar mistakes and add points to your SAT score.

Good luck!

Practice Your Verbal Strategies

Sentence Completion

This set of questions will test your skill in handling sentence completion questions.

1. STRATEGIES No. 1, 2
   Since we have many cornfields in this city, we do not have to _____ corn.
   (A) distribute
   (B) develop
   (C) contain
   (D) import
   (E) eat

2. STRATEGIES No. 1, 2
   Unfortunately, many times insurance companies do not insure the person who really may _____ the insurance.
   (A) sanctify
   (B) appall
   (C) consider
   (D) renege
   (E) need

3. STRATEGIES No. 1, 2
   I never can tolerate a situation which is _____, in other words, where nothing seems to go anywhere.
   (A) abrupt
   (B) uncomfortable
   (C) uncontrollable
   (D) static
   (E) pliant

4. STRATEGY No. 3
   While a television course is not able to _____ a live course, it is still able to teach the _____ aspects of the subject.

   (A) develop . . . necessary
   (B) replace . . . important
   (C) manage . . . relevant
   (D) create . . . negative
   (E) anticipate . . . inconsequential

5. STRATEGY No. 3
   This is a poem which elicits great _____, unlike many which give the impression of utter _____.
   (A) chaos . . . confusion
   (B) understanding . . . happiness
   (C) joy . . . sorrow
   (D) knowledge . . . intelligence
   (E) hatred . . . solemnity

6. STRATEGY No. 4
   By realizing how much _____ the author had, we can how see he created so many books on different subjects.
   (A) intensity
   (B) knowledge
   (C) enthusiasm
   (D) intelligence
   (E) time

7. STRATEGY No. 4
   Although some _____ the performance, most either thought that it was mediocre or actually disliked it.
   (A) enjoyed
   (B) ignored
   (C) belittled
   (D) scrutinized
   (E) considered

8. STRATEGY No. 5

If there is no _____ for the product, _____ promotion alone will not convince people to buy it.

(A) precursor . . . lackadaisical
(B) despondency . . . superficial
(C) need . . . extensive
(D) development . . . stringent
(E) contract . . . expeditious

9. STRATEGY No. 5

Dr. Paul's clear and _____ analysis of the subject won her great literary acclaim.

(A) esoteric
(B) superficial
(C) jaundiced
(D) vestigial
(E) precise

Reading Comprehension

The remainder of the questions in the Verbal Section will test your skill in handling reading comprehension questions. All use the main reading comprehension strategy: STRATEGY No. 1.

Line   Biography is the molding of the disparate and the unshapely facts of an actual life into a coherent form. Writing a biography is an enormously
5 demanding undertaking and the lengthy process of gathering information is only the beginning. The sleuthing must be followed by the incorporation of widely diverse mat-
10 erials into an intelligible and interesting picture—a task that calls for the combined skills of historian, psychologist, and novelist, and for a sense of the multiple contexts within
15 which an individual life enfolds.
  Biographers nowadays are much more interested in the minor characters—because people do not evolve in isolation. The counter picture
20 brings the main character to life. But although all biographers acknowledge the importance of minor characters, and of the small, revealing detail, they seem to be unanimous in
25 their recoil from the "laundry-list" biography, which progresses by massive accumulation of chronolgoical data.
  Attending to the revealing detail, or
30 to the minor characters, does not mean that biographers eschew the more traditional themes of public power and the relationship between important individuals and an era.
35 While there are many different kinds of power—the power of intellect, of literature, the power within relationships—a choice of biographical subjects is usually governed by the
40 desire to show a figure who is a key for her or his generation.

10. Which of these titles best suits the passage?

(A) The Use of Minor Characters in Biography
(B) Current Trends in Biography
(C) Stressing the Main Character in a Biography
(D) The Complex Demands of Writing Biography
(E) Getting the Facts Prior to Writing a Biography

11. According to the passage, which of the following statements is true?

(A) An historian is better equipped than a novelist to write a biography.
(B) A biographer may alter the facts in order to make the book more interesting.
(C) It is proper for a biographer to express freely his/her own opinions about the main character.
(D) Minor characters are generally as important as the main character in a biography.
(E) A duty of a biographer to the reader is to present materials clearly and interestingly.

12. In the passage, a "laundry list" refers to a list of

(A) all the events that a biographer should consider for inclusion in a book.
(B) the unwholesome experiences or actions of some of the characters that are included in the biography.

(C) the day-to-day happenings in the life of the main character in a biography.

(D) the various places that the situations described in a biography have taken place.

(E) the unshapely facts that the biographer reveals in the book.

Line   That one citizen is as good as another is a favorite American axiom, supposed to express the very essense of our Constitution and way
5   of life. But just what do we mean when we utter that platitude? One surgeon is not as good as another. One plumber is not as good as another. We soon become aware of this when
10   we require the attention of either. Yet in political and economic matters we appear to have reached a point where knowledge and specialized training count for very little.
15   A newspaper reporter is sent out on the street to collect the views of various passers-by on such a question as "Should the United States defend El Salvador?" The answer of the barfly
20   who doesn't even know where the country is located, or that it is a country, is quoted in the next edition just as solemnly as that of the college teacher of history. With the basic
25   tenets of democracy—that all men are born free and equal and are entitled to life, liberty, and the pursuit of happiness—no decent American can possibly take issue. But that the
30   opinion of one citizen on a technical subject is just as authoritative as that of another is mainfestly absurd. And to accept the opinions of all comers as having the same value is surely to
35   encourage a cult of mediocrity.

13. Which phrase best expresses the main idea of this passage?
(A) the myth of equality
(B) a distinction about equality

(C) the essence of the Constitution
(D) a technical subject
(E) knowledge and specialized training

14. The author most probably included the example of the question on El Salvador (lines 18–19) in order to
(A) move the reader to rage
(B) show that he is opposed to opinion sampling
(C) show that he has thoroughly researched his project
(D) explain the kind of opinion sampling he objects to
(E) provide a humorous but temporary diversion from his main point

15. The author would be most likely to agree that
(A) Some men are born to be masters; others are born to be servants.
(B) The Constitution has little relevance for today's world.
(C) One should never express an opinion on a specialized subject unless one is an expert on that subject.
(D) Every opinion should be treated equally.
(E) All opinions should not be given equal weight.

Line   Many of the unfavorable changes in the climatic factors in a city can be mitigated or reversed by growing plants, and by installing trees
5   and green belts. Trees have a material effect on the dust content of the city's atmosphere. Comparative measurements taken in thoroughfares lined with trees and those free from trees
10   show that with a comparable traffic flow the dust content in the road lined with trees is about 70% less. The

15 reason for this is mainly that the dust adheres to the surface of the leaves and to the surface of the leaves and branches or settles more easily between the trees because of reduced wind pressure.

20 The reduction in the dust content of the air naturally has an influence on other climatic elements dependent on the dust. As dust is responsible both for the haze canopy (and the consequent reduction in hours

25 in hours of sunshine and other ultraviolet irradiation) and for the increase in fog (due to the condensation of water vapor), a reduction in dust by trees can have a favorable effect on the frequency

30 and density of the haze canopy and fog.

A second important characteristic of trees in city precincts is the influence they exert on temperature

35 and wind movement. Compared with country districts, the temperature in cities is higher. In the hot season of the year, in which the higher temperatures in cities can prove

40 particularly unpleasant, trees can help to ameliorate the climate. In the summer, trees provide areas of shade, which because of the difference in temperature distribution sets

45 up special air currents, which lead, in turn, to a pleasant, gentle wind movement.

Apart from these physically measurable positive characteristics, trees

50 and greenbelts in cities also have an esthetic and psychological function. They make a vital contribution to the beauty of a city and furnish identification points. A public opinion poll

55 in big cities on the question "What appeals to you most about this city?" elicited the reply in most cases that verdure in the city was the prime attraction. Appreciation of this often

60 unconscious attitude of city dwellers toward green belts accounts for the sharp reactions, from representative institutions to the plans of municipal

65 authorities to cut down fine trees to make way for new buildings or to widen streets. As the city dweller is usually able to visit country districts for recreational purposes only on holidays and weekends, trees and parks represent

70 a vital opportunity to install at least a tiny fragment of nature in the city.

16. The most appropriate title for this passage would be

(A) Pollution and City Weather
(B) Trees Go to Town
(C) Can Weather Be Controlled
(D) Trees: Regulators of City Climate
(E) Trees and the Well-Being of Cities

17. Which of the following general differences between city and country climates are stated or implied in the passage?

I. Cities have higher temperatures than the surrounding country areas.
II. Cities have less fog than the surrounding country areas.
III. Cities receive more solar radiation than the surrounding country areas.

(A) I only
(B) III only
(C) I and II
(D) II and III
(E) I, II, and III

18. For what purpose are the two parenthetical statements in the second paragraph used?

(A) To express a cause—then an effect
(B) To express an effect—then a cause
(C) To express two effects
(D) To express two causes
(E) To express neither a cause nor an effect

19. With which of the following statements would the author most likely agree?

(A) Trees are useful and should be planted in cities.

(B) Cars causing pollution should be banned from cities.

(C) Parks in cities waste vital space.

(D) Shade trees cause excess air movement.

(E) Lining streets with trees will result in a minor reduction in airborne dust.

Line   Mist continues to obscure the horizon, but above us the sky is suddenly awash with lavender light. At once the geese respond. Now, as well as
5   their cries, a beating roar rolls across the water as if five thousand housewives have taken it into their heads to shake out blankets all at one time. Ten thousand housewives. It keeps
10   up—the invisible rhythmic beating of all those goose wings—for what seems like a long time. Even Lonnie is held motionless with suspense.
    Then the geese begin to rise. One,
15   two, three hundred—then a thousand at a time—in long horizontal lines that unfurl like pennants across the sky. The horizon actually darkens as they pass. It goes on and on
20   like that, flock after flock, for three or four minutes, each new contingent announcing its ascent with an accelerating roar of cries and wing beats. Then gradually the intervals between
25   flights became longer. I think the spectacle is over, until yet another flock lifts up, following the others in a gradual turn toward the northeastern quadrant of the refuge.
30   Finally the sun emerges from the mist; the mist itself thins a little, uncovering the black line of willows on the other side of the wildlife preserve. I remember to close my
35   mouth—which has been open for some time—and inadvertently shut two or three mosquitoes inside. Only a few straggling geese oar their way across the sun's red surface. Lonnie

40   wears an exasperated, proprietary expression, as if he had produced and directed the show himself and had just received a bad review. "It would have been better with more light," he
45   says; "I can't always guarantee just when they'll start moving." I assure him I thought it was a fantastic sight. "Well," he rumbles,
    "I guess it wasn't too bad."

20. In the descriptive phrase, "shake out blankets all at one time" (line 8), the author is appealing chiefly to the reader's

(A) background
(B) sight
(C) emotions
(D) thoughts
(E) hearing

21. The mood created by the author is one of

(A) tranquility
(B) excitement
(C) sadness
(D) bewilderment
(E) unconcern

22. The main idea expressed by the author about the geese is that they

(A) are spectacular to watch
(B) are unpredictable
(C) disturb the environment
(D) produce a lot of noise
(E) fly in large flocks

23. Judging from the passage, the reader can conclude that

(A) the speaker dislike nature's inconveniences
(B) the geese's timing is predictable
(C) Lonnie has had the experience before
(D) both observers are hunters

(E) the author and Lonnie are the same person

Line   Those who save money are often accused of loving money; but, in my opinion, those who love money most are those who spend it. To them
5   money is not merely a list of dead figures in a bankbook. It is an animate thing, spasmodically restless like the birds in a wood, taking wings to itself, as the poet has said.
10   Money, to the man who enjoys spending, is the perfect companion—a companion all the dearer because it never outstays its welcome. It is responsive to his every mood . . . Age, alas, has
15   blotted out half that world of passionate delight in which I once lived, and to many of the things I once loved I have grown indifferent. The love of money, however, remains. So much
20   do I love it that I feel almost a different person when I have money in my pocket and when I have none. Let me have but money, and, for the time being, I am back among the
25   ardent attachments and illusions of the nursery.
    From all this I am inclined to conclude that the love of money is a form of infantilism. The man who loves
30   money is the man who has never grown up. He has never passed from the world of fairy tales into the world of philosophy (for philosophy, which is the wisdom of the grown man in
35   contrast to the wonder of the child, is as contemptuous of money as it is of jam, sweets, and bubble gum). Money, according to the philosophers, is dross, filthy lucre, an impediment rather
40   than an aid to true happiness. Those who retain the nursery imagination throughout life, however, cannot be persuaded of this. Money they regard as the loveliest gift ever bestowed on

45   a mortal by the wand of a fairy godmother. They are like boys dreaming of a Treasure Island; and their money-bags become almost as dear to them—sometimes,
50   dearer than—their country.

24. According to the first paragraph, money has the quality of

(A) changing a personality
(B) causing restlessness
(C) outstaying its welcome
(D) inspiring greed
(E) retaining the memories of childhood

25. During the author's lifetime, many things have changed for him except his

(A) interest in sports
(B) fear of old age
(C) contempt for philosophy
(D) desire to return to his childhood
(E) love of money

26. Which expression in the second paragraph describes the characteristics of men who like money?

(A) "I am inclined to conclude" (lines 27–28)
(B) "the wisdom of the grown man" (line 34)
(C) "contemptuous of money" (line 36)
(D) "Money . . . is dross, filthy lucre" (lines 37–39)
(E) "like boys dreaming of a Treasure Island" (lines 45–47)

27. The author implies that the "ardent attachments and illusions of the nursery" (lines 25–26) include

(A) bankbooks and checkbooks
(B) animals and birds
(C) jams, sweets, and bubble gum
(D) parents and companions
(E) dross and lucre

Line The theatre is a jungle in which the playwright, the actor, and the director struggle for supremacy. Sometimes the fight goes one way and then, for
5 a time, another. I have lived through the reign of each in turn and now it seems to me the playwright is once more supreme. Pinter, Stoppard, and Gray stalk unchallenged by Olivier
10 and Peter Brook. Once more the audience is invited not only to look and listen but to think as they once thought with Shaw and Galsworthy. There is a rich heritage in the British theatre,
15 but it is not, alas, the heritage of the actor, still less of the director. The playwright must in the final battle always prove the winner. His work, imperishable; his fame, enduring. I
20 write "alas" because although I have tried my hand at both directing and playwriting, I am in essence one of those of whom Shakespeare wrote that we were destined to strut and fret
25 an hour upon the stage and then be heard no more.
   My generation of actors were trained to entice our prey. We kept an eye open, a claw sharpened, even when
30 we professed to slumber. However deep the tragedy or shallow the farce, we never forgot to face front. Nowadays, the relation between player and public tends to be more sophisticated.
35 Together they share a mutual experience of pain and sorrow. Sometimes the actor seems able to dispense

with his audience—to no longer need them. He may choose or chance to
40 perfect his performances on a wet afternoon in Shewsbury, with hardly anyone watching, and thereafter the repetition for him may stale. For me this never happens. I never perfect a
45 performance, though obviously I am sometimes better or worse, but I have learned that without a perfect audience, my struggle to the summit is impossible. I am aware as the curtain
50 rises of the texture of the house.

28. According to the passage, Pinter, Stoppard, and Gray are involved with the theatre as
(A) theatre owners
(B) actors
(C) playwrights
(D) directors
(E) investors

29. The author believes that the audience
(A) is vital
(B) is a necessary evil
(C) is largely irrelevant
(D) would rather not think
(E) prefers comedy to tragedy

30. According to the passage, what is the author's usual occupation in the theater?
(A) playwright
(B) director
(C) reviewer
(D) producer
(E) actor

Line Many archeologists assume that Ice Age animal images represent only a form of hunting magic. The hunter, so the theory runs, made an

5 animal image and "killed" it, then went out and hunted with the power of magic on his side. Still other archeologists theorize that the animals were totems—figures of ancestor animals 10 from which different human groups or clans supposedly descended. The animals have also been interpreted as sexual symbols, with certain species representing the male principle and 15 others the female. I was now to ask new questions.

When I put the Vogelherd horse under the microscope, I discovered that its ear, nose, mouth and eye had 20 been carefully and accurately carved, but that these features had been worn down by long handling. The figure had obviously been kept by its owner and used for a considerable period. 25 Clearly it had not been created for the purpose of being "killed" at once.

But in the shoulder of the horse was engraved one unworn angle that I took to represent a dart or wound. 30 Apparently some time late in the use of this figure, it had been killed. But why? Was the killing intended as hunting magic? Perhaps. But if Cro-Magnon was as sophisticated as I was beginning to 35 find he was, could the killing not have been for some other symbolic purpose, such as initiation, the casting of a spell, the curing of illness, a sacrifice for the coming of winter, or the celebration 40 for the coming spring?

Whatever the meaning, here was an indication that Ice Age images, like notations and certain tools, were made to be kept and used over a long 45 period for specific purposes.

31. In line 9, the dash is used to

(A) take the place of a semicolon

(B) set off a definition
(C) introduce a list
(D) indicate that something has been left out
(E) offer relatively unimportant information

32. What does the passage imply about the author?

(A) He is not familiar with Cro-Magnon man's hunting strategies
(B) He has personally examined numerous Ice Age artifacts
(C) He has found new evidence about Cro-Magnon man from recent diggings
(D) He has known about the significance of the Vogelherd horse for a long time
(E) He was the first scientist to learn of the existence of the Vogelherd horse

33. Which sentence best summarizes the main idea of this passage?

(A) "Many archeologists assume that Ice Age animal images represent only a form of hunting magic." (lines 1 through 3)
(B) "I was now to ask new questions" (lines 15 and 16)
(C) "Clearly it had not been created for the purpose of being 'killed' at once." (lines 25–26)
(D) "But in the shoulder of the horse was engraved one unknown angle that I took to represent a dart or wound." (lines 27 through 29)
(E) "Whatever the meaning, here was an indication that Ice Age images, like notations and certain tools, were made to be kept over a long period or for specific purposes." (lines 41 through 45)

34. The overall tone of this passage may be described as

(A) argumentative
(B) suspended
(C) questioning
(D) humorous
(E) resentful

Line It was at Arles, the small city in the south of France where he stayed from early 1888 to the spring of 1889, that Vincent van Gogh had his first real
5 bout with madness. After a quarrel with Paul Gauguin, he cut off part of his own ear. Yet Arles was also the scene of an astonishing burst of creativity. Over the short span of 15
10 months, van Gogh produced some 200 paintings and more than 100 drawings and watercolors, a record that only Picasso has matched in the modern era. Orchards and wheatfields
15 under the glowing sun, neighbors and townspeople, interiors of the Yellow House where he lived, were all subjects of his frenetic brush. The Arles canvases, alive with color—vermilion,
20 emerald green, Prussian blue and a particularly brilliant yellow—have intensity of feeling that mark the high point of his career, and deeply affected the work of artists to follow, notably the Fauves
25 and the German Expressionists.

Van Gogh went to Arles after two years in Paris, where his beloved younger brother Theo, who supported him psychologically and financially
30 for most of his adult life, was an art dealer. In Paris, Vincent had met Gauguin, and other important artists— Lautrec, Degas, Pissarro, and Seurat. Like the last two, he worked in the
35 Neo-Impressionist or Pointillist style— applying color in tiny dots or strokes

that "mixed" in the viewer's eye to create effects of considerable intensity. But he wanted "gayer" colors than
40 Paris provided, the kind of atmosphere evoked by the Japanese prints he so admired. Then, too, the French capital had exhausted him, mentally and physically. He felt that
45 in Arles, not exactly a bustling art center, he might find serenity, and even establish an artistic tradition.

It was van Gogh's hope of founding a new artists' colony in the south that
50 made him eager to have Gauguin, whose talent van Gogh readily recognized, join him at Arles. The plan, on Vincent's part, was for Gauguin to stay in Arles for maybe a year, working
55 and sharing with him the small living quarters and studio he had found for himself and dubbed the Yellow House. At first, the two men got along well. But they did not at all agree on judg-
60 ments of other artists. Gauguin began pushing the younger artist to paint from memory rather than actuality.

Before the year was up, whether because of Gauguin's attempts to
65 change van Gogh's style, or what, the two men had apparently begun to get on each other's nerves. Gauguin wrote to Theo that he felt he had to return to Paris, citing his and Vincent's
70 "temperamental incompatibility." A letter from Vincent to Theo followed, noting that Gauguin was "a little out of sorts with the good town of Arles, and especially with me."
75 But then, the two apparently made up—but not for long. Gauguin returned to Paris and never saw van Gogh again, although they later had friendly correspondence.

35. Which of the following is the best title for the passage?

   (A) Where Van Gogh's Art Reached Its Zenith

   (B) An Unfortunate Mismatch Between Two Great Artists

   (C) Another Tale of a Genius Unable to Adjust to Society

   (D) A Prolific Painter Whose Art Will Live On

   (E) Van Gogh's Frustration in His Hope to Found a New Artists' Colony

36. According to the passage, which of the following statements is not true?

   (A) Fauvism is a movement in painting typified by vivid colors.

   (B) Gauguin was an older man than Theo.

   (C) Pissarro was a painter associated with the Neo-Impressionist school.

   (D) Van Gogh's work began to deteriorate after Gauguin's departure from Arles.

   (E) Van Gogh's behavior was, at times, quite abnormal.

37. For which of the following reasons did van Gogh decide to leave Paris and go to Arles?

   I. He sought a different environment for the kind of painting he wished to do.

   II. He had hopes of forming a new artists' colony.

   III. He wanted a more peaceful location where there was less stress.

   (A) II only

   (B) III only

   (C) I and II only

   (D) I and III only

   (E) I, II, and III

38. Gauguin's attitude toward van Gogh is best described in the passage as one of

   (A) gentle ridicule

   (B) unallayed suspicion

   (C) tolerant acceptance

   (D) open condescension

   (E) resentful admiration

39. Aside from his quarrel with Gauguin, we may infer that a major contributory reason for van Gogh's going to the extreme of cutting off part of his ear was his

   (A) concern about being able to support himself financially

   (B) inability to get along with Gauguin

   (C) failure to form an artists' colony in Arles

   (D) mental and emotional instability

   (E) being upset by Gauguin's attempts to change his style

Line   As in the case of so many words used by the biologist and physiologist, the word *acclimatization* is hard to define. With increase in knowledge

5   and understanding, meanings of word change. Originally the term *acclimatization* was taken to mean only the ability of human beings or animals or plants to accustom themselves to

10   new and strange climatic conditions, primarily altered temperature. A person or a wolf moves to a hot climate and is uncomfortable there, but after a time is better able to withstand the

15   heat. But aside from temperature, there are other aspects of climate. A person or an animal may become adjusted to living at higher altitudes than those it was originally accus

20   tomed to. At really high altitudes, such as aviators might be exposed to, the

low atmospheric pressure becomes a factor of primary importance.

In changing to a new environment, a person may, therefore, meet new conditions of temperature or pressure, and in addition may have to contend with different chemical surroundings. On high mountains, the amount of oxygen in the atmosphere may be relatively small; in crowded cities, a person may become exposed to relatively high concentrations of carbon dioxide or even carbon monoxide, and in various areas may be exposed to conditions in which the water content of the atmosphere is extremely high or extremely low. Thus in the case of humans, animals, and even plants, the concept of acclimatization includes the phenomena of increased toleration of high or low temperature, of altered pressure and of changes in the chemical environment. Let us define acclimatization, therefore, as the process in which an organism or a part of an organism becomes accustomed or inured to an environment which is normally unsuitable to it or lethal for it. By and large, acclimatization is a relatively slow process. The term should not be taken to include relatively rapid adjustments such as our sense organs are constantly making. This type of adjustment is commonly referred to by physiologists as "adaptation." Thus our touch sense soon becomes accustomed to the pressure of our clothes and we do not feel them; we soon fail to hear the ticking of a clock; obnoxious odors after a time fail to make much impression on us, and our eyes in strong light rapidly become insensitive. The fundamental fact about acclimatization is that all animals and plants have some capacity to adjust themselves to changes in their environment. This is one of the most remarkable characteristics of living organisms, a characteristic for which it is extremely difficult to find explanations.

40. According to the reading selection, all animals and plants

(A) have an ability for acclimatization.
(B) can adjust to only one change in the environment at a time.
(C) are successful in adjusting themselves to changes in their environments.
(D) can adjust to natural changes in the environment but not to artificially induced changes.
(E) that have once acclimatized themselves to an environmental change can acclimatize themselves more rapidly to subsequent changes.

41. It can be inferred from the reading selection that

(A) every change in the environment requires acclimatization by living things.
(B) plants and animals are more alike than they are different.
(C) biologists and physiologists study essentially the same things.
(D) the explanation of acclimatization is specific to each plant and animal.
(E) as science develops the connotation of terms may change.

42. According to the reading selection, acclimatization

    (A) is similar to adaptation.
    (B) is more important today than formerly.
    (C) involves positive as well as negative adjustment.
    (D) may be involved with a part of an organism but not with the whole organism.
    (E) is more difficult to explain with the more complex present-day environment than formerly.

43. By inference from the reading selection, which one of the following would not require the process of acclimatization?

    (A) An ocean fish placed in a lake
    (B) A skin diver making a deep dive
    (C) An airplane pilot making a high-altitude flight
    (D) A person going from daylight into a darkened room
    (E) A businessman moving from Denver, Colorado, to New Orleans, Louisiana

44. According to the passage, a major distinction between acclimatization and adaptation is that acclimatization

    (A) is more important than adaptation.
    (B) is relatively slow and adaptation is relatively rapid.
    (C) applies to adjustments while adaptation does not apply to adjustments.
    (D) applies to terrestrial animals and adaptation to aquatic animals.
    (E) is applicable to all animals and plants and adaptation only to higher animals and human beings.

Social Science Double Passage

Below are two excerpts from speeches that were made more than 2,000 years apart and yet have much in common; both speeches address the issue of democracy and both concern those who had recently given their lives defending their government.

The first was reportedly made in 431 B.C. by the Greek general Pericles shortly after the outbreak of the Peloponnesian War; the second was delivered during the American Civil War at Gettysburg, Pennsylvania, on November 19, 1863, by President Abraham Lincoln.

PASSAGE A—Athens, Greece

Line   Many of those who have spoken here in the past have praised the institution of this speech at the close of our ceremony. It seemed to them

5   a mark of honor to our soldiers who have fallen in war that a speech should be made over them. I do not agree. These men have shown themselves valiant in action, and it would be enough, I think,

10 for their glories to be proclaimed in action, as you have just seen it done at this funeral organized by the state. Our belief in the courage of so many should not be hazarded on the good-
15 ness or badness of any single speech.

Let me say that our system of government does not copy the institutions of our neighbors. It is more the case of our being a model to others
20 than of our imitating anyone else. Our constitution is called a democracy because power is in the hands not of a minority but of the whole people. When it is a question of settling
25 private disputes, everyone is equal before the law; when it is a question of putting one person before another in positions of public responsibility, what counts is not membership
30 in a particular class, but the actual ability that the individual possesses. No one who could be of service to the state is kept in political obscurity because of poverty. And, just
35 as our political life is free and open, so is our day-to-day life in our relations with each other. We do not get into a state with our neighbors if they enjoy themselves in their own
40 way, nor do we give anyone the kind of frowning looks that, though they do no real harm, still hurt people's feelings. We are free and tolerant in our private lives; but in public affairs
45 we keep to the law. This is because it commands our great respect . . .

They gave Athens their lives, to her and to all of us, and for their own selves they won praises that
50 never grow old, the most splendid of sepulchers—not the sepulcher in which their bodies are laid, but where their glory remains eternal in others' minds, always there on the right
55 occasion to stir them to speech or to action. For the famous have the whole earth for their tomb: it is not only the inscriptions on their graves in their own country that marks

60 them out; no, in foreign lands also, not in any visible form but in people's hearts, their memory abides and grows. It is for you to try to be like them. Make up your minds that
65 happiness depends on being free, and freedom depends on being courageous. Let there be no relaxation in the face of the perils of war . . .

PASSAGE B—Gettysburg, Pennsylvania

Line   But, in a larger sense, we cannot dedicate—we cannot consecrate—we cannot hallow—this ground. The brave men, living and dead, who struggled
5 here, have consecrated it far above our poor power to add or detract. The world will little note nor long remember what we say here, but it can never forget what they did here. It is for
10 us, the living, rather, to be dedicated here to the unfinished work which they who fought here have thus far so nobly advanced. It is rather for us to be here dedicated to the great task
15 remaining before us—that from these honored dead we take increased devotion to the cause for which they gave their last full measure of devotion; that we here highly resolve that these
20 dead shall not have died in vain; that this nation under God, shall have a new birth of freedom; and that government of the people, by the people, for the people, shall not perish from
25 the earth.

45. Why does Pericles "not agree" (line 7) that a speech such as the one he is giving can further honor fallen soldiers?

(A) Public officials give too many boring speeches.
(B) Fallen soldiers are seldom the subject of speeches.
(C) Past speakers concentrated too much on winning personal fame.

(D) The potential inadequacies of the speech could detract from the glory of the fallen soldiers.

(E) The glory achieved in battle is best remembered by loved ones, not by public officials.

46. The word "state" in line 38 means

(A) stage of development
(B) political unit
(C) declaration
(D) luxury
(E) furor

47. In the second paragraph of Passage A, Pericles primarily stresses that

(A) a democratic spirit will help Athens win the war.
(B) Athens will always be remembered.
(C) people in neighboring countries envy Athenians.
(D) the customs of others seem strange to Athenians.
(E) the Athenian form of government is an admirable one.

48. Which best summarizes the reason given in Passage A for the soldiers having earned "praises that never grow old" (lines 49–50)?

(A) People in foreign lands will praise the Greeks for ages.
(B) Memorials dedicated to heroic events will always be honored.
(C) The Athenians will honor their military heroes annually.
(D) The memory of great feats will repeatedly inspire others.
(E) Relatives and friends of the heroes will never forget them.

49. It can be inferred from the content and tone of Passage A that Pericles' primary feeling was one of

(A) sadness because Athens had lost so many courageous soldiers.
(B) dismay at his responsibility to guide the Athenians safely.
(C) annoyance because the Athenians might not appreciate the sacrifices that had been made for them.
(D) concern about whether the audience would agree with his views.
(E) pride in Athens and determination that it would continue into the future.

50. In Passage B, the word "consecrate" (line 2) means

(A) absolve
(B) adore
(C) make sacred
(D) begin praising
(E) enjoy properly

51. The "unfinished work" referred to in line 11 is the

(A) battle of Gettysburg
(B) defense of freedom
(C) establishment of a government
(D) dedication of the battlefield
(E) honoring of the fallen soldiers

52. Which statement from Passage A does NOT have a parallel idea conveyed in Passage B?

(A) "These men have shown themselves valiant in action" (lines 7–8)
(B) "our system of government does not copy the institutions of our neighbors" (lines 16–18)
(C) "They gave Athens their lives, to her and to all of us" (lines 47–48)

(D) "It is for you to try to be like them" (lines 63–64)

(E) "freedom depends on being courageous" (lines 66–67)

53. Which statement is best supported by a comparison of the two excerpts?

(A) Both excerpts urge an end to existing hostilities.

(B) Both excerpts are appeals to the audience for personal political support.

(C) Both excerpts emphasize the cruelty of the opponents of the state.

(D) The intent and the development of ideas in both excerpts are similar.

(E) The purpose of both excerpts is to prepare the audience for the eventual outbreak of war.

Answers to Sentence Completion Questions

1. D. Key words: *since, have.* We don't have to import corn since we have cornfields.

2. E. Key words: *unfortunately, really*

3. D. Key words: *in other words.* Translate the words following the key-word phrase: "where nothing seems to go anywhere" into the word *static.*

4. B. Use the positive-negative approach. Key words: *while* (meaning "although"), *still.* The key words tell you that the two clauses of the sentence are being contrasted. The first clause is negative, with a *not* in it. The second clause must therefore be positive. Choice B makes the best sense with this construction.

5. C. Also a sentence with two contrasting parts, as shown by the key word *unlike.* Choice C, with two words that are antonyms, fits the bill.

6. B. Work backwards from the second part of the sentence. The key words *we*

can see how . . . show that the second part of the sentence must follow logically from the first. Since the author created books on many different subjects, he must have had a lot of *knowledge.*

7. A. Again, work backwards. Key words: *although, most, mediocre, disliked.* If most people disliked the performance, the obvious contrast is that some *enjoyed* it.

8. C. Don't be scared or led astray by difficult words in choices, like *lackadaisical, stringent,* and *expeditious.* They may not be correct. The sentence seems to make most sense using the easy words *need* and *extensive.*

9. E. Again, don't be scared by difficult words like *esoteric, jaundiced, vestigial. Precise* is correct (since the missing word is joined by *and* to the word *clear,* the word is probably a near-synonym of *clear). Precise* fits the bill.

Answers to Reading Comprehension Questions

10. D	19. A	28. C	37. E	46. E
11. E	20. E	29. A	38. C	47. E
12. A	21. B	30. E	39. D	48. D
13. B	22. A	31. B	40. A	49. E
14. D	23. C	32. B	41. E	50. C
15. E	24. A	33. E	42. A	51. B
16. E	25. E	34. C	43. D	52. B
17. A	26. E	35. A	44. B	53. D
18. B	27. C	36. D	45. D	

MATH PREP, SHORTCUTS, AND STRATEGIES

Math Prep

This chapter contains material specifically designed to prepare you for the detailed math strategies that follow. The chapter is organized with three sections:

- **Test Yourself** enables you to find out quickly where you need to brush up on your math.
- **Correct Yourself** gives you the answers to the test questions—plus instructions on each test problem so that you can tutor yourself on any problem area.
- **Arm Yourself** contains instructional summaries of the principal math formulas and equivalencies that you need to know to use the math strategies effectively.

Test Yourself

Spend 30 minutes or less taking the test on the following pages. The questions on this test are much easier than the ones on the actual SAT. Nevertheless, do not skip over this section! The test is a review and summary of the principal mathematical operations that the SAT test-makers use as the basis for constructing their test questions! So this entire section is actually a *giant basic strategy.* You must know *all* this material to perform successfully on the SAT and to understand—and use—the specific math strategies outlined in the rest of this book.

When you have finished the test, go on to the next section, **Correct Yourself.** There you will find the answers to the **Test Yourself** questions, plus additional instruction.

Remember: you must be able to get every question correct, and understand why, before you go on with the rest of the book.

These questions test your ability and background in working with FACTORS.

1. $(x + 5)(x - 4) =$ _____

2. $(x - y)^2 =$ _____

3. $-(x - y) =$ _____

4. Factor: $a^2 - b^2$ _____

These questions test your ability and background in working with EXPONENTS.

5. $10^4 =$ _____

6. $x^3 \times x^8 =$ _____

7. $(xy)^5 =$ _____

8. $a^{-4} \times a^{+5} =$ _____

9. What is x^{-4} written with no negative signs? _____

10. If $x^2 = 4$, what is x? _____

11. Find: $2^2 + 4^2$ _____

These questions test your ability and background in working with PERCENTS.

12. 22% of 100 = _____

13. What is 8% of 4? _____

14. What percent of 7 is 14? _____

These questions test your ability and background in working with EQUATIONS.

15. What is y in terms of x given $y - x = 5$? _____

16. Find the value of x and y:

$x + 2y = 3; x - 2y = 1$ _____

These questions test your ability and background in working with ANGLES.

17.

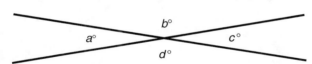

In the diagram above, what is the value of

    (1) $a + b$ (2) $a - c$
    (3) $a + b + c + d$ (4) $b - d$?

    (1) _____ (2) _____ (3) _____
    (4) _____

18. What is the value of $a + b + c$ in the diagram below?

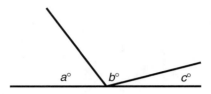

These questions test your ability and background in working with TRIANGLES.

19. In the diagram below, is $a + b$ greater than c?

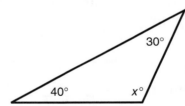

20. In the diagram below, what is the value of x?

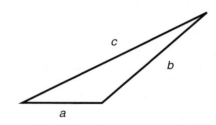

21. In the diagram below, what is y?

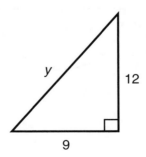

22. In the diagram below, what is *a*?

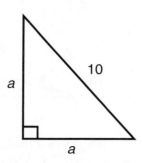

23. What is the area of the triangle below?

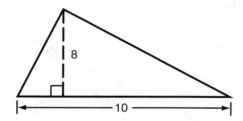

These questions test your ability and background in working with CIRCLES.

24. Find the area and the circumference of the circle:

area = _____

circumference = _____

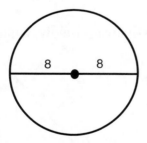

25. If *AB* is a diameter of the circle, what is *y*?

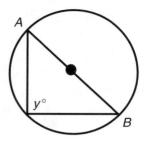

This question tests your ability and background in working with PARALLEL LINES.

26. In the diagram below, where l_1 and l_2 are parallel, what is the value of *a, b, c, d,* and *e*?

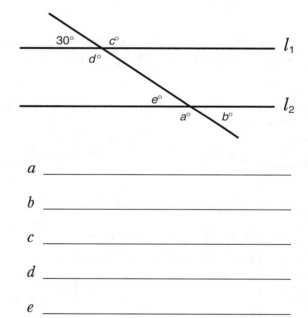

a _____

b _____

c _____

d _____

e _____

This question tests your ability and background in working with NUMBER LINES.

27. Use the signs > (greater than), < (less than), or = (equal) to determine the relative values of a and b:

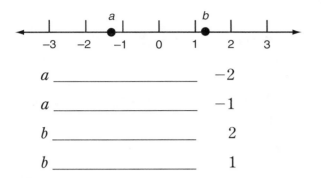

a _____ -2

a _____ -1

b _____ 2

b _____ 1

This question tests your ability and background in working with COORDINATES.

28. From the diagram below, determine which variables (a, b, c, d) are positive or negative:

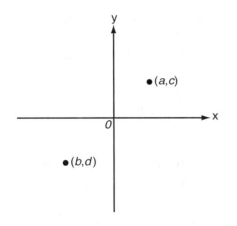

a (positive or negative?) _____

b (positive or negative?) _____

c (positive or negative?) _____

d (positive or negative?) _____

29.

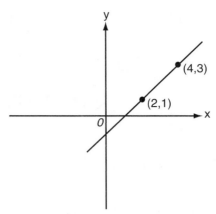

What is the slope of the line above?

_____

These questions test your ability and background in working with INEQUALITIES.

30. If $a > b$, is $3a > 3b$? _____

31. If $a + b > c$, is $a > c - b$? _____

32. If $-3 < p < +3$, is $+3 > -p > -3$? _____

33. If $a < b$, is $na < nb$? _____

These questions test your ability and background in working with AVERAGES.

34. What is the average score in a class of 3 students whose scores are 45, 60, and 90 on an exam? _____

35. What is the average rate of speed of a bicycle traveling 30 miles in 3 hours?

_____

Explanatory Answers with Shortcuts, Strategies, and General Math Review

Correct Yourself

FACTORS

1.

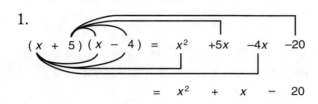

$$= x^2 + x - 20$$

Multiply *each* quantity in the first factor with *each* quantity in the second factor. That is,

- Multiply x by x to get x^2
- Multiply 5 by x to get $5x$
- Multiply x by -4 to get $-4x$
- Multiply 5 by -4 to get -20

  Then add:

  $$x^2 + 5x - 4x - 20 = x^2 + x - 20$$

  In general,

  $$(x + y)(s + t) = xs + ys + xt + yt$$

2. Memorize (after working out to convince yourself):

   $$(x - y)^2 = x^2 - 2xy + y^2$$
   $$(x + y)^2 = x^2 + 2xy + y^2$$

3. Memorize (after working out to convince yourself):

   $$-(x - y) = -x + y$$
   $$x(y + z) = xy + xz$$

$$-(x + y) = -x - y$$
$$x(y - z) = xy - xz$$

4. Memorize (after working out to convince yourself):

   $$a^2 - b^2 = (a + b)(a - b)$$

EXPONENTS

5. $10^4 = 10\,000$ $10^5 = 1\,00\,000$
      4 zeros   *5 zeros*

6. $x^3 \times x^8 = x^{11}$
   In general, for any a, b, and x:
   $x^a \times x^b = x^{a+b}$
   (To multiply, add exponents.)

7. $(xy)^5 = x^5 y^5$
   In general, for any n, x, and y:
   $(xy)^n = x^n y^n$

8. $a^{-4} \times a^{+5} = a^{(-4+5)} = a^{+1} = a$
   In general, for any n, m and a:

   $$a^{-n} \times a^{+m} = a^{m-n}; \frac{a^m}{a^{m-n}}$$

9. $x^{-4} = \frac{1}{x^4}$

   Don't be afraid of negative exponents.

   In general, for any n, $x^{-n} = \frac{1}{x^n}$

10. If $x^2 = 4$, $x = \pm\sqrt{2} = \pm 2$ (Read as "plus or minus two.")

    If $x^2 = n$, then $x = \pm\sqrt{n}$ (Don't forget the $\pm$ sign!)

11. $2^2 + 4^2 = 2 \times 2 + 4 \times 4 = 4 + 16 = 20$

    $2^2 = 2 \times 2$; $2^3 = 2 \times 2 \times 2$; etc.

    $n^4 = n \times n \times n \times n$ (four times)

PERCENTS

12. 22% of $100 = \dfrac{22}{100} \times 100$

    of becomes $\times$, % becomes $\dfrac{1}{100}$

    So, we get

    22% of 100 =

    $22 \quad \dfrac{1}{100} \quad \times \quad 100 = \dfrac{22}{100} \times 100 = 22$

13. What is 8% of 4? Remember to *translate:*

    What becomes x variable x or unknown x)

    %   becomes $\times$ $\dfrac{1}{100}$

    is   becomes $=$ (equals)

    of   becomes $\times$ (times)

    So, what is 8   %   of 4

    $\quad\quad\quad\quad 8 \quad (\frac{1}{100})$

    $x \quad = \quad \dfrac{8}{100} \quad \times \quad 4 = \dfrac{32}{100}$ or .32

    (You could reduce the fraction further, if you wished, to $\dfrac{8}{25}$.)

14.

    What percent of 7 is 14?

    $(x) \quad (\frac{1}{100}) \quad \times \quad 7 \quad = \quad 14$

    $\dfrac{x}{100} \times 7 = 14; \dfrac{x}{100} = 2; x = \mathbf{200\%}$

EQUATIONS

15. If $y - x = 5$ and we want to solve for y alone, let's *add x* to both sides of the equation:

    $y - x + x = 5 + x$

    $\quad\quad y = 5 + x$

    If we had to find what x was in terms of y, we would still add x to both sides:

    $y - x + x = 5 + x$

    $\quad\quad y = 5 + x$

    Then we would subtract 5 from both sides:

    $y - 5 = 5 + x - 5$

    $y - 5 = x$

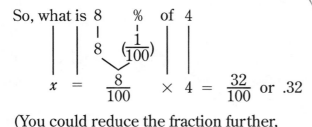

16. What is the value of x and y if:

    $x + 2y = 3$

    $x - 2y = 1$

    Let's add both equations:

    $\quad x + 2y = 3$

    $+ \ x - 2y = 1$

    Adding left sides we get:

    $x + x + 2y - 2y = 2x$

Adding right sides we get: $3 + 1 = 4$

Now we equate left and right sides:
$2x = 4; x = 2.$

Now take the value $x = 2$, and put this value *back* into any one of the equations. Let's work with $x + 2y = 3$. If $x = 2$, then we get:

$$2 + 2y = 3$$
$$2y = 3 - 2$$
$$2y = 1$$
$$y = \frac{1}{2}$$

ANGLES

17.

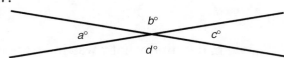

Vertical angles are equal, so $a = c$, and $b = d$.

a and b are *supplementary* angles. So are c and d, a and d, and c and b. So we get:

$a = c, b = d$

$a + b = 180; c + d = 180; a + d = 180; c + b = 180$
Thus:

(1) $a + 0 = \mathbf{180°}$

(2) $a - c = 0°$ (since $a = c$)

(3) $a + b + c + d = 180 + 180 = \mathbf{360°}$

(4) $b - d = \mathbf{0°}$ (since $b = d$)

18.

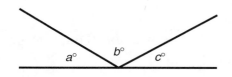

$a + b + c = \mathbf{180°}$

TRIANGLES

19. For any triangle,
$a + b > c,$

$c + a > b; b + c > a$

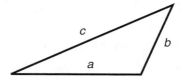

Look at the following triangle:

If $\angle A > \angle B$ then $a > b$

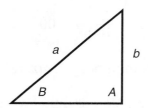

20.

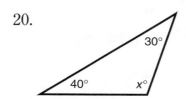

The sum of the interior angles in a triangle $= 180°$

So,

$$30 + 40 + x = 180°$$

$$70 + x = 180$$

$$x = 180 - 70 = \mathbf{110°}$$

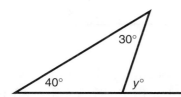

Another useful thing for you to know is that an *exterior angle* (like $y°$ above) is *equal* to the *sum of the remote interior angles* (that is, in the above diagram, $y = 30 + 40$).

Suppose we have the following triangle:

If sides are equal, base angles are equal.

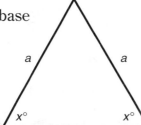

21.

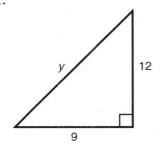

The Pythagorean Theorem:

for a right triangle (one angle = 90°)

$$9^2 + 12^2 = y^2$$

$$81 + 144 = y^2$$

$$225 = y^2$$

$$\sqrt{225} = y$$

$$15 = y$$

In general:

$$a^2 + b^2 = c^2$$

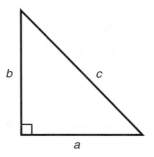

Memorize these right triangles:

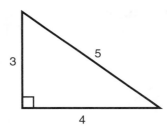

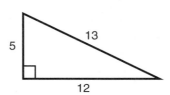

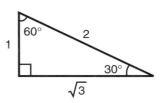

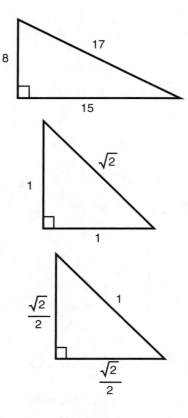

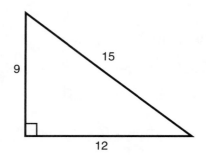

The reason it is important to be familiar with these right triangles (9,12,15; 3,4,5, etc.) is the following. You may be given a right triangle with sides, for example, of 9 and 12. And you may have to find what the third side is. Well, if you know there's a right triangle that has sides 9,12, and 15, you will immediately realize that the third side of a right triangle of sides 9 and 12 is 15. And so you don't have to do any calculation.

22. $a^2 + a^2 = 10^2$

$$2a^2 = 10^2$$

$$a^2 = \frac{100}{2}$$

$$a^2 = 50$$

$$a^2 = \sqrt{50}$$

$$= \sqrt{25 \times 2}$$

$$= \mathbf{5\sqrt{2}}$$

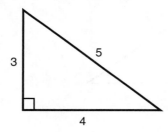

Note that you may multiply each side of the above triangles by a **constant:**

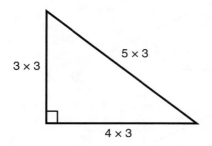

or look at the following triangle: Multiply each side by 10:

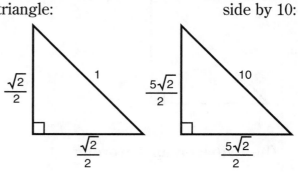

So we get $a = 5\sqrt{2}.$

23.

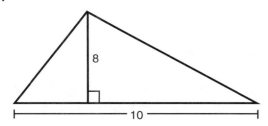

Area = $\frac{1}{2}$ (8) × 10 = 4 × 10 = 40

In general:

Area = $\frac{1}{2}$ hb

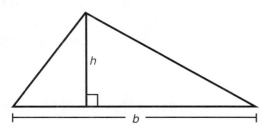

or if we have:

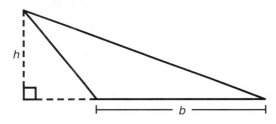

Area is still $\frac{1}{2}$ hb

Area of rectangle = h × b

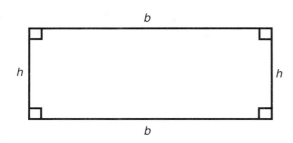

Area of parallelogram = $h \times b$

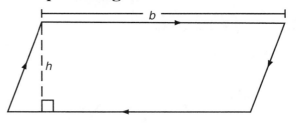

CIRCLES

24. **Area** = πr^2 = $(8)^2$ = **64π**

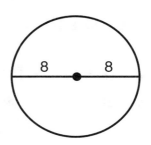

Circumference = $2\pi r$

$= 2\pi(8) = \mathbf{16\pi}$

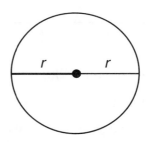

25. If AB is diameter of circle, then arc AB is 180°.

$y°$ is measured by $\frac{1}{2}$ arc

so $y = \frac{1}{2}$ (180) = **90°**.

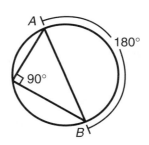

In general: An inscribed angle is measured by $\frac{1}{2}$ the arc it cuts.

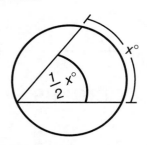

PARALLEL LINES

26. $f + d = 180$; $f + c = 180$;

$e + d = 180$; $a + e = 180$;

$a + b = 180$; $e = g$, $d = h$,

$e = b$, $f = g$, $f = e$, $c = h$

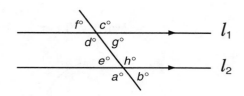

So if we have $f = 30$,

then $d = 150$ and $e = 30$

$a = d = \mathbf{150}$, $b = e = \mathbf{30}$,

$c = d = \mathbf{150}$, $d = 150$, $e = \mathbf{30}$

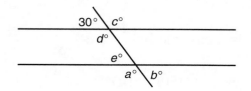

NUMBER LINES

27.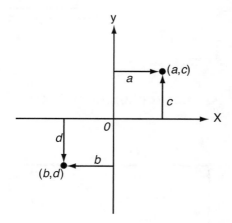

a is between -1 and -2 so $-2 < a < -1$ and so $a < -1$, $a > -2$

b is between $+1$ and $+2$ so, $1 < b < 2$, and so $b < 2$, and $b > 1$

If you have trouble remembering the difference between $>$ and $<$, try remembering that the "open mouth" of the symbol is always on the side of the greater quantity. So $a > b$ means that a is greater; $a < b$ means that b is greater than a.

COORDINATES

28. a is to the *right* so it is **positive**

b is to the *left* so it is **negative**

c is *up* so it is **positive**

d is *down* so it is **negative**

In general:

$$m > 0; n > 0; p < 0;$$

$$q > 0; a < 0;$$

$$b < 0; c > 0; d < 0$$

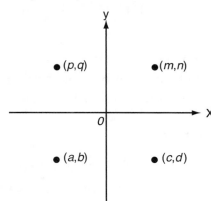

From the graph at right the

length $AB = = \sqrt{3^2 + 4^2} = \sqrt{5^2} = 5$

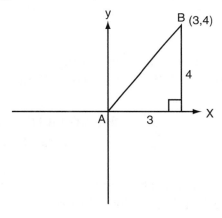

29.

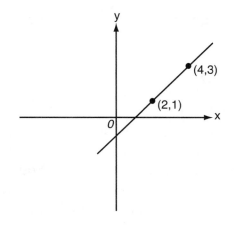

The slope of a line $y = mx + b$ is m. If two points (x_1, y_1) and (x_2, y_2) are on

the line then the slope is $\dfrac{y_2 - y_1}{x_2 - x_1} = m$.

Here $x_1 = 2, y_1 = 1, x_2 = 4, y_2 = 3$ so

$$\frac{y_2 - y_1}{x_2 - x_1} = \frac{3 - 1}{4 - 2} = 1$$

If two lines are perpendicular, the slope of one is the negative reciprocal of the other.

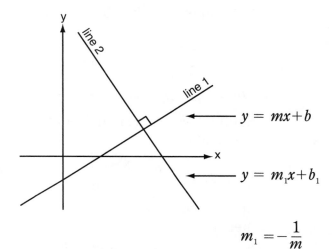

$$m_1 = -\frac{1}{m}$$

Example: What is the slope of a line perpendicular to the line $y = -3x + 4$? Since the slope of the line $y = -3x + 4$ is -3, the slope of the line perpendicular to that line is the negative reciprocal or $-1/-3 = + 1/3$.

INEQUALITIES

30. If $a > b$, is $3a > 3b$?

We work with **inequalities** almost the same way that we work with **equalities**. For example:

$$3 = 3$$

Multiply both sides by 2:

We get: $\qquad 2 \times 3 = 2 \times 3$

So suppose we have

$$3 > 2$$

We can multiply (or divide) both sides of the inequality by the same positive number and still get the same inequality sign. Let's multiply both sides of the inequality $3 > 2$ by 5.

We get: $5 \times 3 > 5 \times 2$

So, as an example, if $a > b$, then **$3a > 3b$**.

Note that if we multiply an inequality by $a -$ (minus) sign we must *reverse* the order of the inequality. That is, if $a > b$ and we multiply by -1, we get $-a < -b$.

31. If $a + b > c$, is $a > c - b$?

Work as if we have an $=$ sign

Subtract b from both sides of the inequality:

$$a + b - b > c - b$$
$$\boldsymbol{a > c - b}$$

In general, i f $a + b > c$
then, $a + b - d > c - d$
Also if $a > b$ then $a - m > b - m$
or if $a > b$ then $a + m > b + m$

That is, you can also add a number to both sides of an inequality and still get the same relationship of the inequality.

32. If $-3 < \mathrm{p} < + 3$ is $3 > -\mathrm{p} > -3$?

Multiply by (-1): Remember to *reverse* the order! Multiply by -1:

$(-1)(-3 \quad < \quad p \quad < \quad + 3) =$
$(-1)(-3) \quad > (-1)(p) > \quad (-1)(+3)$

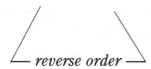
reverse order

So we get $\boldsymbol{+3 > -p > -3}$

33. If $a < b$ then is $na < nb$?

This is true only if n > 0 *(or if* n *is positive)*.

AVERAGES

34. Average score is defined as total scores divided by number of students (or number of tests taken).

In other words:

$$\text{Average Score} = \frac{\text{Total Score}}{\text{No. of Students (Tests)}}$$

$$\text{Total Scores} = 45 + 60 + 90$$
$$= 195$$
$$\text{No. Students} = 3$$
$$\text{So } \frac{195}{3} = \boldsymbol{65}$$

35. Average rate is defined as Total Distance divided by Total Time.

$$\text{So Average Rate} = \frac{\text{Total Distance}}{\text{Total Time}}$$

Since Total Distance was given as 30 miles and Time was 3 hours,

$$\text{Average Rate} = \frac{30}{3} = \boldsymbol{10 \text{ mph}}$$

Arm Yourself

Below are summaries of factors, equivalencies, exponents, roots, etc., that are frequently encountered on the SAT. You should arm yourself for the SAT by making sure you know them all. Know them literally backwards and forwards. Whenever you see just one side of any of these equations and equivalencies, the other side should immediately spring to mind. If you do not arm yourself with this material, you will not be able to use the math strategies effectively.

FACTORS

$(a + b)^2 = a^2 + 2ab + b^2$
$(a - b)^2 = a^2 - 2ab + b^2$

The expression $a^2 + b^2$ is not factorable into anything useful. But the expression $a^2 - b^2$ contains a very important pair of factors.

$a^2 - b^2 = (a + b)\ (a - b)$

(Don't confuse this with $(a - b)^2$, above!)

Here are examples of how $a^2 - b^2$ sometimes appears:

$a^2 - 1 = (a + 1)(a - 1)$

$a^2 - 4 = (a + 2)\ (a - 2)$

etc.

Notice how number pairs like the following, whose difference is an even number, fit the $a^2 - b^2$ pattern:

$101 \times 99\ = (100 + 1)\ (100 - 1)$
$\qquad\qquad = 100^2 - 1$
$802 \times 798 = (800 + 2)(800 - 2)$
$\qquad\qquad = 800^2 - 2^2$

Watch out for these. They may fool you:

$(a + b)^2$ is *not* the same as $a^2 + b^2$ (See above)

$(a - b)^2$ is *not* the same as $a^2 - b^2$ (See above)

SQUARE ROOTS

$\sqrt{x}\ \sqrt{y} = \sqrt{xy}$
$(\sqrt{x} + \sqrt{y})^2 = x + 2\sqrt{xy} + y$
$(\sqrt{x} - \sqrt{y})^2 = x - 2\sqrt{xy} + y$
$(\sqrt{x + y}\ )^2 = x + y$
$(\sqrt{xy})^2 = xy$

Be very careful of these. They may fool you.

$\qquad \sqrt{x} + \sqrt{y}$ is *not* equal to $\sqrt{x + y}$
$\qquad \sqrt{x} - \sqrt{y}$ is *not* equal to $\sqrt{x - y}$
$\qquad (\sqrt{x} + \sqrt{y})^2$ is *not* equal to $x + y$ (See above)
$\qquad (\sqrt{x} - \sqrt{y})^2$ is *not* equal to $x - y$ (See above)

EXPONENTS

$x^0 = 1 \qquad x^1 = x$
$\qquad\qquad$ (Both are very important!)
$x^3 \times x^5 = x^{3+5} = x^8$
$\qquad\qquad$ (To multiply, add exponents)
$x^n \times x^m = x^{n+m}$

$\dfrac{x^n}{x^m} = x^{n-m}$ (To divide, subtract exponents)

$(ab)^n = a^n \times b^n$

$(a^m)^n = a^{mn}$ (It does *not* equal a^{m+n})

Here are examples involving factoring with exponents. Study them carefully until you thoroughly understand them.

$2^7 - 2^6 = 2^6(2^1 - 2^0) = 2^6(2 - 1) = 2^6(1) = 2^6$

$10^7 - 10^6 = 10^6(10^1 - 10^0) = 10^6(10 - 1)$
$\qquad\qquad\qquad\qquad = 10^6(9)$ or 9×10^6

$x^5 + x^3 = x^3\ (x^2 + x^0) = x^3\ (x^2 + 1)$

$x^5 - x^3 = x^3(x^2 - x^0)$
$\qquad\quad = x^3\ (x^2 - 1) = x^3\ (x + 1)(x - 1)$

Here's a very important equivalency involving exponents: $a^{-x} = \dfrac{1}{a^x}$

RECIPROCALS

$$\frac{1}{\frac{a}{b}} = \frac{b}{a} \qquad \frac{a}{\frac{b}{c}} = a \times \frac{c}{b} = \frac{ac}{b}$$

$$\frac{1}{\frac{1}{x}} = \frac{x}{1} = x \qquad \frac{\frac{a}{b}}{c} = \frac{a}{b} \div c = \frac{a}{b} \times \frac{1}{c} = \frac{a}{bc}$$

$$\frac{1}{x} + \frac{1}{y} = \frac{x+y}{xy} \qquad a^{-x} = \frac{1}{a^x}$$

$$\frac{x}{y} + \frac{y}{x} = \frac{x^2 + y^2}{xy}$$

RATES

rate $\times$ time = distance

$$r \times t = d \qquad r = \frac{d}{t} \qquad t = \frac{d}{r}$$

$$\text{Average rate} = \frac{\text{Total Distance}}{\text{Total Time}}$$

ODDS AND EVENS

e = any even integer

o = any odd integer

$$\left.\begin{matrix} o \pm o \\ e \pm e \end{matrix}\right\} = e \qquad o \times o = o \qquad \frac{o}{o} = o \text{ or a fraction}$$

$$\left.\begin{matrix} o \pm e \\ e \pm o \end{matrix}\right\} = o \qquad \left.\begin{matrix} e \times e \\ e \times o \end{matrix}\right\} = e \qquad \frac{o}{e} = \text{a fraction}$$

$$e^2 = e \qquad \frac{e}{o} = e \text{ or a fraction}$$

$$o^2 = o \qquad \frac{e}{e} = e \text{ or } o \text{ or a fraction}$$

SIGNS

$$\left.\begin{matrix} \text{minus} \times \text{minus} \\ \text{plus} \times \text{plus} \end{matrix}\right\} = \text{plus}$$

$$(-x)(-y) = +xy \; ; \; (+x)(+y) = +xy$$

$$\frac{1}{x} = \frac{-1}{-x} = -\left(\frac{1}{-x}\right) = -\left(\frac{-1}{x}\right)$$

minus $\times$ plus = minus

$$(-x)(+y) = -xy$$

$$-\left(\frac{1}{x}\right) = \frac{1}{-x} = \frac{-1}{x} = -\left(\frac{-1}{-x}\right)$$

INEQUALITIES

$a > b$ means a is greater than b.

$a < b$ means b is greater than a (or a is less than b).

REMEMBER: THE OPEN MOUTH OF THE SYMBOL IS ON THE SIDE OF THE *GREATER* QUANTITY.

$a \leq b$ — means b is greater than or equal to a.

$a < b < c$ — means that the value of b is between a and c (or, b is greater than a, and c is greater than b).

$a \leq b \leq c$ — means that the lowest possible value of b is a; the highest possible value is c; and it may be anywhere in between.

$0 < x < 1$ — means that x is a positive fraction less than one.

$a > b$ — also means $b < a$.

MEDIANS

The median of a set of numbers is the number which is in the *middle* of the set. For example:

Find the median of 20, 0, 80, 12, and 30.

Solution: Arrange the numbers in increasing order:

0

12

20

30

80

The *middle* number is 20, so 20 is the *median*.

Note: If there is an *even* number of items, such as:

0

12

20

24

30

80

there is no *middle* number. In this case we take the average of the two middle numbers, 20 and 24, and get 22, which is the *median*.

MODES

The mode of a set of numbers is the number that occurs most frequently.

If we have the numbers 0, 12, 20, 30, and 80 there is no mode, since no one number appears with the greatest frequency. But consider this:

Example: Find the mode of 0, 12, 12, 20, 30, and 80.

Solution: 12 appears most frequently, so it is the mode.

Example: Find the mode of 0, 12, 12, 20, 30, 30, and 80.

Solution: Here, *both* 12 and 30 are modes.

IMPORTANT NOTE ON THE ALLOWED USE OF CALCULATORS ON THE SAT

You are allowed to use a calculator when you take the SAT. But there will be times when another problem-solving method or shortcut may be faster. So you must be selective about when and when not to use a calculator on the test.

Here's an example of when a calculator should *not* be used.

$$\frac{2}{5} \times \frac{5}{6} \times \frac{6}{7} \times \frac{7}{8} \times \frac{9}{10} \times \frac{10}{11} =$$

(A) $\frac{9}{11}$ (B) $\frac{2}{11}$ (C) $\frac{11}{36}$

(D) $\frac{10}{21}$ (E) $\frac{244}{360}$

Here using a calculator may take some time. However, if you use the strategy of canceling numerators and denominators as shown, you can see that the answer comes easily.

CANCEL NUMERATORS/ DENOMINATORS:

$$\frac{2}{5} \times \frac{5}{6} \times \frac{6}{7} \times \frac{7}{8} \times \frac{9}{10} \times \frac{10}{11} \times \frac{2}{11}$$

Later on, I will show you an example in the new *grid-type* question, where using a calculator will also take you a longer time to solve a problem than *not* using a calculator.

Here's an example where using a calculator may get you the solution *as fast* as using a strategy without the calculator:

25 percent of 16 is equivalent to $\frac{1}{2}$ of what number?

(A) 2   (B) 4   (C) 8   (D) 16   (E) 32

Using a calculator, you'd use the strategy of translating *of* to *times* and *is* to *equals*. Then you'd say, 4 = half of what number? and you'd find that number to be 8.

Without using a calculator, you'd still use Math Strategy 7 (the translation strategy), but you could write 25% as $\frac{1}{4}$, so you'd figure out what $\frac{1}{4}$ of 16 was (4). Then you'd call the number you want to find x, and say $4 = \frac{1}{2} \times (x)$. You'd find $x = 8$.

Note that both methods, with and without a calculator, are about equally efficient. However, the technique in the second method can be used for many more problems and hones more thinking skills.

IMPORTANT NOTES ON MATH QUESTIONS ON THE SAT

The SAT math sections have two types of questions:

1. **Regular Math** (total of 44 counted questions)
   Each question has five choices. The strategies for Regular Math start on the next page.

2. **"Grid-Type" Math Questions** (total of 10 counted questions)

   These questions are described on page 114.

Regular Math Strategies

Before we illustrate strategies and shortcuts with specific SAT type examples, you ought to know some important math shortcuts. Here they are in Strategies 1–4.

To Find Which of Two Fractions Is Larger, Use the Criss-cross Multiplication Method

Many times you will find a question in which you must compare the values of two fractions. For example, suppose you want to find which fraction is greater:

$$\frac{5}{13} \quad \text{or} \quad \frac{3}{8}$$

Many students would try to get a common denominator and then compare the fractions. That's the long way! Here's how to do it the short way, using the technique called **criss-cross multiplication** (multiplying the numerator of each fraction by the denominator of the other).

Multiply the 8 by the 5 and put the result under the $\frac{5}{13}$. Then multiply the 13 by the 3 and put the result under the $\frac{3}{8}$. Like this:

multiply:

Since 40 is greater than 39, and 40 was under the $\frac{5}{13}$, then $\frac{5}{13}$ is greater than $\frac{3}{8}$. This works every time, and of course you can prove this, but that's not our purpose here.

Notice how much simpler it is to compare fractions this way than by getting a common denominator and then comparing them.

Remember, when you criss-cross multiply a denominator times a numerator, you must put your answer under the fraction whose numerator you used in multiplying. Remember it this way: *put your answer under the numerator.*

Try these examples. Which is greater?

$$\text{(A) } \frac{7}{9} \text{ or } \frac{5}{7} \qquad \text{(B) } \frac{3}{5} \text{ or } \frac{4}{7} \qquad \text{(C) } \frac{11}{13} \text{ or } \frac{7}{8}$$

Answers: (A) $\frac{7}{9}$, (B) $\frac{3}{5}$, (C) $\frac{7}{8}$

To Add or Subtract Fractions Rapidly, Use the Criss-cross Multiplication Method

Suppose you have the following problem: Find the value of $\frac{3}{4} + \frac{5}{6}$. Most people would try to find the common denominator and then add. Here's a shorter way when you don't want to get the common denominator.

Multiply

$$\frac{3}{4} + \frac{5}{6} \qquad \frac{3 \times 6 + 4 \times 5}{4 \times 6} = \frac{18 + 20}{24} = \frac{38}{24}$$

multiply

What we have done is to multiply the 6 by the 3, and add that result to the product of the numbers 4 by 5. The result is our answer's *numerator.* Then multiply the 4 by the 6 and the result is our answer's *denominator.* So our answer is:

$$\frac{38}{24} = \frac{19}{22} = 1\frac{7}{12}$$

If we want to subtract: $\frac{5}{7} - \frac{3}{10}$ we would do the following:

Multiply

multiply

Try these examples. Add the following fractions:

(A) $\dfrac{4}{5} + \dfrac{5}{7}$ (B) $\dfrac{7}{9} + \dfrac{3}{4}$ (C) $\dfrac{x}{y} + \dfrac{y}{x}$ *(Remember this one!)*

Answers: (A) $\dfrac{53}{35}$ or $1\dfrac{18}{35}$ (B) $\dfrac{55}{36}$ or $1\dfrac{19}{36}$ (C) $\dfrac{x^2 + y^2}{xy}$

Try these now. Subtract:

(A) $\dfrac{2}{3} - \dfrac{1}{2}$ (B) $\dfrac{3}{4} - \dfrac{1}{7}$ (C) $\dfrac{x}{y} - \dfrac{y}{x}$

Answers: (A) $\dfrac{1}{6}$, (B) $\dfrac{17}{28}$, (C) $\dfrac{x^2 + y^2}{xy}$ or $\dfrac{(x + y)(x - y)}{xy}$ *(by factoring)*

STRATEGY 3

To Find the Sale Price in Discount Problems, Start by Subtracting the Discount % from 100%

Sometimes you have to figure what selling price you would pay for an item discounted a certain percent. Here's an example:

What is the selling price of an article that lists for $5.00 and is discounted 20%?

Most of you would probably multiply 20% by $5.00 and then subtract that result from $5.00. There's a faster way.

First, always *subtract the percent from 100%*. In this case you would subtract 20% from 100% and get 80%. Now multiply this 80% by the $5.00. You get $4.00, and that's the answer.

So, in summary, subtract the percent discount from 100%, then multiply that number by the list price to get the sale price.

Try these examples:
1. What is the selling price of an item discounted 30% whose list price (before discount) is $8.00?
2. What is the selling price of an item discounted 40% whose list price is $4.00?

Answers: 1. $5.60; 2. $2.40

To Turn a Fraction into a Percent, Try Multiplying Instead of Dividing

Suppose you have a number like $\dfrac{3}{25}$ and want to find what percent that is. You may be tempted, as most students are, to divide 25 into 3. That sure is the long way! Now just do some thinking: Isn't it easier to work with simple denominators than hard ones? So let's make the denominator 25 into a simpler one. But since you are going to multiply the denominator by 4 you must also multiply the numerator, 3, by 4 so you don't change the value of the fraction! Like this:

$$\frac{3 \times 4}{25 \times 4} = \frac{12}{100}$$

Thus we get $\dfrac{12}{100}$ which is just 12%. That's our answer.

This method works on fractions with any of the following denominators: 2, 4, 5, 10, 20, 25, 50

Try these examples. Write each of the following fractions as a percent (or as an integer over 100):

(A) $\dfrac{1}{2}$ (B) $\dfrac{1}{4}$ (C) $\dfrac{2}{5}$ (D) $\dfrac{3}{10}$ (E) $\dfrac{3}{20}$ (F) $\dfrac{4}{25}$ (G) $\dfrac{1}{50}$

Answers: (A) 50% or $\dfrac{50}{100}$ (E) 15% or $\dfrac{15}{100}$

(B) 25% or $\dfrac{25}{100}$ (F) 16% or $\dfrac{16}{100}$

(C) 40% or $\dfrac{40}{100}$ (G) 2% or $\dfrac{2}{100}$

(D) 30% or $\dfrac{30}{100}$

STRATEGY 5

Read Math Questions Very Carefully, So That You Solve What Is Asked For

Telling you to read questions carefully may seem like an obvious piece of advice. But SAT questions often seem to ask for one thing while actually asking for another. For example:

If a is not 0 or 1 and b is not 0 or 1, what is the reciprocal of $\dfrac{1}{\frac{1}{a} + \frac{1}{b}}$?

(A) $\dfrac{ab}{a + b}$ (B) $\dfrac{1}{a + b}$ (C) $a + b$ (D) ab (E) $\dfrac{a + b}{ab}$

If you are not careful, you might simplify the expression $\dfrac{1}{\frac{1}{a} + \frac{1}{b}}$ and get the answer $\dfrac{ab}{a + b}$, Choice A. That's the correct simplification of the expression.

And it's the wrong answer. The question asked for the **reciprocal** of the expression. So the correct answer is Choice E. Many students get tricked because they either don't notice that the question asks for a reciprocal, or they forget after they have simplified the expression. Don't get so rushed that you do the math correctly but put down the wrong answer!

If You Must Test *All* Choices, Work from Choice E Backward

Many questions ask you to work through many of the choices before coming to the correct one. And many students would start with Choice A first. Is that the best approach? Here's an example:

Which fraction is less than $\dfrac{2}{3}$?

(A) $\dfrac{3}{4}$ (B) $\dfrac{13}{19}$ (C) $\dfrac{15}{22}$ (D) $\dfrac{9}{13}$ (E) $\dfrac{7}{11}$

In this question, where you essentially have to *look through* the choices and cannot necessarily zero in on the correct choice, the test-maker will expect you to work through Choices A, B, C, etc. in that order. And the chances are that if you're careless, you'll make a mistake before you get to the right choice. That's how the test-maker makes up the choices. So, in cases such as this, *start with Choice E and work backwards* with Choice D, C, etc., in that order. The chances are that Choice E or D is the correct answer! So in the above question let's compare $\dfrac{2}{3}$ with $\dfrac{7}{11}$ in Choice E. Remember our shortcut way?

Multiply:

Since 22 is greater than 21, $\dfrac{2}{3}$ is greater than $\dfrac{7}{11}$; so Choice E is in fact the correct answer.

Here's another SAT-type question that involves the same strategy:

> If p is an even integer and q is an odd integer, which of the following could be an even integer?
>
> (A) $q - p$ (B) $q + p$ (C) $\dfrac{p + q}{2}$ (D) $\dfrac{q}{2} + p$ (E) $\dfrac{p}{2} + q$

Note the words *could be* in the question. So, we just have to find one set of numbers that makes the choice an even number. Again, *work with Choice E first.* Since p is **even,** let $p = 2$ (for example). Since q is **odd,** let $q = 3$ (for example). Then Choice E, which is $\dfrac{p}{2} + q$, becomes $\dfrac{2}{2} + 3 = 1 + 3 = 4$.

So we see that Choice E *could be even,* so it is the correct answer.

So remember, when you have to work with all the choices or have to substitute numbers in the choices (that is, when you cannot just arrive at a correct answer without looking through all the choices) *work with Choice E first,* then Choice D, etc., in that order. Chances are that Choice E or Choice D is correct.

Use the "Translation Technique" on Verbal Problems to Turn Words into Math Symbols

A verbal problem is simply a question in which you must translate words into mathematical terms. Many students have difficulty with such problems. Here's a way to make them quite simple and direct. If you master this technique, you should be able to do verbal problems almost mechanically, with very little anxiety and brain-racking. We call this the **Translation Technique.**

Here's a typical SAT-type question measuring verbal abilities in mathematics:

> John is three times as old as Paul, and Paul is two years older than Sam. If Sam is y years old, find an expression for the age of John:
>
> (A) $6 - 3y$ (B) $6 + 3y$ (C) $3y + 2$ (D) $3y - 2$
>
> (E) $3y - 6$

The key thing to remember about verbal problems is to translate the *key words:*

is becomes = (equals)

of becomes × (times)

more than, older than, etc. become + (plus)

less than, younger than, etc. become − (minus)

% becomes $\overline{100}$

What becomes *x, y,* etc.

So let's look at the first part of the question: "John is three times as old as Paul . . ." This translates (with John = J, and P = Paul) as

1. $J = 3 \times P$

    The next part, "and Paul is two years older than Sam . . ." is translated as (Let S = Sam or Sam's age):

2. P = 2 + S

Now look at the second sentence: "If Sam is y years old, find an expression for the age of John." We translate this as:

$S = y$

Now substitute $S = y$ into Equation 2 above:

We get: P = 2 + y. Now substitute P = 2 + y into Equation 1. We get:
J = 3 × P = 3 × (2 + y) = 3 × 2 + 3 × y

$$= 6 + 3y$$

Thus, Choice B is correct.

Here's another very tricky typical problem of this kind:

> Bill bought 4 times as many apples as Harry and 3 times as many apples as Martin. If Bill, Harry, and Martin purchased less than a total of 190 apples, what is the greatest number of apples that Bill could have purchased?
>
> (A) 168   (B) 120   (C) 119   (D) 108   (E) 90

Translate: The number of apples that Bill bought = B
The number of apples that Harry bought = H
The number of apples that Martin bought = M

The phrase "Bill bought 4 times as many apples as Harry" is translated to:
1. $B = 4 \times H$

The phrase " . . . and 3 times as many apples as Martin" is translated to:
2. $B = 3 \times M$

The phrase "If Bill, Harry, and Martin purchased less than a total of 190 apples . . ." is translated to:
3. $B + H + M < 190$

Now the question asks for the greatest number of apples that Bill could have purchased. Translated, it asks for the *maximum value of the variable B*. So let's just get some equation involving B and get rid of the H and the M. We can do this by substituting what H is in terms of B and what M is in terms of B in Equation 3.

That is, from Equation 1 we have: $B = 4H$ or $\dfrac{B}{4} = H$, and from Equation 2 we have

B = 3M or $\dfrac{B}{3} = M$.

Now look at Equation 3: $B + H + M < 190$. Substitute $\dfrac{B}{4} = H$ and $\dfrac{B}{3} = M$.

$$B + \frac{B}{4} + \frac{B}{3} < 190$$

$$\text{Factor}: B \left(1 + \frac{1}{4} + \frac{1}{3}\right) < 190$$

$$\text{or} \qquad B \left(\frac{12}{12} + \frac{3}{12} + \frac{4}{12}\right) < 190$$

$$B \left(\frac{19}{12}\right) < 190$$

Get the B alone (multiply both sides of the inequality by 12 and divide by 19):

$$B < 190 \times \frac{12}{19} \qquad \text{So} \quad B < 120$$

You might think the answer is Choice C: 119. But $\frac{B}{4} = H$ and $\frac{B}{3} = M$, so $B \neq 119$, since $\frac{B}{4}$ and $\frac{B}{3}$ must be integers. So B must be exactly divisible by 12 and thus the greatest value of $B = 12 \times 9 = 108$ (Choice D).

STRATEGY 8

In Problems with More Than One Unknown, Take Special Care with Substitutions

Sometimes you will have to substitute numbers or variables in a problem with two unknowns. It is very important for you to make the right substitution—one that will lead you rapidly to the correct answer. In general, substitute to get rid of the unknown that is *not* part of the answer that the question asks for.

Let's look at another SAT-type verbal problem:

> Matt and Phil have combined salaries of $1500 a week. Matt's salary is three-fifths Phil's. What is four-fifths of Matt's salary per week?
>
> (A) $250.00 (B) $350.00 (C) $450.00 (D) $500.00
> (E) $550.00

Make sure that you immediately write M for Matt, P for Phil (you can, of course, use m and p). The first sentence translates to

1. $M + P = 1500$

The second sentence translates to

2. $M = \dfrac{3}{5} P$

The question asks you to find the value of:

3. $\dfrac{4}{5} M$

Since the second equation tells you that $M = \dfrac{3}{5}$, you may be tempted to substitute $\dfrac{3}{5} P$ for M in the first equation and solve from there. Don't do it! Remember, the question asks you to find the value of $\dfrac{4}{5} M$. Since we want to find the value of $\dfrac{4}{5}$ M, let's get rid of P in the equations, and keep the M.

The best way to do this is to write P in terms of M in Equation 2:

$$M = \frac{3}{5} P; \quad 5M = 3P; \quad \text{so} \quad \frac{5M}{3} = P$$

Then substitute $P = \dfrac{5M}{3}$ into Equation 1:

$$M + P = 1500; \quad M + \dfrac{5M}{3} = 1500;$$

$$\dfrac{3M + 5M}{3} = 1500; \quad \dfrac{8M}{3} = 1500$$

Now let's get the M alone by multiplying the last equation by $\dfrac{3}{8}$:

$$\dfrac{8M}{3} \times \dfrac{3}{8} = 1500 \times \dfrac{3}{8}$$

$$M = 1500 \times \dfrac{3}{8}$$

We have to find the value of $\dfrac{4}{5}$ M, so we multiply the last equation by $\dfrac{4}{5}$:

$$\dfrac{4}{5} \times M - 1500 \times \dfrac{3}{8} \times \dfrac{4}{5} = 450$$

So, Choice C is correct.

STRATEGY 9

In Solving a Problem with Several Parts, Start with the Part That Gives You the Most Information

The worst thing you can do on the SAT is to exhaust yourself by thinking too hard on a particular question. Many times you will see a question that you know there is a definite answer for, but you also know that it will take you a long time to solve it. Furthermore, you may really rack your brains trying to solve the question. In every case that I have seen, there's a fast, almost mechanical way to do such problems. Here's a typical problem:

If $mnq = 0$, $mcr = 0$ and $nrc = 1$, which must be necessarily 0?

(A)n (B)r (C)m (D)q (E)c

Take a quick look at the first two equations: $mnq = 0$ and $mcr = 0$. You should immediately notice that *any or all* of the unknowns could be 0. Not much information there! Now go to the third equation: $nrc = 1$. This tells us that neither *n, r,* nor c can be 0. Now with this information, you can go back to Equation 2: $mcr = 0$. What you learned from Equation 3 tells you that c and r cannot be 0, so *m* must be. The correct answer is Choice C—and you didn't even need Equation 1 to find it!

Incidentally, don't jump to the conclusion that since *m* is common to Equations 1 and 2, then $m = 0$. Your answer would be right—but for the wrong reason. In Equation 1, *q* might have been 0 and in Equation 2, *r* might have been 0. Only by going to Equation 3 can you see that *r, c,* and *n cannot* be 0. (*q* could still be 0, but it doesn't have to be.)

Here's another SAT question where you want to go right away to the information that lets you start off the problem.

If $0.1 \leq m \leq 1$
and $0.001 \leq n \leq 0.01$
then the maximum value of $\dfrac{m}{n}$ is

(A)1   (B)10   (C)100   (D)1000   (E) 10.000

After reading through the question, look for the piece of information you must use first. Note when reading the statements that the information contained in them alone does not enable us to start the problem.

There is additional "information" hidden in the question. To get the maximum value of $\frac{m}{n}$, you must look for the *greatest* value of m and the *least* value of n. That is what will make the fraction $\frac{m}{n}$ greatest. So m must be 1 and n must be .001.

$$\frac{m}{n} = \frac{1}{.001} = \frac{1}{\frac{1}{1000}} = 1 \times \frac{1000}{1} = 1000$$

Choice D is correct.

STRATEGY 10

To Find Irregular or Unusual Lengths, Areas, or Volumes, Try Subtracting from a Quantity You Know or Can Calculate

Let's look at another example:

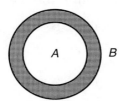

In the above figure, Circle A has a radius of *a* and Circle B has a radius of *b*. What is the area of the region which is shaded?

(A) $\pi (a + b)$ (B) $\pi(b - a)$ (C) $\pi (b^2 - a^2)$ (D) $\pi(b^2 + a^2)$
(E) $\pi(b - a)^2$

You can see that the area of the shaded region is just the *difference of the area of the big circle* (radius *b*) *and the area of the small circle* (radius a). The area of the small circle is just a^2, and the area of the big circle is just b^2. So the difference is:

$$\pi b^2 - \pi a^2 = \pi (b^2 - a^2) \text{ (Choice C)}$$

Some questions ask you to subtract two *lengths* in order to find the unknown length. Here's an example:

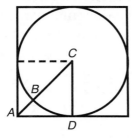

A circle is inscribed in the square above. Point *C* is the center of the circle. What is the ratio of *AB* to *AC*?

(A) $\dfrac{2 - \sqrt{2}}{2}$ (B) $\dfrac{\sqrt{2} + 1}{\sqrt{2}}$ (C) $\dfrac{\sqrt{2}}{2}$ (D) $\dfrac{2}{\sqrt{2}}$ (E) Cannot be determined

In the diagram above, call $AB = s$, and the radius of the circle, r. Since CB is also the radius, $CB = r$. You should also realize that triangle ADC is an isosceles right triangle, and that therefore $AD = r$. Therefore side $CA = r\sqrt{2}$ (by the Pythagorean theorem).

We want to find what the ratio to $r + s$ is but we don't know what s is. Here's the main strategy:

SUBTRACT LINES FROM LINES TO GET UNKNOWN LINES.

$CA - CB = BA$ (unknown) noting that $BA = s$.

But $CA = r\sqrt{2}$ (from before) and $CB = r$

So $CA - CB = r\sqrt{2} - r$

and since $CA - CB = s$,

$s = r\sqrt{2} - r$

So the ratio,

$$\frac{s}{r + s} = \frac{r\sqrt{2} - r}{r + r\sqrt{2} - r} \text{ (substituting } r\sqrt{2} - r \text{ for } s \text{ in } \frac{s}{r + s})$$

The r's cancel and we get

$$\frac{r\sqrt{2} - r}{r + r\sqrt{2} - r} = \frac{\sqrt{2} - 1}{1 + \sqrt{2} - 1} = \frac{\sqrt{2} - 1}{\sqrt{2}}$$

But what? There's no answer in the choices like that! What do we do now? Don't panic—and above all, don't choose Choice B just because it looks sort of like your answer with only one sign changed! Simplify your fraction by getting rid of $\sqrt{2}$ in the denominator. Multiply both numerator and denominator above by $\sqrt{2}$ to simplify the fraction. We get:

$$(\frac{\sqrt{2} - 1}{\sqrt{2}}) \frac{\sqrt{2}}{\sqrt{2}} = \frac{\sqrt{2}\sqrt{2} - \sqrt{2}}{\sqrt{2}\sqrt{2}} = \frac{2 - \sqrt{2}}{2}$$

Choice A is then correct.

STRATEGY 11

Beware of "Average Rate" Problems! Don't Average Rates. Divide Total Distance by Total Time.

"Average Rate" problems are very tricky. Here's a typical example:

> What is the average rate of a car initially traveling at 20 miles per hour and then traveling twice the initial distance at 60 miles per hour?
>
> (A) 25mph   (B) 30mph   (C) 36mph   (D) 40mph   (E) 50mph

Some students would be lured into thinking that they should average 20 and 60 to get 40, which is Choice D. Or some may be lured into thinking that they should divide 60 by 2 because of the word "twice" and then average that result with 20 to get 25, which is Choice A. But here's the method: *average rate is total distance divided by total time:*

$$\frac{\text{TOTAL DISTANCE}}{\text{TOTAL TIME}}$$

Now what is the total distance? Since distance is not given in the question, let's just *pick a value for initial distance.* Since we have numbers like 20 and 60 in the question, let's choose the initial distance as a simple multiple of 20, like 20. This will make things simpler when you calculate. Let's proceed to find the TOTAL DISTANCE traveled. The initial distance (which we chose) is **20 miles.** The car then traveled *twice* that distance. This means that the car *next* traveled $20 \times 2 = $ **40 miles.** So the TOTAL DISTANCE is $20 + 40 = $ **60 miles.** Now let's find out what the TOTAL TIME is. If the car traveled 20 miles at 20 mph, the initial time would be

$$\frac{\text{initial distance}}{\text{initial rate}} = \frac{20 \text{ miles}}{20 \text{ miles per hour}} = 1 \text{ hour}$$

The final time would be

$$\frac{\text{final distance}}{\text{final rate}} = \frac{40 \text{ miles}}{60 \text{ miles per hour}} = \frac{4}{6} \text{ hours}$$

So the TOTAL TIME would be initial time + final time =

$$1 + \frac{4}{6} \text{ hours}$$

And now we may calculate the average rate:

$$\frac{\text{TOTAL DISTANCE}}{\text{TOTAL TIME}} = \frac{60 \text{ miles}}{1 + \frac{4}{6} \text{ hrs}} = \frac{60}{\frac{10}{6}} =$$

$$60 \times \frac{6}{10} = 36 \text{ mph}$$

Therefore the correct answer is Choice C.

STRATEGY 12

In Averaging Scores, Make Sure That You Separate Terms in Order to Use Information on Averages

Remember: *The average is equal to the sum of the scores divided by the number of scores* (tests or students).

Let's look at another "average" problem:

> The average exam score, y, of a class of 20 students was below 68. If 8 students had increased their exam scores by 10 points each, the average exam score of the class would have been 68 or over. Which of the following describes the values of y?
>
> (A) $56 \leq y < 68$
>
> (B) $64 < y \leq 68$
>
> (C) $64 < y < 68$
>
> (D) $64 \leq y < 68$
>
> (E) $64 \leq y \leq 68$

Now there is a really tricky way to do this problem based on the choices. I'll show you this way now, but I'd prefer you learn the honest way so that you may do many more problems based on the actual strategy.

First Method: It seems pretty obvious that the choices one should consider are B, C, D, and E. Choice A with the 56 looks like a "dark horse," and the chances are that if 56 was in the answer, it would also be in many of the other choices. Now look at the first statement in the question: It says that the score, y, was below 68. This means mathematically that $y < 68$. So already, we see that the only correct possibilities are Choices C and D. Now the phrase "the average exam score would have been *68 or over* gives a feeling that we have a *greater/equal sign* ($\geq$ or $\leq$) because of the words *68 or over*. The only choice that fits the bill (from C or D) is Choice D.

Second Method: Let's see how a knowledge of *separation of terms* would help solve this problem.

Let T stand for the total of all the class's exam scores. Then y (the average score) is T divided by 20 students:

$$\frac{T}{20} = y$$

If 8 students had increased their exam scores by 10 points each, the new total score would be:

$$T + (8 \times 10) = T + 80$$

And the new average score would be:

$$\frac{T + 80}{20}$$

Here's where the **separation of terms** strategy comes in. We can separate this last expression as follows:

$$\frac{T + 80}{20} = \frac{T}{20} + \frac{80}{20}$$
$$= \frac{T}{20} + 4$$

And since we know already that $\dfrac{T}{20} = y$

$$T + \frac{80}{20} = y + 4 \,(\text{substituting } y \text{ for} \frac{T}{20})$$

This expression, $y + 4$, is the *new* average score (when 8 students increase their score by 10 points each).

The problem states that the new average score is 68 or over. In mathematical terms:

$$y + 4 \geq 68$$

Subtract 4 from both sides of the inequality/equality:

$$y + 4 - 4 \geq 68 - 4$$

$$y \geq 64 \ (\text{or, } 64 \leq y)$$

Since the problem stated that $y < 68$, we combine inequalities to get:

$$64 \leq y \leq 68$$

Thus Choice D is correct.

The key to solving this problem is the knowledge that the expression $\dfrac{T + 80}{20}$ can be separated into $\dfrac{T}{20} + \dfrac{80}{20}$. This may at first seem like a rather unimportant point to make into a strategy. But this type of problem, involving an increase (or decrease) in an average, is one of the commonest types of SAT problems. Master this one strategy, and you'll probably add at least 10 points to your SAT score.

STRATEGY 13

Be Constantly on the Lookout for Standard, "Classic" Factors or Similar Equivalencies

A very large number of SAT math questions are designed so that they can be solved by factoring or by writing an expression in another form. Sometimes this method gives you a shortcut way to a quick solution. Sometimes it is the *only* way to solve a problem. For example:

> If $2 \leq x \leq 3$
> $1 \leq y \leq 4$
>
> What is the maximum possible value of $\dfrac{x+y}{xy}$?
>
> (A) $\dfrac{7}{12}$ (B) $\dfrac{3}{2}$ (C) $\dfrac{5}{4}$ (D) $\dfrac{4}{3}$ (E) $\dfrac{6}{8}$

Lots of students, seeing the word *maximum* in the problem, would rush ahead and substitute the maximum values of $x(3)$ and $y(4)$ in the expression $\dfrac{x+y}{xy}$. They would come up with Choice A as the answer. Don't do this! As you will see, it's wrong.

Look at the expression $\dfrac{x+y}{xy}$. And notice that it is the equivalent of the expression

$\dfrac{1}{x} + \dfrac{1}{y}$. (Remember: $\dfrac{x+y}{xy} = \dfrac{x}{xy} + \dfrac{y}{xy} = \dfrac{1}{y} + \dfrac{1}{x}$.)

To make a fraction as large as possible, make its denominator a small number. So you should substitute the *smallest* possible values of x and y to get the largest value of $\dfrac{1}{x} + \dfrac{1}{y}$:

$$\frac{1}{2} + \frac{1}{1} = 1\frac{1}{2} \text{ or } \frac{3}{2}$$

So the correct answer is Choice B.

Here's another example of the factoring strategy:

> Where x is an integer, $x^2 + 2x + 1$ is always
>
> (A) an odd integer
>
> (B) an even integer
>
> (C) a prime number
>
> (D) an integer divisible by 3
>
> (E) the square of an integer

Immediately notice that you can factor $x^2 + 2x + 1$ into the factors $(x + 1)(x + 1)$. Since x is an integer, $(x + 1)(x + 1)$ is always the square of an integer. Choice E is correct.

> Here's a final example of this very important strategy:
>
> If $999 \times 1001 = 10^n - x$
>
> where N is an integer, the pair n, x could be:
>
> (A) 3,2   (B) 6,3   (C) 6,1   (D) 3,1   (E) none of these

Note that the numbers 999×1001 are separated by 2. There's your clue, right there:

$$999 \times 1001 = (1000 + 1)(1000 - 1)$$

And, since $1000 = 10^3$, you can substitute:

$$(1000 + 1)(1000 - 1) = (10^3 + 1)(10^3 - 1)$$

Multiply the last expression out. Remember—to multiply, *add exponents.*

$$(10^3 + 1)(10^3 - 1) = 10^6 - 1$$

And your answer is C, the pair 6,1.

STRATEGY 14

> **When a Question Asks You to Find a *Compound* Expression (Like $x + 1$, or $\frac{y}{3}$, or $a^2 + b^2$), Look for a Way to Find This Compound Expression from What Is Given**

Sometimes an SAT math question asks you to find a quantity like $x + y$ instead of x; or $\frac{y}{x}$ instead of y or x; or $a^2 + b^2$ instead of a and b. Whenever you are asked to find a compound expression like these, look for a way to find the expression directly. You want to avoid going through the trouble of finding the individual variables x, or y, or a, or whatever, and then constructing the compound expression from these variables.

Below are three powerful strategies for you to consider when faced with this type of problem. The problem will usually yield to one of the three.

METHOD 1: TRY ADDING OR SUBTRACTING QUANTITIES

Look at the following example:

> If $3x + y = 7$ and $x + 3y = 13$, what is $x + y$?
>
> (A) 3   (B) 4   (C) 5   (D) 6   (E) 7

Don't solve for x or y! Try adding the two equations:

$$
\begin{aligned}
3x + y &= 7 \\
\underline{x + 3y} &= \underline{13} \\
4x + 4y &= 20
\end{aligned}
$$

Dividing each expression by 4:

$$x + y = 5$$

So your answer is Choice C.

METHOD 2: LOOK FOR POSSIBLE FACTORS

Here's a typical example:

> If $xy + 4y - x - 4 = 0$, and $x + 4 = -9$ then $y - 1 =$
>
> (A) +1   (B) +2   (C) 0   (D) −1   (E) −2

Here you can certainly solve for x and get $x = -13$, plug that value of $x = -13$ into the first equation, $xy + 4y - x - 4 = 0$, and then solve for x. Then you would calculate what $x - 1$ is once you solve for the value of x. But ask yourself—Why did the test-maker give you what $x + 4$ was and not what x alone was? And also, why did the test-maker ask you to solve for $y -1$ and not just for x? I mean, you should be pretty sure that the test-maker was not testing to see whether once you knew what y was you could solve for $x - 1$. So what I would do is to do something with the $x + 4$ and the $y - 1$. You should suspect that they are factors of something else you could use to solve the problem. Try multiplying them:

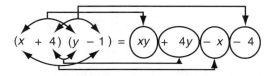

It turns out that $x + 4$ and $y - 1$ are the factors of the first equation in the problem! So therefore:

$$(x + 4)(y - 1) = 0$$

Since the two factors, multiplied together, equal 0, then one or both of the factors must equal 0. But the problem states that $x + 4 = -9$, not 0. So the other factor, $y - 1$, must be 0. Choice C is the correct answer.

METHOD 3: EXPAND ONE OF THE EXPRESSIONS

This is a third way of solving directly for the value of a compound expression. Look at the example:

> If $ab = -2$ and $(a + b)^2 = 8$, what is the value of $a^2 + b^2$?
>
> (A) 4   (B) 6   (C) 8   (D) 10   (E) 12

You first may be tempted to solve for the values of both a and b, and then substitute those values into the expression $a^2 + b^2$. That's the long way to do it. You should ask yourself: if the test-maker wanted you to find out what the value of a and b was, that is, if the test-maker wanted you to solve for both a and b, the test-maker would have probably asked you to find the values of a and b and not a quantity like $a^2 + b^2$. So, you should think, Is there something that I can do with the quantities $ab = -2$ and $(a + b)^2 = 8$ so that I can somehow *produce* $a^2 + b^2$ from them? First, I would be tempted to expand $(a + b)^2$:

$$(a + b)^2 = a^2 + 2ab + b^2 \text{ (Remember that relation?)}$$

Now $ab = -2$ so I substitute $ab = -2$ into the above:

But $(a + b)^2 = 8$ (given), so

$$8 = a^2 + 2(-2) + b^2$$

and we get

$$8 = a^2 - 4 + b^2$$
$$12 = a^2 + b^2$$

So our answer is Choice E. Note why the first few choices are inserted:

Choice A is 4 because in the last step of our solution above, when you bring the -4 over to the other side (in $8 = a^2 - 4 + b^2$) you may subtract $8 - 4$ to get 4.

Choice B is 6 because someone may just add: $8 + (-2)$.

Choice C is 8 because someone may think that $(a + b)^2 = a^2 + b^2 = 8$

Choice D is 10 because someone may subtract: $8 - (-2)$.

Here's another SAT-type example of this strategy:

If $a + b = 4$ and $ab = 2$, what is the value of $a^2 + b^2$?

(A) 12   (B) 14   (C) 16   (D) 18   (E) 20

Expand the equation $a + b = 4$ by squaring both sides. That will yield an equation with the a^2 and the b^2 that you are looking for:

$$(a + b)^2 = 4^2$$
$$a^2 + 2ab + b^2 = 16$$

Now, if $ab = 2$ (the second equation in the problem), you can substitute:

$$a^2 + 2(2) + b^2 = 16$$

Now solve for $a^2 + b^2$:

$$a^2 + 4 + b^2 = 16$$
$$a^2 + b^2 = 16 - 4$$
$$= 12$$

And your answer is Choice A.

STRATEGY 15

Simplify Expressions by Factoring out Common Quantities Before You Multiply

Often, an equation in which compound expressions are multiplied can be solved by factoring out common quantities from each compound expression.

Here's an SAT-type example, using exponents for a change:

If $(2^7 - 2^6)(2^4 - 2^3) = 2^y$, then $y =$

(A) 6   (B) 7   (C) 8   (D) 9   (E) 10

Here you may be tempted to multiply:

$(2^7 - 2^6)(2^4 - 2^3)$

But be a little observant: Factor out the 2^6 from the first factor.

We get $(2^7 - 2^6) = 2^6(2^1 - 2^0) = 2^6(2^1 - 1)$

(Remember: you *add* exponents when multiplying.)

Now factor out 2^3 from $(2^4 - 2^3)$

We get $(2^4 - 2^3) = 2^3(2^1 - 1)$

So we obtain $(2^7 - 2^6)(2^4 - 2^3) = 2^6(2^1 - 1) \times 2^3(2^1 - 1)$

But $2^1 = 2$ and since $2 - 1 = 1$, we find the above is just $2^6 \times 2^3$

which is just 2^9 (add exponents)

Thus the relation,

$(2^7 - 2^6)(2^4 - 2^3) = 2^y$ is equal to 2^9 and $2^y = 2^9$

so $y = 9$ and Choice D is correct.

Many times, factoring such as we did above simplifies the solution tremendously.

STRATEGY 16

In Problems Containing Unfamiliar Symbols, Use Simple Substitution

From my experience, many students have problems with questions containing unfamiliar symbols. For example, here's a problem containing an unfamiliar symbol: a small square. This is not a standard math symbol at all. It is an arbitrary symbol invented by the test-maker to express a particular relationship between the quantities A and B. However, symbols like these can be "translated" and used fairly easily:

> If for all real numbers $A \square B = A^2 + B^2 - AB$, then what is the value of $(2 \square 3) \square 3$?
>
> (A) 6   (B) 18   (C) 37   (D) 64   (E) 108

All that $A \square B$ means is that every time you see a quantity on the left of the box (an A quantity) and a quantity on the right (a B quantity) you write the following:

Now the question asks what is $(2 \square 3) \square 3$?

$$A \; \square \; B \; = \; A^2 + B^2 - AB$$

Calculate what $(2 \square 3)$ is first, since this is inside the parentheses.

It is

$$(2 \; \square \; 3) \; = \; 2^2 + 3^2 - (2)(3) = 4 + 9 - 6 = 7$$

Now we are asked to find what $(2 \square 3) \square 3$ is. We know that $(2 \square 3) = 7$, so $(2 \square 3) \, 3 = 7 \square 3$. But $7 \square 3 = 7^2 + 3^2 - (7)(3) = 49 + 9 - 21 = 37$

Choice C is then correct.

Here's another SAT sample of the same type. In this problem, the arbitrary symbol is $\varnothing$.

If x, y, z, m, n, q are all positive numbers, and if

$$xyz \varnothing mnq = \frac{xyz}{mnq} + \frac{mnq}{xyz}, \quad \text{then}$$

$$xxy \varnothing xyz =$$

(A) $\dfrac{zx}{mn}$ (B) $\dfrac{zx}{x^2+y^2}$ (C) $\dfrac{zx}{x^2+z^2}$ (D) $\dfrac{x^2+z^2}{zx}$ (E) none of these

Now remember to substitute as shown in the diagram:

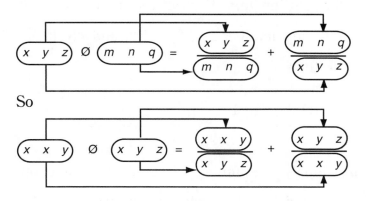

So

Now cancel like terms:

$$\frac{\cancel{x}\, x\, \cancel{y}}{\cancel{x}\, \cancel{y}\, z} + \frac{\cancel{y}\, \cancel{y}\, z}{\cancel{x}\, x\, \cancel{y}} = \frac{x}{z} + \frac{z}{x}$$

But, what? There is no answer in the choice with the form $\dfrac{x}{z} + \dfrac{z}{x}$!

You may at this point be tempted to choose Choice E (none of these), but what I'd do first is to *add:*

$$\frac{x}{z} + \frac{z}{x}$$

Remember the shortcut way?

Multiply

$$\frac{x}{z} + \frac{z}{x} = \frac{x^2 + z^2}{zx}$$

Multiply

So, $\dfrac{x}{z} + \dfrac{z}{x} = \dfrac{x^2 + z^2}{zx}$ which is Choice D.

Try to Get Rid of Fractions

In many examples, you will not have to carry out a tedious solution, but through common sense or logic, you can get an answer readily. Here's an SAT-type example:

> a, b, c, d, and e are different integers. Each of the numbers is equal to one of the following numbers: 1, 2, 4, 12, and 48. If
>
> $6a = \dfrac{1}{4} b = 12c = d = 3e$ then $c =$
>
> (A) 48   (B) 12   (C) 4   (D) 2   (E) 1

The first thing to do is to simplify the numbers: Get rid of the fraction. Remember to multiply instead of divide where you can—we went over this before. So I would try to get rid of the $\dfrac{1}{4}$ from $\dfrac{1}{4} b$. Since we want to find the value of c, we work with $\dfrac{1}{4} b = 12 c$

Multiply both sides of the above by 4. We get

$b = 4 \times 12c = 48c$

This says that b is 48 times another number, c. Look at the numbers for a, b, c, d, and e: 1, 2, 4, 12, and 48. *The only numbers such that one is 48 times another are the numbers 1 and 48.* So, b must be 48 and c must be 1! Thus Choice E is correct. This method is the most direct way of doing this problem and also the fastest way.

STRATEGY 18

When a Question Asks You to Find an Exception, Look for Some Element Common to Four of the Five Choices. The Choice *Without* That Element Is Your Answer.

Here's a fairly common type of SAT question—a question that asks you to find a choice that is *different from* all its neighbors:

> If the dimensions of a rectangular box are represented by the choices, which box has a *different* volume from the other four? The box that has dimensions
>
> (A) 5 by 8 by 12   (D) 3 by 4 by 40
> (B) 15 by 16 by 2   (E) 2 by 6 by 36
> (C) 3 by 32 by 5

There are three ways to do this problem, and one is better than the others. The worst way to do it would be to calculate all the volumes by multiplying the numbers in each of the choices. *Since you are looking for a choice that is different from the other four choices, there must be something in four of the choices that the correct choice doesn't contain.* One way of spotting the correct choice is to notice that Choices A, B, C, and D are such that the product of the numbers in each of those choices ends in 0. Choice E's product does not. But the *best* way to notice the difference is to see that there is a 5 or you can get a 5 from each of the choices, A, B, C, or D, but there is no way to extract a 5 from Choice E. Therefore Choice E is the answer. (Notice that if you had looked for 4's first, you wouldn't have found the answer!)

Note that in the above SAT example, those who would calculate the product in each of the choices would probably go through the first four choices before coming to the correct last one. So here the best strategy would be to start with Choice E and work backwards, calculating the product in Choice D next, etc.

STRATEGY 19

Look out for Unnecessary Information!

Many times there will be a question that presents more information than you absolutely need to solve the problem. It is better not to make use of this "extraneous" information (which I think is very unfair to the test-maker to present to you). You can avoid this trap if you use the right strategy and approach.

Here's an SAT-type example:

In this diagram, $a + b =$

(A) 90   (B) $180 - (c + d)$ (C) $c + d$

(D) $c + d + 90$ (E) 180

Here the key strategy is to try to be observant and use the information that will give you the *fastest* result. If you use the fact that one of the angles of the triangle is 90°, you'll be playing around with angles and trying to figure them out. However, just look at the diagram. Aren't angles a and d vertical angles, and aren't angles b and c vertical angles? So, $a = d$ and $b = c$. Then $a + b = c + d$ because equals added to equals are equal. So, Choice C is correct, and you really didn't have to calculate specifically what the angles were by using the fact that one of the angles of the triangle was 90°. So don't let the test-maker lure you into using unnecessary information or lead you on the wrong road by providing you with such information!

Here's another SAT-type example:

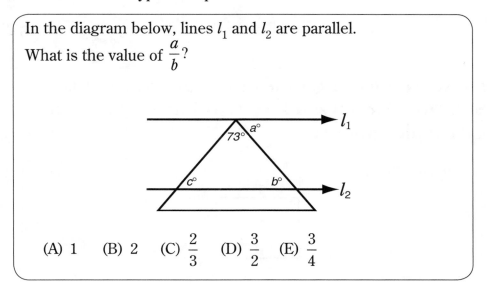

In the diagram below, lines l_1 and l_2 are parallel. What is the value of $\dfrac{a}{b}$?

(A) 1   (B) 2   (C) $\dfrac{2}{3}$ (D) $\dfrac{3}{2}$ (E) $\dfrac{3}{4}$

Here you would be foolish to use the angle 73° and the base angle $c°$ in the triangle. You will spend too much time if you do, calculating angles. Instead look at the parallel lines. What do they tell you? Parallel lines tell you that a lot of angles are related and equal. For example, they tell you that $a° = b°$ (alternate interior angles of parallel lines are equal). Therefore $\dfrac{a}{b}$ must be equal to 1! Choice A is the correct answer. And you didn't even need to use that strange angle 73° or the other angle $a°$!

STRATEGY 20

Draw Connecting Lines in Order to Find the Solution More Quickly. Also Label Quantities Like Sides and Angles.

Here's an example:

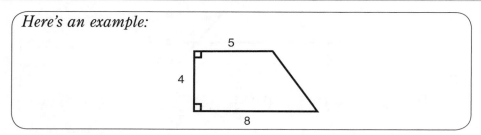

In the diagram above, the perimeter of the quadrilateral

(A) is 21   (B) is 22   (C) is 23   (D) is 24   (E) cannot be determined

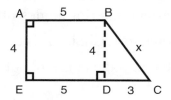

In order to find the perimeter we must find all the sides. So drop a perpendicular line from B to side EC, as shown above and then label sides with BC = x.

Notice that you have thus created a parallelogram ABDE.

Thus ED = AB = 5. Since EC = 8 (given), and ED = 5, *DC must be 3.* Now AE = BD (because ABDE is a parallelogram), so AE = *4 = BD*. Triangle BDC is a right triangle with sides 3 and 4. Call side BC = x.

Then

$$3^2 + 4^2 = x^2 \text{ (Pythagorean Theorem)}$$

$$25 = x^2$$

$$5 = x$$

Thus the perimeter is

$$4 + 5 + 8 + 5 = 22$$

Choice B is correct.

> *Here's another example:*
>
> The maximum distance between two points on or inside a square of side 3 is
>
> (A) $3\sqrt{2}$
>
> (B) 6
>
> (C) $3\sqrt{3}$
>
> (D) 9
>
> (E) 3.5

One should draw a diagram of the square:

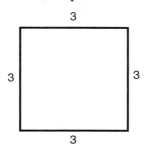

Now you should draw the diagonal:

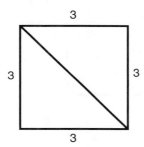

At this point you should be able to see that the maximum distance of two points is the length of the diagonal since the points at the ends of the diagonal are furthest from each other than any other points on or inside the square. The length of the diagonal is (by the Pythagorean Theorem) $\sqrt{3^2 + 3^2} = \sqrt{18} = 3\sqrt{2}^*$. Thus Choice A is correct.

* You should memorize that the diagonal of a square with side x is $x\sqrt{2}$.

A third example:

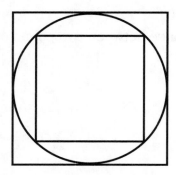

A square is inscribed in a circle above and the circle above is inscribed in a square. What is the ratio of the area of the larger square to that of the smaller?

(A) $\sqrt{2} : 1$

(B) $2 : 1$

(C) $\sqrt{3} : 1$

(D) $3 : 1$

(E) $4 : 1$

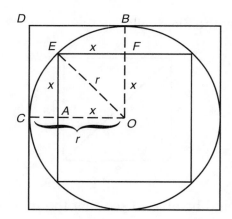

Draw from center of circle O, lines OC, OB, and OE. You have created two squares (OAEF and OCDB) exactly one-quarter the size (area) of the respective smaller and larger squares of the original question. Thus the ratio of the areas of these " $\frac{1}{4}$ " squares is the same ratio of areas of the original squares.

Now the *area of OCDB* is $r \times r = r^2$. (r is the radius of the circle.)
The *area of the square OAEF* is

$$x \times x = x^2$$

But we know by the Pythagorean Theorem (since OAE is a right triangle) that

$$x^2 + x^2 = r^2$$
$$2x^2 = r^2$$
$$x^2 = \frac{r^2}{2}$$

The ratio of the area of the large square to the small square is

$$\frac{r^2}{x^2}$$

and since $x^2 = \dfrac{r^2}{2}$, the ratio becomes

$$\frac{r^2}{\frac{r^2}{2}} = r^2 \times \frac{2}{r^2} = 2$$

Therefore Choice B is correct.

The Grid-Type Math Questions

There are 10 questions on the SAT for which you have to "grid" in your answer rather than choose from a set of choices. Here are the directions to the "grid-type" question. Make sure that you understand these directions completely before you answer any of the grid-type questions.

Directions: Each of the 10 questions in this part requires you to solve the problem and enter your answer by marking the ovals in the special grid, as shown in the examples below.

Answer: $\frac{7}{12}$ or 7/12   Answer: 2.5   Answer: 201
                                                          Either position is
                                                          correct.

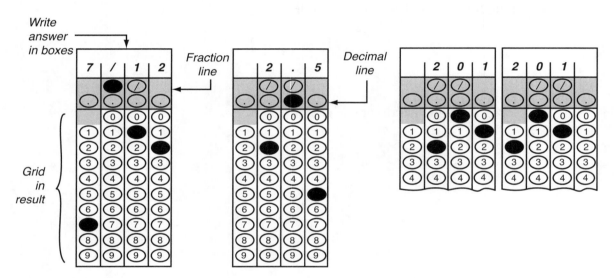

Note: You may start your answers in any column, space permitting. Columns not needed should be left blank.

- Mark no more than one oval in any column.
- Because the answer sheet will be machine-scored, *you will receive credit only if the ovals are filled in correctly.*
- Although not required, it is suggested that you write your answer in the boxes at the top of the columns to help you fill in the ovals accurately.
- Some problems may have more than one correct answer. In such cases, grid only one answer.

- No question has a negative answer.

- *Mixed numbers* such as $2\frac{1}{2}$ must be gridded as 2.5 or 5/2.

If 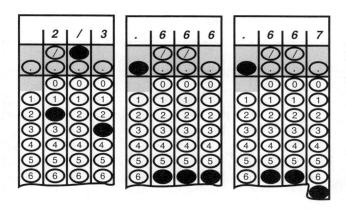 is gridded, it will be interpreted as $\frac{21}{2}$, not $2\frac{1}{2}$.

- *Decimal Accuracy.* If you obtain a decimal answer, *enter the most accurate value the grid will accommodate.* For example, if you obtain an answer such as 0.6666 . . . , you should record the result as .666 or .667. *Less accurate results such as .66 or .67 are not acceptable.*

Acceptable ways to grid $\frac{2}{3}$ = .6666 . . .

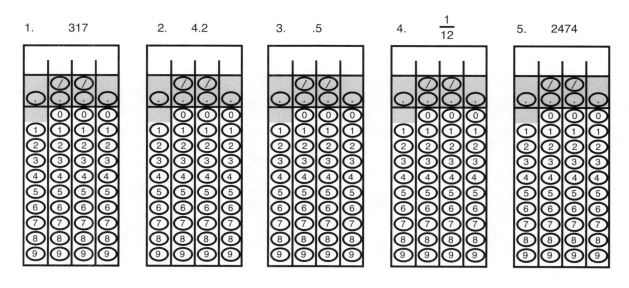

According to the directions on the previous page, grid the following values in grids 1–15:

1. 317   2. 4.2   3. .5   4. $\frac{1}{12}$ 5. 2474

6. $3\frac{1}{2}$ 7. $\frac{57}{3}$ 8.   0   9.   .346   10. $4\frac{3}{4}$

11.   39   12.   1   13. $\frac{3}{8}$ 14.   45.3   15. $8\frac{1}{7}$

Answers

1. 317 2. 4.2 3. .5 4. $\frac{1}{12}$ 5. 2474

6. $3\frac{1}{2}$ 7. $\frac{57}{3}$ 8. 0 9. .346 10. $4\frac{3}{4}$

11. 39 12. 1 13. $\frac{3}{8}$ 14. 45.3 15. $8\frac{1}{7}$

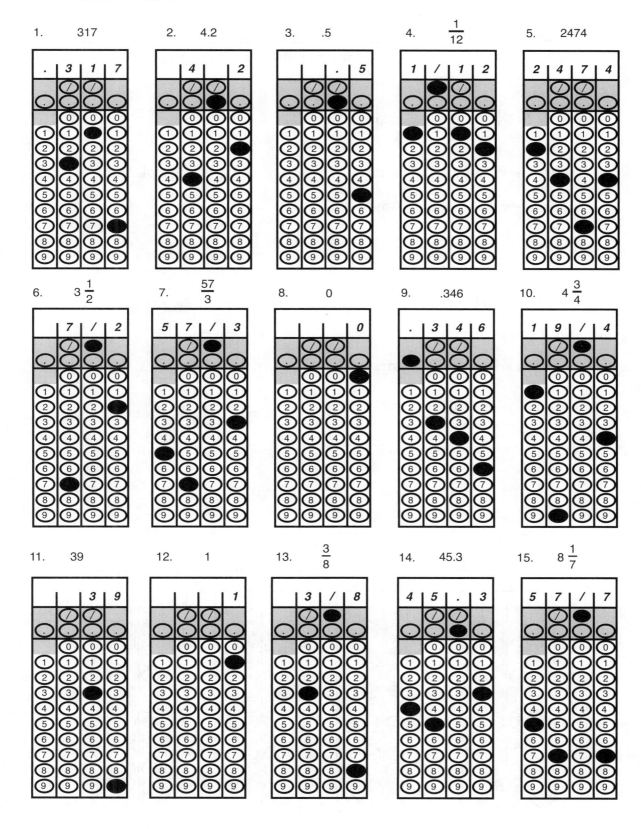

Using a Calculator in the Grid-type Question

In solving the following problem, you can either use a calculator or not. However, the use of a calculator will require a different gridding.

Example:

If $\dfrac{2}{7} < x < \dfrac{3}{7}$ find one value of x.

Solution without a Calculator:

Get some value *between* $\dfrac{2}{7}$ and $\dfrac{3}{7}$.

Write $\dfrac{2}{7} = \dfrac{4}{14}$ and $\dfrac{3}{7} = \dfrac{6}{14}$

So we have $\dfrac{4}{14} < x < \dfrac{6}{14}$.

And x can be $\dfrac{5}{14}$

Solution with a Calculator:

Calculate on calculator:

$$\dfrac{3}{7} = .4285714\ldots$$

$$\dfrac{2}{7} = .2857142\ldots$$

So $.2857142 < x < .4285714$

The grid will look like:

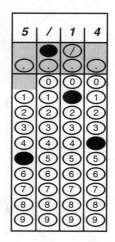

The answer on the grid could look like the following . . . all the way to:

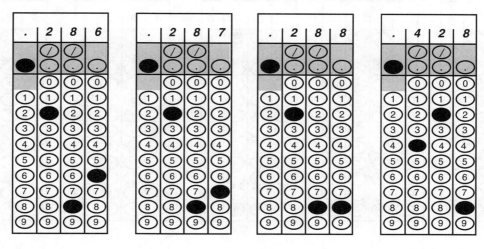

About Calculators

Bring a calculator to the test, but be aware that every math question on the SAT can be solved *without* a calculator; in many questions, it's actually easier not to use one.

Acceptable Calculators:

Graphing calculators,

Scientific calculators, and

Four-function calculators (not recommended) are all permitted during testing

If you have a calculator with characters that are one inch or higher, or if your calculator has a raised display that might be visible to other test takers, you will be seated at the discretion of the test supervisor.

Unacceptable Calculators:

- Laptops or portable/handheld computers,

- Calculators that have a QWERTY keyboard, make noise, use an electrical outlet, or have a paper tape,

- Electronic writing pads or stylus-driven devices,

- Pocket organizers, and

- Cell phone calculators will not be allowed during the test.

MATH PRACTICE EXERCISES

This section contains SAT-type math problems. They will give you the opportunity to practice the strategies you have learned. Each problem is modeled after a specific SAT question that appeared on a recent exam. Before each problem you will see the number of the strategy in this book that will be useful in solving it.

When you work with these problems, see if you can solve each one without looking back first. Look back only if you find you don't know how to approach a problem. It's a good idea to put off starting on these practice problems until you are reasonably sure that you have mastered the strategies.

The discussions after the answers will help you if you find you got an answer wrong. When this happens, work on the problem until you find out where you went wrong. If you don't understand how a particular strategy can be used to solve the problem, work at it until you do understand. Remember, each problem is based on an actual SAT question. If you get a problem wrong, you'll get any similar SAT question wrong too. If you learn where you went wrong, and can handle the problem the next time you see it, you'll add points to your SAT score. Good luck!

Regular Math

Problems 1–11 will give you practice in using two very important math strategies: working backward from Choice E when you must test all choices, and using the "translation technique" in rendering verbal problems into mathematical form. Both strategies require you to analyze the problem before you actually start working on it. So, as you look at each problem, make sure you understand why its particular strategy applies.

1. Strategy No. 6
When you divide a number by $\frac{1}{3}$ you get the same result as if you multiplied that number by

(A) $\frac{1}{3}$ (B) 0.3

(C) 6   (D) $33\frac{1}{3}\%$

(E) 3

2. Srategy No. 6
Of the following, which number is odd?

(A) 6×7

(B) $71 - 17$

(C) $57 + 27$

(D) $75 \div 5$

(E) 4^3

3. Strategy No. 6
The ratio of two whole numbers is NOT equal to which of the following?

(A) $\frac{1}{5}$ (B) 0.50

(C) 5%   (D) $\frac{5^2}{2}$

(E) $\frac{\sqrt{5}}{1}$

4. Strategy No. 6
Which of the following pairs of numbers are UNEQUAL?

(A) $\frac{1}{125}$, 0.008   (B) 4.3, $\frac{43}{10}$

(C) $\frac{5}{7}, \frac{55}{77}$ (D) $\frac{18}{96}, \frac{3}{16}$

(E) $\frac{68}{16}, \frac{32}{6}$

5. Strategy No. 6
x is a number less than 0. Which of the following must be true?

(A) $2 \div 2 = x$ (B) $x \div 2 = 2$
(C) $2 \div x = x$ (D) $x \div x = x$
(E) $x \div x = 1$

6. Strategy No. 6
If $x\,(2/y) = 2$, which is not always true?

(A) $xy = x^2$

(B) $x - y = 0$

(C) $x^2 + y^2 = 2y^2$

(D) $x + y = 2y$

(E) $x = \frac{1}{y}$

7. Strategy No. 7
Mr. Harris is P years old. He is also 4 years older than Mrs. Jones. How many years old was Mrs. Jones 3 years ago?

(A) $P - 7$ (B) $P - 1$

(C) $P + 1$ (D) $P + 7$

(E) $P - 4$

8. Strategy No. 7
Harry and Paul were playing a certain card game. Harry scored 35% more points than Paul scored. If Paul scored 60 points, what was Harry's score?

(A) 60   (B) 70

(C) 65   (D) 81

(E) 92

9. Strategy No. 7
If p is divided by q and this result is then subtracted from the sum of p and q, the final result is

(A) $\frac{q}{p} - (p+q)$ (B) $\frac{p}{q} - (p+q)$

(C) $(p + q) - \frac{p}{q}$ (D) $(p + q) - \frac{q}{p}$

(E) 1

10. Strategy No. 7

Cindy is three times as old as Jeffrey. Two years ago, she was 4 times as old as Jeffrey was then. What is Jeffrey's age now?

(A) 4   (B) 5

(C) 6   (D) 7

(E) 8

11. Strategy Nos. 7, 8

$\frac{3}{5}$ of the people at a party are married and $\frac{2}{3}$ of the married are over 30 years of age. What fraction of the people at the party are married who are under or equal to 30 years of age?

(A) $\frac{6}{15}$ (B) $\frac{3}{5}$

(C) $\frac{2}{3}$ (D) $\frac{1}{5}$

(E) Cannot be determined

The next pair of problems also illustrates an important analytical strategy: looking for the part of the problem that gives you the most information before you actually start working on it.

12. Strategy No. 9

If $\frac{a}{2}$ is an even integer and $\frac{a}{4}$ is an odd integer, then it is possible that a could equal

(A) 104   (B) 88

(C) 44   (D) 16

(E) 14

13. Strategy No. 9

If m ranges in value from 0.01 to 0.1 and n ranges in value from 1.0 to 100.0, then the minimum value of $\frac{m}{n}$ is

(A) 0.0001   (B) 0.001

(C) 0.01   (D) 0.1

(E) 1.0

Here is a group of problems that have in common the strategy of finding an unknown area or length by subtraction from a known quantity or length.

14. Strategy No. 10

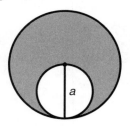

In the figure above, the larger circle has radius a and the smaller circle has diameter a. What is the area of the region that is shaded?

(A) πa^2 (B) 0

(C) $\frac{3\pi a^2}{4}$ (D) $\frac{\pi a^2}{4}$

(E) $\frac{1}{2}\pi a^2$

15. Strategy No. 10

The area of the unshaded area in the figure below in terms of a, b, and c is

(A) $ba - 8c^2$

(B) $4c - ba$

(C) $ba - 4c^2$

(D) $ba + 4c^2$

(E) ba

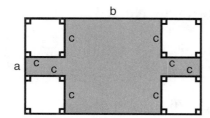

16. Strategy No. 10

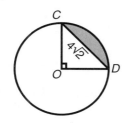

In the above figure, the center of the circle is 0, angle $COD = 90°$, and side CD of triangle COD is $4\sqrt{2}$. What is the area of the shaded region?

(A) $4\pi - 8$

(B) $4\pi + 8$

(C) 16π

(D) $32\pi - 16$

(E) This cannot be determined from the information given.

17. Strategy No. 10

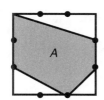

The sides of the square above are divided into three equal segments. The area of the shaded region is A and the area of the square is B. What is the ratio A/B?

(A) $\dfrac{1}{3}$ (B) $\dfrac{2}{3}$

(C) $\dfrac{3}{4}$ (D) $\dfrac{7}{16}$

(E) $\dfrac{5}{8}$

The grouping of problems that comes next utilizes a couple of strategies, but the problems themselves have one thing in common: They were designed by the test-makers to fool you. Read them carefully, and don't be fooled!

18. Strategy No. 5

A car travels K kilometers in h hours and m minutes. What is the car's average speed in kilometers per hour?

(A) $\dfrac{K}{h + m}$ (B) $\dfrac{K + m}{h}$

(C) $(h + \dfrac{m}{60})K$ (D) $\dfrac{K}{h + \dfrac{m}{60}}$

(E) $\dfrac{K}{h + \dfrac{m}{60}}$

19. Strategy No. 5

A space shuttle travels at an average rate of 150 miles every x seconds. How many minutes will it take the rocket to travel 3000 miles?

(A) $\dfrac{3}{x}$ (B) $\dfrac{x}{3}$

(C) $200x$ (D) $\dfrac{200}{x}$ (E) $\dfrac{x}{200}$

20. Strategy No. 11

What is the average rate in miles per hour of a car going uphill at a rate of 20 mph and downhill the same distance at 30 mph?

(A) 21

(B) 23

(C) 24

(D) 25

(E) 28

21. Strategy No. 12

Test scores of 12 students have an average of 70. When the three highest and the three lowest scores are not computed in the average, the new average becomes 64. The average of the scores eliminated is

(A) 76

(B) 77

(C) 78

(D) 79

(E) impossible to determine

22. Strategy No. 12

Twenty students averaged t on a test. Test scores ranged from 0 to 100 inclusive. The average score for the first 15 papers graded was 70. What is the difference between the greatest and least possible values of t ?

(A) 20

(B) 25

(C) 30

(D) 35

(E) 40

23. Strategy No. 12

A weekly test had a range in scores from 0 to 100. John got a score of 60 on the first test and 70 on the second test. What is the lowest score John can get on the next test to average 70 on the first five tests?

(A) 20

(B) 40

(C) 50

(D) 60

(E) 70

24. Strategy No. 14

If $(y + \dfrac{1}{y}) = 9$ then $y^2 + \dfrac{1}{y^2} =$

(A) 76 (B) 77

(C) 78 (D) 79

(E) 81

25. Strategy No. 14

If $a + b = c$ and $a - b = \dfrac{2}{c}$ $(c \neq 0)$, then $a^2 - b^2 =$

(A) $2c$ (B) $\dfrac{c^2 - 2}{c}$

(C) 1 (D) 2

(E) $\dfrac{1}{4}$

26. Strategy No. 14
If $4m - n = 9$ and $2m - 3n = 5$, then $m + n =$

(A) 2 (B) 4

(C) $\dfrac{5}{9}$ (D) -4

(E) -2

27. Strategy No. 14

If $7a + 4b = 21$ and $2a + 2b = 9$, then $\dfrac{9a + 6b}{15} =$

(A) 1

(B) 2

(C) 7

(D) 9

(E) 18

Now try a group of problems whose solution involves factoring. (You may also wish to look back at the material involving exponents in the section titled "Arm Yourself" in the Math Prep chapter.)

28. Strategy No. 13

What is the minimum value of $\dfrac{a+b}{ab}$ if $1 \leq a < b \leq 12$ and a and b are integers?

(A) $\dfrac{13}{12}$ (B) 1

(C) $\dfrac{23}{132}$ (D) $\dfrac{39}{135}$

(E) $\dfrac{24}{144}$

29. Strategy Nos. 15, 13

If $30 \times 4000 = 12 \times 10^x$, $x =$

(A) 3

(B) 4

(C) 5

(D) 6

(E) 7

30. Strategy Nos. 15, 13

If $(2^6)(5^7) = 5(10^p)$, $p =$

(A) 4   (B) 5

(C) 6   (D) 7

(E) 8

31. Strategy No. 15

$(3^4 - 3^5)(3^2 - 3) =$

(A) 186

(B) $-3^3 \times 15$

(C) $-3^2 \times 120$

(D) $-3^4 \times 12$

(E) $-3^4 \times 15$

32. Strategy No. 16

If $\boxed{m}\ \boxed{n}\ \boxed{q} = \dfrac{mn}{q}$ for all nonzero real numbers of m, n, and q then $\boxed{\dfrac{1}{4}}\boxed{\dfrac{1}{3}}\boxed{\dfrac{1}{15}} =$

(A) $\dfrac{4}{5}$

(B) $\dfrac{1}{12} \times \dfrac{1}{15}$

(C) $\dfrac{5}{4}$

(D) $\dfrac{5}{9}$

(E) $\dfrac{9}{5}$

33. Strategy No. 16

For all real numbers where $a \neq 0$, $b \neq 0$, $c \neq 0$

$(m, p, z \oplus a, b, c) = \dfrac{m}{a} + \dfrac{p}{b} + \dfrac{z}{c}$

then

$(1, 2, 3 \oplus -1, -2, -3) \times (1, 4, 1 \oplus 1, 2, 1) =$

(A) -6

(B) $+6$

(C) -12

(D) $+12$

(E) None of these

34. Strategy No. 16

Where a and b are real and where $a \neq 0$ and $b \neq 0$ and $a \neq b$, the following definition applies:

$\emptyset\ \begin{matrix} a \\ \\ b \end{matrix} = \dfrac{a + b}{a - b}$

Which of the following is necessarily true?

Here's a set of problems that deal with the use of arbitrary symbols:

I. $\dfrac{a^2}{\emptyset}\ =\ \dfrac{a^2\ +\ b^2}{a^2\ -\ b^2}$
b^2

II. $\dfrac{a}{\emptyset}\ =\ -\emptyset\dfrac{b}{a}$

III. $\dfrac{\frac{1}{a}}{\emptyset}\ =\ -\emptyset\dfrac{a}{b}$
$\frac{1}{b}$

(A) I only

(B) II only

(C) III only

(D) II and III only

(E) I, II, III

Each of the following questions contains some unnecessary information. See if you can spot the unnecessary information in each question and can solve the problem without using it.

35. **Strategy No. 17**
Given the following relations, which of the choices is equal to a?
Relations:
$$b = \frac{2}{5}c$$
$$f = \frac{2}{3}b$$
$$c = \frac{d}{4}$$
$$d = 3e$$
$$c = \frac{3}{4}a$$

(A) b

(B) c

(C) d

(D) e

(E) f

36. **Strategy No. 19**

If $\dfrac{3}{4}$ the area of an equilateral triangle is 12, what is the area of the triangle?

(A) 6   (B) 16

(C) 9   (D) 20

(E) 12

37. **Strategy No. 20**

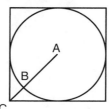

The circle with center A and radius AB is inscribed in the square above. AB is extended to C. What is the ratio of AB to AC?

(A) $\sqrt{2}$

(B) $\dfrac{\sqrt{2}}{4}$

(C) $\dfrac{\sqrt{2}-1}{2}$

(D) $\dfrac{\sqrt{2}}{2}$

(E) None of these

38. Strategy No. 20

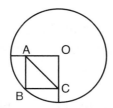

In the figure above, O is the center of a circle with a radius of 6, and $AOCB$ is a square. If point B is on the circumference of the circle, the length of $AC =$

(A) $6\sqrt{2}$
(B) $3\sqrt{2}$
(C) 3
(D) 6
(E) $6\sqrt{3}$

40. Strategy No. 20

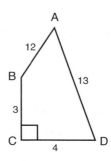

(Note: Figure is not drawn to scale.)

The area of the above figure $ABCD$

(A) is 36
(B) is 108
(C) is 156
(D) is 1,872
(E) Cannot be determined.

39. Strategy No. 20

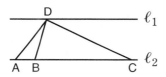

Lines ℓ_1 and ℓ_2 are parallel. $AB = \frac{1}{3}AC$.

$$\frac{\text{The area of triangle } ABD}{\text{The area of triangle } DBC} =$$

(A) $\dfrac{1}{4}$

(B) $\dfrac{1}{3}$

(C) $\dfrac{3}{8}$

(D) $\dfrac{1}{2}$

(E) Cannot be determined.

41. Strategy No. 20

In the above figure, two points, B and C, are placed to the right of point A such that $4AB = 3AC$. The value of $\dfrac{BC}{AB}$

(A) equals $\dfrac{1}{3}$

(B) equals $\dfrac{2}{3}$

(C) equals $\dfrac{3}{2}$

(D) equals 3

(E) Cannot be determined.

Grid Questions

Problems 42–51 give you practice in recording your answers on a grid. Most of the problems in this set can be solved using basic math skills and logic. Where a particular strategy would be appropriate, a strategy number is included for reference.

Directions: Each of the 10 questions in this part requires you to solve the problem and enter your answer by marking the ovals in the special grid, as shown in the examples below.

Answer: $\frac{7}{12}$ or 7/12   Answer: 2.5   Answer: 201

Either position is correct.

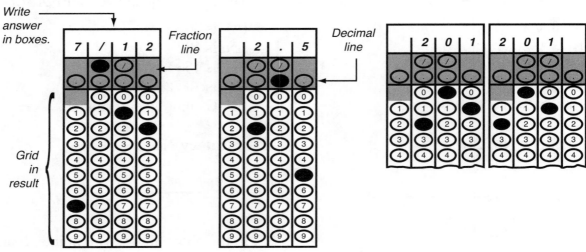

Note: You may start your answers in any column, space permitting. Columns not needed should be left blank.

- Mark no more than one oval in any column.
- Because the answer sheet will be machine-scored, *you will receive credit only if the ovals are filled in correctly*
- Although not required, it is suggested that you write your answer in the boxes at the top of the columns to help you fill in the ovals accurately.
- Some problems may have more than one correct answer. In such cases, grid only one answer.
  - No question has a negative answer.
  - *Mixed numbers* such as $2\frac{1}{2}$ must be gridded as 2.5 or 5/2.

    If [2|1|/|2] is gridded, it will be interpreted as $\frac{21}{2}$, not $2\frac{1}{2}$.

- *Decimal Accuracy.* If you obtain a decimal answer, *enter the most accurate value the grid will accommodate.* For example, if you obtain an answer such as 0.6666 . . . , you should record the result as .666 or .667. *Less accurate results such as .66 or .67 are not acceptable.*

42. Strategy No. 7

Susan has 3 times as many jellybeans as Mary, and Rose has 18 times as many jellybeans as Mary. What is the ratio

$$\frac{\text{Rose's jellybeans}}{\text{Susan's jellybeans}}?$$

43. Strategy: Know Volumes of Figures

If two cubes have edges of 1 and 2, what is the sum of their volumes?

44. Strategy No. 16

If the numerical value of the binomial coefficient $\binom{n}{2}$ is given by the formula $\frac{n(n-1)}{2}$, then the numerical value of is $\binom{15}{2}$

45. Strategy No. 19

The letters r and s represent numbers satisfying $r^2 - 9$ and $s^2 - 25$. The difference between the greatest possible values of $s - r$ and $r - s$ is

46. Strategy No. 7

According to the graph, what percent of the people in the group had brown eyes?

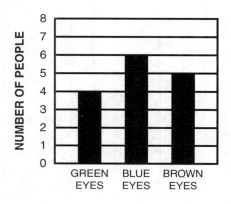

47. Strategy No. 19

$$
\begin{array}{r}
N\ 5 \\
L\ M \\
\hline
3\ 8\ 5 \\
3\ 8\ 5 \\
\hline
4,\ 2\ 3\ 5
\end{array}
$$

In the multiplication problem above, L, M, and N each represent one of the digits 0 through 9. If the problem is computed correctly, find N.

48. Strategy No. 16

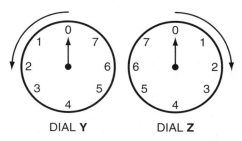

DIAL **Y**   DIAL **Z**

In the figure above, the hand of dial Z moves in a clockwise direction. When its hand makes one complete revolution, it causes the hand of dial Y to move 1 number in the counterclockwise direction. How many complete revolutions of the hand of dial Z are needed to move the hand of dial Y 3 complete revolutions?

49. Strategy No. 19

To make enough paste to hang 6 rolls of wallpaper, a $\frac{1}{4}$-pound package of powder is mixed with $2\frac{1}{2}$ quarts of water. How many pounds of powder are needed to make enough of the same mixture of paste to hang 21 rolls of paper?

50. Strategy No. 12

On a mathematics test, the average score for a certain class was 90. If 40 percent of the class scored 100 and 10 percent scored 80, what was the average score for the remainder of the class?

51. Strategy: Know Facts about Triangles

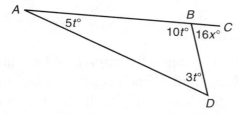

In the figure above, *ABC* is a line segment. What is the value of *x*?

Grids for Sample Questions

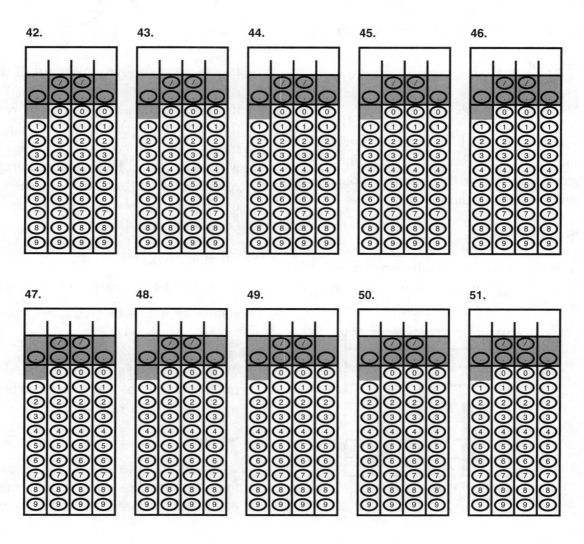

Answers to Regular Math Questions

1–6. In testing choices (Questions 1–6), always work from Choice E backwards.

1. E

2. D

3. E

4. E

5. E

6. E

7. A. Translate: $P = 4 + J$; $P - 4 = J$; $P - 7 = J - 3$.

8. D. Translate: $H = (\frac{35}{100})P + P$; $H = (\frac{35}{100})60 + 60$; $H = 21 + 60 = 81$

9. C. Translate: If p is divided by $q \to \frac{p}{q}$; the sum of p and $q \to p + q$; subtracted $\to -$.

   So the answer is $p + q - \frac{p}{q}$.

10. C. Translate: $C = 3J$; $C - 2 = 4(J - 2)$; $3J - 2 = 4J - 8$; $6 = J$

11. D. Translate: $(\frac{3}{5})P = M, \dfrac{\frac{1}{3}M}{P} = \dfrac{\frac{1}{3}M}{\frac{5}{3}M} = (\frac{1}{3}) \times (\frac{3}{5}) = \frac{1}{5}$

12. C. The information that $\frac{a}{4}$ is an odd integer is the most important information.

13. A. Minimum of $\frac{m}{n}$ occurs when m is minimum and n is maximum. This is when $m = .01$ and
    $n = 100$. So minimum of $\frac{m}{n} = \frac{.01}{100} = 0.0001$

14. C. Shaded area = large circle area − small circle area $= \pi a^2 - \pi(\frac{a}{2})^2$

    $= \pi a^2 - \frac{\pi a^2}{4} = \frac{3\pi a^2}{4}$

15. C. Unshaded area = area of rectangle − area of four squares $= ba - 4c^2$

16. A. Shaded area = area of $\frac{1}{4}$ of circle − area of triangle.

    $= \frac{\pi(\overline{OD})^2}{4} - \frac{(\overline{OD})^2}{2} = \frac{\pi 4^2}{4} - \frac{4^2}{2} = 4\pi - 8$

17. B. $B = 3 \times 3 = 9$;

$A = B -$ area of 3 of the triangles.

So $A = B - \dfrac{1 \times 2 + 1 \times 1 + 3 \times 1}{2} = 9 - 3 = 6$

$\dfrac{A}{B} = \dfrac{6}{9} = \dfrac{2}{3}$

18. E. You are asked to find speed in kilometers *per hour*. You must divide minutes by 60 to get hours. So m minutes $= \dfrac{m}{60}$ hours.

19. B. $\dfrac{150}{\frac{x}{60}} = \dfrac{3000}{y}$ $\qquad\qquad y = \dfrac{3000}{150} \times \dfrac{x}{60} =$

20. C. Let distance uphill (or downhill) = 60 miles. (We choose this number because it can be evenly divided by both 20 and 30). Uphill time then $= \dfrac{60}{20} =$ hours. Dowhill time $= \dfrac{60}{30} =$ hours. Total time is then 5 hours. Total distance is $60 + 60 = 120$ miles.

So average rate = total distance/total time $= \dfrac{120}{5} = 24$ mph.

21. A. $\dfrac{\text{Sum of scores}}{12} = 70$

$\dfrac{\text{Sum of scores} - (\text{three highest and three lowest})}{6} = 64$

Separate this last expression:

$\dfrac{\text{Sum of scores}}{6} - \dfrac{(\text{three highest and three lowest})}{6} = 64$

Average of scores eliminated $=$

$\dfrac{\text{three highest} + \text{three lowest}}{6} = \dfrac{\text{sum of scores}}{6} - 64$

Now $\dfrac{\text{sum of scores}}{12} = 70$, so $\dfrac{\text{sum of scores}}{6} = 140$

$140 - 64 = 76$

22. B. $\dfrac{\text{Sum of scores}}{20} = t$

$\dfrac{\text{Sum of 15 papers}}{15} = 70$

(Although you don't really need to use this figure.)

$$\frac{\text{Sum of 15 papers} + \text{sum of 5 papers}}{20} = t$$

$$\frac{\text{Sum of 15 papers}}{20} + \frac{\text{sum of 5 papers}}{20} = t$$

$$\text{greatest} = 100 \times \frac{5}{20} = \frac{500}{20}$$

$$\text{least} = 0 \times \frac{5}{20} = 0$$

$$\text{greatest} - \text{least} = \frac{500}{20} - 0 = \frac{500}{20} = 25$$

23. A. To get the lowest score on the next test John will have to score 100 on each of the last two tests. So:

$$\frac{60 + 70 + x + 100 + 100}{5} = 70;$$
$$330 + x = 350;$$
$$x = 20$$

For questions 24–27—*Don't* solve for individual variables first! Try to find value of a complete expression directly.

24. D. Start by squaring both sides of the first equation; then expand the expression.

$(y + \frac{1}{y})^2:$

$(y + \frac{1}{y})^2 = 9 \times 9 = 81; \; y^2 + \frac{1}{y^2} + 2 = 81; \; y^2 + \frac{1}{y^2} = 79$

25. D. $a + b = c; \; a - b = \frac{2}{c}; \; (a + b)(a - b) = a^2 - b^2 = \frac{2}{c} \times c = 2$

26. A. $4m - n = 9$

$\frac{-(2m - 3n = 5)}{2m + 2n = 4} \qquad m + n = 2$

27. B.

$$7a + 4b = 21$$
$$\underline{+2a + 2b = 9}$$
$$9a + 6b = 30$$

$$\frac{9a + 6b}{15} = \frac{30}{15} = 2$$

28. C. $\dfrac{a+b}{ab} = \dfrac{a}{ab} + \dfrac{b}{ab} = \dfrac{1}{b} + \dfrac{1}{a}$

Minimum occurs when b and a are maximum.

So max of $\dfrac{1}{b} + \dfrac{1}{a}$ is $\dfrac{1}{12} + \dfrac{1}{11}$ (since $12 \geq b > a$ and b and a are integers)

$$\frac{1}{12} + \frac{1}{11} = \frac{12 + 11}{12 \times 11} = \frac{23}{132}$$

29. B. $30 \times 4000 = 12 \times 10^4$. Thus $x = 4$.

30. C. $2^6 \times 5^7 = (2 \times 5)^6 \times 5^1$. Thus $p = 6$.

31. D. $(3^4 - 3^5)(3^2 - 3) = 3^4(3^0 - 3^1)(3^2 - 3)$
$$= 3^4(1 - 3)(6)$$
$$= 3^4(-2)(6) = -3^4(12)$$

Note: 32, 33, 34 require simple substitution.

32. C. $\boxed{\dfrac{1}{4}} - \boxed{\dfrac{1}{3}} - \boxed{\dfrac{1}{15}} = \dfrac{\frac{1}{4} \times \frac{1}{3}}{\frac{1}{15}} = \dfrac{\frac{1}{12}}{\frac{1}{15}} = \dfrac{1}{12} \times 15 = \dfrac{5}{4}$

33. C. $(1,2,3 \oplus -1, -2 -3) = \dfrac{1}{-1} + \dfrac{2}{-2} + \dfrac{3}{-3}$

$(1,4,1 \oplus 1,2,1) \qquad = \dfrac{1}{1} + \dfrac{4}{2} + \dfrac{1}{1}$

Product: $(1,2,3 \oplus -1, -2, -3) \times (1,4,1 \oplus 1,2,1)$

$$= \frac{1}{-1} + \frac{2}{-2} + \frac{3}{-3} \times \frac{1}{1} + \frac{4}{2} + \frac{1}{1}$$
$$= (-3) \times 4 = -12$$

34. **E.** I.
$$\frac{a^2}{\varnothing\ b^2} = \frac{a^2+b^2}{a^2-b^2}; \text{ I is correct.}$$

II.
$$-\frac{b}{\varnothing\ a} = -\frac{b+a}{b-a} = +\frac{a+b}{a-b}; \text{ II is correct}$$

III.
$$\frac{\frac{1}{a}}{\varnothing} = \frac{\frac{1}{a}+\frac{1}{b}}{\frac{1}{b}-\frac{1}{b}} = \frac{\frac{b+a}{ab}}{\frac{b-a}{ab}} = \frac{b+a}{b-a} = -\frac{a}{\varnothing\ b}$$

III is correct

35. **D.** Get rid of fractions:

$5b = 2c$

$3f = 2b$

$\left.\begin{array}{l} 4c = \\ d = \end{array}\right\} \begin{array}{l} d \\ 3e \end{array} \rightarrow 3e = d = 4c$

$4c = 3a \rightarrow 4c = 3a$, So $3a = 3e; a = e$

36. **B.** $\frac{3}{4} A = 12; A = 16$

Note: You do not need to use the fact that you are working with an *equilateral* triangle.

37. **D.** Always draw or extend lines to get more information. Also label unknown lengths, angles, or arcs with letters.

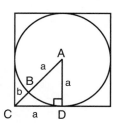

Label $AB = a$ and $BC = b$.

Draw a perpendicular AD. Note it is just the radius, a. CD also $= a$, because each side of the square is length $2a$ (the diameter) and CD is $\frac{1}{2}$ the side of the square.

We want to find $\dfrac{AB}{AC} = \dfrac{a}{a+b}$

Now $\triangle ADC$ is an isosceles right triangle so $AD = CD = a$.

By the Pythagorean Theorem, $a^2 + a^2 = (a + b)^2$ where $a = b$ is hypotenuse of right triangle.

We get: $2a^2 = (a + b)^2$
Divide by $(a + b)^2$:
$$\frac{2a^2}{(a + b)^2} = 1$$
Divide by 2:
$$\frac{a^2}{(a + b)^2} = \frac{1}{2}$$

Take square roots of both sides:
$$\frac{a}{(a + b)} = \frac{1}{\sqrt{2}} =$$
$$= \frac{1}{\sqrt{2}}\left(\frac{\sqrt{2}}{\sqrt{2}}\right)$$
$$= \frac{\sqrt{2}}{2} \quad (\textit{Answer})$$

38. D.

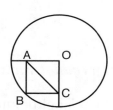

This is tricky if not impossible if you don't draw OB. So draw OB:

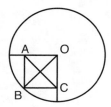

Since $AOCB$ is a square, $OB = AC$; and since $OB = $ radius $= 6$, $AC = 6$.

39. D.

$$AB = \frac{1}{3}AC$$

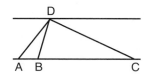

Ask yourself, what is the area of a triangle? It is $\frac{1}{2}$ (height x base). So let's get the heights and the bases of the triangles *ABD* and *DBC*. First draw the altitude (call it *h*).

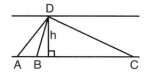

Now label $AB = \frac{1}{3}AC$ (given)

This makes $BC = \frac{2}{3} AC$, since $AB + BC = AC$

Thus the area of $\triangle ABD = \frac{1}{2}h\,(AB) = \frac{1}{2}h\left(\frac{1}{3}AC\right)$

Area of $\triangle DBC = \frac{1}{2}h\,(BC) = \frac{1}{2}h\left(\frac{2}{3}AC\right)$

$$\frac{\text{Area of } ABD}{\text{Area of } DBC} = \frac{\frac{1}{2}h\left(\frac{1}{3}AC\right)}{\frac{1}{2}h\left(\frac{2}{3}AC\right)}$$

$$= \frac{\frac{1}{3}}{\frac{2}{3}} = \frac{1}{3} \times \frac{3}{2} = \frac{1}{2}$$

40. **A.**

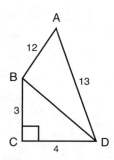

Draw *BD*. *BCD* is a 3-4-5 right triangle, so *BD* = 5. Now remember that a 5-12-13 triangle is also a right triangle, so angle *ABD* is a right angle. The area of triangle *BCD* is (3 × 4)/2 = 6 and the area of triangle *BAD* is (5 × 12)/2 = 30, so the total area is 36.

41. **A.**

Place *B* and *C* to the right of *A:*

$$\overset{\textstyle\bullet}{\underset{\text{A}}{}}\quad\overset{\textstyle\bullet}{\underset{\text{B}}{}}\quad\overset{\textstyle\bullet}{\underset{\text{C}}{}}\quad\ell$$

Now label AB = a and BC = b:

$$\overset{\textstyle\bullet}{\underset{\text{A}}{}}\overset{a}{}\overset{\textstyle\bullet}{\underset{\text{B}}{}}\overset{b}{}\overset{\textstyle\bullet}{\underset{\text{C}}{}}\quad\ell$$

$\dfrac{BC}{AB} = \dfrac{b}{a}$ ($\dfrac{b}{a}$ is what we want to find)

We are given $4AB = 3AC$

So, $4a = 3(a + b)$.

Expand: $4a = 3a + 3b$

Subtract 3a: $a = 3b$

Divide by 3 and *a*: $\dfrac{1}{3} = \dfrac{b}{a}$

But remember $\dfrac{BC}{AB} = \dfrac{b}{a}$, so $\dfrac{BC}{AB} = \dfrac{1}{3}$

Answers to Grid Questions

42. Let M = number of Mary's jellybeans   (1)
    Let S = number of Susan's jellybeans   (2)
    And R = number of Rose's jellybeans   (3)

We are looking for $\dfrac{\text{Rose's jellybeans}}{\text{Susan's jellybeans}}$ (4)

According to the given, S = 3M
Also given, R = 18M   (5)

Dividing (6) by (5), we get $\dfrac{R}{S} = \dfrac{6}{1}$ (6)

43. Volume of cube = $(\text{side})^3$
    Thus, the volume of a cube whose
        edge has length of $1 = 1^3 = 1$.
    The volume of a cube whose edge
        has the length of $2 = 2^3 = 8$.
    Thus the sum of the volumes of the
        two cubes = 8 + 1 = 9.

44.   Given: $\binom{n}{2} = \dfrac{n(n-1)}{2}$

    Thus $\binom{15}{2} = \dfrac{15(15-1)}{2}$

           $= \dfrac{15(14)}{2}$

           $= 105$

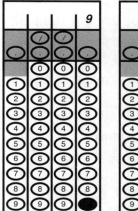

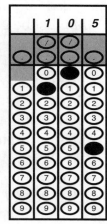

45. *Given:* $r^2 = 9$ (1)
    $s^2 = 25$ (2)
    From (1) and (2), we have
    $r = 3$ or -3 (3)
    $s = 5$ or -5 (4)

The greatest possible value of $s - r$ occurs
when s is a maximum and r is a minimum or
    $5 - (-3) = 8$ (5)

The greatest possible value of $r - s$ occurs
when r is a maximum and s is a minimum or
    $3 - (-5) = 8$ (6)

The answer to this question is the difference between (5) and (6): $8 - 8 = 0$

46. According to the graph, 4 people had green eyes, 6 people had blue eyes, and 5 had brown eyes, so there were 15 people in the group. The percentage, x, can be found by setting up the ratio

$$\frac{x}{100} = \frac{5}{15} = \frac{1}{3}, \text{ or } x = 33\frac{1}{3}. \ 33\frac{1}{3}\% \text{ had brown eyes.}$$

Note that $33\frac{1}{3}$ translates to 33.3 on the grid.

47. From the given problem we see that $N5 \times M = 385$
Try $N = 1$
  $15 \times M = 385$
M must be greater than 10, which is incorrect.
Try $N = 2$:
  $25 \times M = 385$
M must be greater than 10, which is incorrect.
Try $N = 3$
  $35 \times M = 385$
M must be greater than 10, which is incorrect.
Try $N = 4$
  $45 \times M = 385$
M is not an integer.
Try $N = 5$
  $55 \times M = 385.$ Thus, $M = 7$
Therefore, L can be equal to 7 to give:

$$
\begin{array}{r}
N\ 5 \\
L\ M \\
\hline
3\ 8\ 5 \\
3\ 8\ 5 \\
\hline
4,2\ 3\ 5
\end{array}
$$

Alternate Method:

The number $N5$ can be written as $10N + 5$.
  For example: $25 = 10 \times 2 + 5$.
So we have $(10N + 5) \times M = 385$ in the multiplication example given.
Factor to make problem simpler.
  $10N + 5 = 5(2N + 1)$
So: $5(2N + 1) \times M = 385$
Now divide by 5: $(2N + 1)M = 77$
The only two pairs of integers that can be multiplied to produce 77 are 11 and 7, or 77 and 1.
It is given that N and M must be less than 10.
So either $2N + 1 = 11, M = 7$

MATH PRACTICE EXERCISES • 141

or $2N + 1 = 7$, $N = 11$ (which is impossible)
If $2N + 1 = 11$, then $N = 5$.

48. By definition, the hand of dial Y moves
one number for each complete
revolution of the hand of dial Z. (1)

The hand of dial Y must move 8 numbers to
complete one of its own
revolutions. Therefore it must
move 24 numbers to complete 3 of its revolutions.

From (1) above, 24 numbers on dial y correspond
to 24 complete revolutions on dial Z.

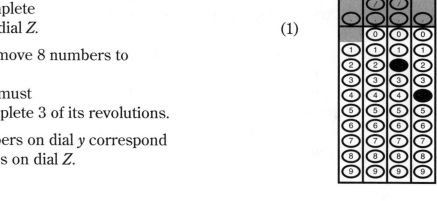

49. Given: 6 rolls uses $\frac{1}{4}$ pound of powder (1)

6 rolls uses $2\frac{1}{2}$ quarts of water (2)

Number (2) is not necessary to solve the problem!
We need to know how much powder is needed for
the same mixture for 21 rolls.
Let x = number of pounds for 21 rolls. We set up a proportion:
Multiply (3) by 1/6. We get

$$\frac{6 \text{ rolls}}{\frac{1}{4} \text{ pound}} = \frac{21 \text{ rolls}}{x}$$

$$(6 \text{ rolls})x = (21 \text{ rolls}) \times (\tfrac{1}{4} \text{ pound})$$

$$6x = 21 \times \tfrac{1}{4} \text{ pound} \tag{3}$$

Multiply (3) by $\frac{1}{6}$. We get

$$\frac{1}{6}(6x) = \frac{1}{6}(21 \times \frac{1}{4} \text{ pound})$$

$$x = \frac{1}{6} \times 21 \times \frac{1}{4} \text{ pound}$$

$$x = \frac{21}{24} \text{ pound}$$

$$x = \frac{7}{8} \text{ of a pound.}$$

Note that answer may be gridded as either 7/8 or .875.

50. Let x = Total number of students (1)
    Then
       $.40x$ = Number of students scoring 10 (2)
       $.10x$ = Number of students scoring 80 (3)
          y = Average score of remaining students (4)
    We know the whole class is 100%. (5)
    From (2) and (3) we know: 40% + 10% = 50%
    have been accounted for. (6)
    Subtracting (6) from (5), we get remaining
    students represent 50% of the class. (7)
    Using (7) and (1), we get:
       Number of remaining students = $.5x$ (8)
    We know:

$$\text{Average} = \frac{\text{Sum of the values}}{\text{Total number of values}}$$

(9)

Given: Average = 90 (10)
Substituting (1), (2), (3), (4), (8) and (10) into (9),
we get:

(11)

$$90 = \frac{.40x(100) + .10x(80) + .5x(y)}{x}$$

Multiply (11) by x. We get:
$90x = 40x + 8x + .5xy$
$90x = 48x + .5xy$
$42x = .5xy$
$42 = .5y$
$84 = y$

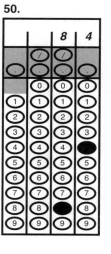

50.

51. The sum of the angles in a triangle = 180°
    Therefore:

$3t° + 5t° + 10t° = 180$
$\qquad\qquad 18t = 180$
$\qquad\qquad\quad t = 10$ (1)

Since ABC is a line segment,
straight angle $ABC = 180°$ (2)
$< ABC = < ABD + < DBC$ (3)
Substituting the given and (2) in (3) gives:
$180 = 10t + 16x$ (4)
Substituting (1) in (4) we have:
$180 = 10(10) + 16x$
$180 = 100 + 16x$
$\ \ 80 = 16x$
$\ \ \ 5 = x$

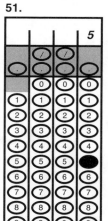

51.

THE SAT WRITING TEST

The Writing test will include a direct writing sample and multiple-choice questions that require recognition of the conventions of standard written English, appropriate diction, and effective and logical expression.

The SAT Writing Test will include:

- An essay that will provide a direct measure of writing ability;

- Essay topics which will not assume any specific subject-matter knowledge;

- Revision-in-context passages which will present a context larger than a discrete sentence and therefore permit questions on logic, coherence, and organization;

- Revision-in-context tasks which are similar to common in-class exercises in which students revise their own essays;

- Usage questions which will require students to recognize errors. Sentence-correction questions will require recognition of errors and selection of the correct rephrasing.

The SAT Writing Section

The SAT Writing section will measure a student's mastery of developing and expressing ideas effectively. It will include both multiple-choice items and an essay. The multiple-choice component of the writing section will measure the student's understanding of how to use language in a clear, consistent manner and how to improve a piece of writing through revision and editing. Students will be asked to recognize sentence errors, to choose the best version of a piece of writing, and to improve paragraphs within a writing context. However, they will not be asked to define or to use grammatical terms, and spelling or capitalization will not be tested.

For the essay, students will have 25 minutes to write a first draft of an original essay. This will be a direct measure of their ability, under timed conditions, to do the kind of writing required in most college courses—writing that emphasizes precise use of language, logical presentation of ideas, development of a point of view, and clarity of expression.

The combination of the multiple-choice items and the essay will provide an assessment of writing that takes into account both the student's understanding of the conventions of language and his or her ability to develop ideas in a thoughtful, coherent, and cogent essay.

The scores for the SAT Writing section will range from 200 to 800. Two subscores will be given for the writing section: a multiple-choice subscore that will range from 20 to 80 and an essay subscore that will range from 2 to 12. Essays not written on the essay assignment will be given a score of zero. The essay component will count toward roughly one-third of the total writing score, and the multiple-choice component will count toward two-thirds of the total writing score.

Content of the Writing Test

Multiple-Choice Questions: 35 Minutes, 49 Questions*

- Usage—Identifying Sentence Errors: 18 questions

- Sentence Correction—Improving Sentences: 25 questions

- Revision-in-Context—Improving Paragraphs: 6 questions

Essay (Writing Exercise): 25 Minutes
Scoring the Writing Test

All essays will be scored holistically. Two readers will independently read each essay and score according to agreed-upon criteria.

Essay Reporting Service

Students may request that copies of essays be sent to high schools and/or colleges.

*The PSAT will include items in this multiple-choice writing section.

The Essay on the SAT Writing Test

On the SAT, you will be required to write an essay. Here's an example of the directions to the Essay:

SECTION 2	Time—25 minutes	ESSAY
	1 Question	

Directions: Consider carefully the following excerpt and the assignment below it. Then plan and write an essay that explains your ideas as persuasively as possible. Keep in mind that the support you provide—both reasons and examples—will help make your view convincing to the reader.

Please note the essays are considered "first drafts" and are scored holistically. This means readers will award a score according to the overall quality of the essay. They will take into account aspects of writing such as the development of ideas, supporting examples, organization, word choice, and sentence structure.

> The principle is this: each failure leads us closer to deeper knowledge, to greater creativity in understanding old data, to new lines of inquiry. Thomas Edison experienced 10,000 failures before he succeeded in perfecting the lightbulb. When a friend of his remarked that 10,000 failures was a lot, Edison replied, "I didn't fail 10,000 times, I successfully eliminated 10,000 materials and combinations that didn't work."
>
> *Myles Brand, "Taking the Measure of Your Success"*
>
> **Assignment:** What is your view on the idea that it takes failure to achieve success? In an essay, support your position using an example (or examples) from literature, the arts, history, current events, politics, science and technology, or your experience or observation.

WHEN THE SUPERVISOR ANNOUNCES THAT 25 MINUTES HAVE PASSED, YOU MUST STOP WRITING THE ESSAY. DO NOT GO ON TO ANY OTHER SECTION IN THE TEST.

YOU MAY MAKE NOTES ON THIS PAGE, BUT YOU MUST WRITE YOUR ESSAY ON THE ANSWER SHEET.

Here are some more sample Essay topics:

Consider carefully the following statement and the assignment below it. Then, plan and write your essay as directed.

"Outrageous behavior is instructive. It reveals to us the limits of our tolerance."

Assignment: The quotation implies that those who go beyond accepted standards help us to clarify our own standards. Do you agree or disagree with the quotation? Discuss, supporting your position with examples from current affairs, literature, history, or your own experience.

Consider carefully the following quotation and the assignment following it. Then, plan and write your essay as directed.

"People seldom stand up for what they truly believe; instead they merely go along with the popular view."

Assignment: Do you agree or disagree with this statement? Write an essay in which you support your opinion with specific examples from history, contemporary affairs, literature, or personal observation.

Consider carefully the following statement and the assignment below it. Then, plan and write your essay as directed.

"Everything has its cost."

Assignment: Choose an example from literature, current affairs, history, or from personal observation in which a cause, an ideal, or an object had to be paid for at some cost. What was that cost? Was what was gained worth it, or was the cost too high? Give reasons for your position.

A Few Words about Scoring the Essay. Even with some errors in spelling, punctuation, and grammar, a student can get a top score on the essay. The highly trained high school and college composition teachers who score the essays will follow a rubric that focuses upon content, organization, and language usage and sentence structure. Each essay will be scored independently by two such readers on a 1–6 scale. If the readers' scores differ by more than two points, the test will be evaluated by a third reader. We know from our experience with the SAT II: Writing test that fewer than 2 percent of all scored essays require a third reader.

The rubric for the SAT Writing section will be similar to the one used for the previous SAT II: Writing Test, which follows:

The SAT Scoring Guide

Score of 6	Score of 5	Score of 4
An essay in this category is *outstanding*, demonstrating *clear and consistent mastery*, although it may have a few minor errors. A typical essay	An essay in this category is *effective*, demonstrating *reasonably consistent mastery*, although it will have occasional errors or lapses in quality. A typical essay	An essay in this category is *competent*, demonstrating *adequate mastery*, although it will have lapses in quality. A typical essay
• effectively and insightfully develops a point of view on the issue and demonstrates outstanding critical thinking, using clearly appropriate examples, reasons, and other evidence to support its position	• effectively develops a point of view on the issue and demonstrates strong critical thinking, generally using appropriate examples, reasons, and other evidence to support its position	• develops a point of view on the issue and demonstrates competent critical thinking, using adequate examples, reasons, and other evidence to support its position
• is well organized and clearly focused, demonstrating clear coherence and smooth progression of ideas	• is well organized and focused, demonstrating coherence and progression of ideas	• is generally organized and focused, demonstrating some coherence and progression of ideas
• exhibits skillful use of language, using a varied, accurate, and apt vocabulary	• exhibits facility in the use of language, using appropriate vocabulary	• exhibits adequate but inconsistent facility in the use of language, using generally appropriate vocabulary
• demonstrates meaningful variety in sentence structure	• demonstrates variety in sentence structure	• demonstrates some variety in sentence structure
• is free of most errors in grammar, usage, and mechanics	• is generally free of most errors in grammar, usage, and mechanics	• has some errors in grammar, usage, and mechanics

Essays not written on the essay assignment sheet will receive a score of zero.

Score of 3	Score of 2	Score of 1
An essay in this category is *inadequate*, but demonstrates *developing mastery*, and is marked by ONE OR MORE of the following weaknesses:	An essay in this category is *seriously limited*, demonstrating *little mastery*, and is flawed by ONE OR MORE of the following weaknesses:	An essay in this category is *fundamentally lacking*, demonstrating *very little* or *no mastery*, and is severely flawed by ONE OR MORE of the following weaknesses:
• develops a point of view on the issue, demonstrating some critical thinking, but may do so inconsistently or use inadequate examples, reasons, or other evidence to support its position	• develops a point of view on the issue that is vague or seriously limited, demonstrating weak critical thinking, providing inappropriate or insufficient examples, reasons, or other evidence to support its position	• develops no viable point of view on the issue, or provides little or no evidence to support its position
• is limited in its organization or focus, or may demonstrate some lapses in coherence or progression of ideas	• is poorly organized and/or focused, or demonstrates serious problems with coherence or progression of ideas	• is disorganized or unfocused, resulting in a disjointed or incoherent essay
• displays developing facility in the use of language, but sometimes uses weak vocabulary or inappropriate word choice	• displays very little facility in the use of language, using very limited vocabulary or incorrect word choice	• displays fundamental errors in vocabulary
• lacks variety or demonstrates problems in sentence structure	• demonstrates frequent problems in sentence structure	• demonstrates severe flaws in sentence structure
• contains an accumulation of errors in grammar, usage, and mechanics	• contains errors in grammar, usage, and mechanics so serious that meaning is somewhat obscured	• contains pervasive errors in grammar, usage, or mechanics that persistently interfere with meaning

Essays not written on the essay assignment will receive a score of zero.

The Writing Sample

Writing sample essays are read and scored by "readers," high school and college teachers who have experience with the writing demonstrated by students at the end of high school. They do not expect polished compositions. Two readers score each essay on a 6-point scale, with 6 as the highest score and 1 as the lowest. The total writing sample score is the sum of the two readers' scores. It is weighted to equal one-third of the total SAT Writing Test score. If the two readers' scores are more than two points apart, a third reader resolves the discrepancy.

Sample Essays

Reproduced below is a topic used on an SAT Writing Test. You will also see the Scoring Guide for Readers of Student Responses to the Writing Subject Test and actual students' essays. The Scoring Guide, shown on page 149, is used to instruct essay readers. The directions that follow are identical to those in the test.

You have twenty-five minutes to write an essay on the topic assigned below. DO NOT WRITE ON ANOTHER TOPIC. AN ESSAY ON ANOTHER TOPIC IS NOT ACCEPTABLE.

The essay is assigned to give you an opportunity to show how well you can write. You should, therefore, take care to express your thoughts on the topic clearly and effectively. How well you write is much more important than how much you write, but to cover the topic adequately you will probably need to write more than one paragraph. Be specific.

Your essay must be written on the lines provided on your answer sheet. You will receive no other paper on which to write. You will find that you have enough space if you write on every line, avoid wide margins, and keep your handwriting to a reasonable size. It is important to remember that what you write will be read by someone who is not familiar with your handwriting. Try to write or print so that what you are writing is legible to the reader.

Consider carefully the following statement. Then plan and write your essay as directed.

Nothing requires more discipline than freedom.

> **Assignment:** In an essay, discuss your view of the statement above. Support your view with an example or examples from literature, the arts, history, politics, science and technology, current events, or your experience or observation.

Essay with a Total Score of 12

(Each reader gave the essay a score of 6.)

Although essays in this category differ in approach, style, and opinion, and have slight differences in quality, they all demonstrate the *clear and consistent competence* specified in the scoring guide. These essays are characterized by good organization, good command of the language, pertinent support for the ideas being developed, and an effective presentation. These essays are not perfect, nor are they expected to be, for each is only a first draft written in the twenty minutes allotted. The essay below is representative of essays in this category.

The ultimate freedom does not require discipline because to be entirely free, one must have no restrictions created by them or the world around them. But ultimate freedom exists only as a concept and while humans can strive to be free, in reality it can never be achieved. Discipline is therefore inescapable.

In William Shakespeare's *King Lear*, the theme of madness plays a major role in Lear's life. Lear's madness becomes his freedom from the rules around him. In the first scene, Lear gives up his land and therefore, power to his daughters, supposedly freeing himself from obligations in his old age. Yet Lear soon finds that his life and the people in his life are not as he once thought them to be. His daughters Regan and Goneril each display cruelty towards him and place restrictions of Lear. By giving up his power, Lear was in fact giving away his freedom. He can no longer do as he pleases, for example, he must beg each daughter to let him live with them. If discipline is taken to mean restrictions and rules placed upon oneself, then Lear in fact has more as a free man than a powerful man. Lear's freedom, or rather his lack of power, ends up promoting his madness. This madness removes him from obligations, but at the same time creates a different kind of restriction on him. Lear in his mad state may not have restrictions and discipline in the sence generally thought of, but he does in a new sence. The discipline of madness consumes him.

Lear, in both his powerful state and his weakened yet free state has freedom and discipline. And while the concept of ultimate freedom is without discipline, Lear's freedom in both cases is an example of how imperfect freedom does involve discipline. When Lear had power, he was free to make decisions, but these decisions were disciplined choices. When Lear had madness instead of power, he had freedom to do what he wanted, without concern of the consequences, but he had discipline forced upon him by his situation. Because ultimate freedom cannot be attained, freedom as we see it and refer to daily does involve discipline. Only the unachievable, ultimate freedom does not require discipline.

Essay with a Total Score of 10

(Each reader gave the essay a score of 5.)

Essays in this category demonstrate the *reasonably consistent competence* described in the scoring guide. They present pertinent examples and a developed argument. These essays, however, do contain lapses that keep them out of the top category. These lapses range from an awkward sentence or two to a failure to maintain a consistent tone. Still, whatever the flaws, they do not detract from the overall impression that the writing is well done.

In society today, as well as histories past, we have seen that "nothing requires more discipline than freedom". Freedom was a principle that people fought and died for. It was an undisputable right that was sometimes put to the test. However, Adeline Yen Mah and Martin Luther King Jr. prove that nothing isn't worth fighting for.

In "Falling Leaves" by Adeline Yen Mah, we can easily sympathize with her struggle for freedom and rights of passage. Ever since she was a young Chinese girl growing up in a male-dominated world, Adeline had to prove to herself and others that she deserved the praise, affection, and education that her three brothers easily attained. With much determination and introspective spirit, she soon learned the power of her will. By speaking out for her wanting to be rid of her provincial education and moving on to higher learning through attending England's Universities did she recognize that "nothing requires more discipline than freedom."

In addition to Adeline's opposition, Martin Luther King Jr. was a prominent figure in America's history that proved that his efforts were not wasted. He was a firm believer of equal rights for his fellow African American people. Without Martin's unerring attempts at breaking the barriers, there would not have been such a great uproar to stop the injustices.

From time to time, people have felt the restraint and oppression, but Adeline and Martin proved that their voices could not go on unheard. They attacked all obstacles and grew strong enough to realize the importance of their cause. The attainment of freedom have bonded these figures into our nation.

Essay with a Total Score of 8

(Each reader gave the essay a score of 4.)

As the scoring guide describes, essays in this category demonstrate *adequate competence* with occasional errors and lapses in quality. Although the papers show that the writers have adequate command of the skills needed for good writing, the papers have the kinds of flaws that keep them out of the top ranges.

In today's world almost all people are granted certain freedoms in relation to behavior or emotions. In the United States of America this privilege is especially prevelant through it's democratic government and the constitution it provides to protect the people's rights. Because too much unrestricted freedom can hurt a nation, the freedoms granted to the people must be regulated by each person's self-discipline. As with most things in life, freedom can be taken for granted if responsibility is not taken for one's own actions.

One major freedom given to most teenagers is the privilege to go away from home for college. This is a major commitment and responsibility because in many cases a student will be living away from his/her parents for the first time. His/her mother and father are no longer around to hassle the youth about homework, going to sleep, or other decisions. It is a beginning college student's own discipline or practicality that must aid the teen in making such lifestyle choices. In order to succeed and keep the new freedom of living away from home, the student must prove that he or she is mature enough to handle it. The student must organize his/her time appropriately, take care of himself/herself, and act like an adult.

Many personal freedoms and liberties are granted to people in life. In exchange for these rights, human beings must show they are worthy of receiving them by showing discipline and maturity in their actions and decision. If people were to live carelessly without regard for the preciousness of their freedom, the world would be full of chaos and injustice.

Important Tips on How to Write the Best Essay

Making Your Sentences Effective

What Is Style?

Many good ideas are lost because they are expressed in a dull, wordy, involved way. We often have difficulty following—and we may even ignore—instructions that are hard to read. Yet we find other instructions written in such a clear and simple way that a child could easily follow them. This way of writing—the words we choose and the way we use them—we call *style*.

No two people write exactly alike. Even when writing about the same thing, they probably will say it differently. Some will say it more effectively than others, of course; what they say will be more easily read and understood. But there is seldom any one best way to say something. Rather, there are usually several equally good ways. This flexibility is what makes English such a rich language.

Style can't be taught; each person's style is like personality—it is unique to him or her. But we can each improve our style. Let us consider how we can improve our writing style by improving our sentences.

How to Write Effective Sentences

We speak in sentences; we write in sentences. A single word or phrase sometimes carries a complete thought, but sentences are more often the real units of thought communication.

Writing good sentences takes concentration, patience, and practice. It involves much more than just stringing words together, one after another, as they tumble from our minds. If writers aren't careful, their sentences may not mean to the reader what they want them to; they may mean what they *didn't* want them to—or they may mean nothing at all.

This section discusses five things writers can do to write better sentences—or improve sentences already written. These are:

1. Create interest
2. Make your meaning clear
3. Keep your sentences brief
4. Make every word count
5. Vary your sentence patterns

Let's consider interest first.

1. Create Interest

We can make our writing more interesting by writing in an informal, conversational style. This style also makes our writing easier to understand and our readers more receptive to our thoughts.

Listen to two men meeting in the coffee shop. One tells the other, "Let me know when you need more paper clips." But how would he have written it? Probably as follows:

Request this office be notified when your activity's supply of paper clips, wire, steel gem pattern, large type 1, stock No. 7510-634-6516, falls below 30-day level prescribed in AFR 67-1, Vol. II, Section IV, subject: Office Supplies. Requisition will be submitted as expeditiously as possible to preclude noncompliance with appropriate directives.

Judging from the formal, academic style of much of our writing, we want to *impress* rather than *express*. There seems to be something about writing that brings out our biggest words, our most complex sentences, and our most formal style. Obviously this is not effective writing. We wouldn't dare say it aloud this formally for fear someone would laugh at us, but we will write it.

WRITE TO EXPRESS

One of the best ways to make our writing more interesting to the reader and, hence, more effective is to write as we talk. Of course we can't write *exactly* as we talk, and we shouldn't want to. We usually straighten out the sentence structure, make our sentences complete rather than fragmentary or run-on, substitute for obvious slang words, and so on. But we can come close to our conversational style without being folksy or ungrammatical or wordy. This informal style is far more appropriate for the kind of writing we do and for the kind of readers we have than the old formal style. And it certainly makes better reading.

BE DEFINITE, SPECIFIC, AND CONCRETE

Another way—and one of the surest—to arouse and hold the interest and attention of readers is to be definite, specific, and concrete.

2. Make Your Meaning Clear

You do not need to be a grammarian to recognize a good sentence. After all, the first requirement of grammar is that you focus your reader's attention on the meaning you wish to convey. If you take care to make your meaning clear, your grammar will usually take care of itself. You can, however, do three things to make your meaning clearer to your reader: (1) emphasize your main ideas, (2) avoid wandering sentences, and (3) avoid ambiguity.

EMPHASIZE THE MAIN IDEAS

When we talk we use gestures, voice changes, pauses, smiles, frowns, and so on to emphasize our main ideas. In writing we have to use different methods for emphasis. Some are purely mechanical; others are structural.

Mechanical devices include capital letters, underlining or italics, punctuation, and headings. Printers used to capitalize the first letter of a word they wanted to emphasize. We still occasionally capitalize, or use a heavier type to emphasize words, phrases, or whole sentences. Sometimes we underline or italicize words that we want to stand out. Often we label or head main sections or subdivisions, as we have done in this book. This effectively separates main ideas and makes them stand out so that our reader doesn't have to search for them.

But mechanical devices for emphasizing an idea—capitalization, particularly—are often overused. The best way to emphasize an idea is to place it effectively in the sentence. The most emphatic position is at the end of the sentence. The next most emphatic position is at the beginning of the sentence. The place of least importance is anywhere in the middle. Remember, therefore, to put the important clause, phrase, name, or idea at the beginning or at the end of your sentences, and never hide the main idea in a subordinate clause or have it so buried in the middle of the sentence that the reader has to dig it out or miss it altogether.

Unemphatic: People drive on the left side instead of the right side in England.

Better: Instead of driving on the right side, people in England drive on the left.

AVOID WANDERING SENTENCES

All parts of a sentence should contribute to one clear idea or impression. Long, straggling sentences usually contain a hodgepodge of unrelated ideas. You should either break them up into shorter sentences or put the subordinate thoughts into subordinate form. Look at this sentence:

The sergeant, an irritable fellow who had been a truck driver, born and brought up in the corn belt of Iowa, strong as an ox and 6 feet tall, fixed an angry eye on the recruit.

You can see that the main idea is "The sergeant fixed an angry eye on the recruit." That he was an irritable fellow, strong as an ox, and 6 feet tall adds to the main idea. But the facts that he had been a truck driver and had been born in Iowa add nothing to the main thought, and the sentence is better without them.

The sergeant, an irritable fellow who was strong as an ox and 6 feet tall, fixed an angry eye on the recruit.

AVOID AMBIGUITY

If a sentence can be misunderstood, it will be misunderstood. A sentence that says that "The truck followed the jeep until its tire blew out" may be perfectly clear to the writer, but it will mean nothing to the reader until the pronoun *its* is identified.

MAKE SURE THAT YOUR MODIFIERS SAY WHAT YOU MEAN

"While eating oats, the farmer took the horse out of the stable." This sentence provides little more than a laugh until you add to the first part of the sentence a logical subject ("the horse"): "While the horse was eating oats, the farmer took him out of the stable." Sometimes simple misplacement of modifiers in sentences leads to misunderstanding: "The young lady went to the dance with her boyfriend wearing a low-cut gown." You can clarify this sentence by simply rearranging it: "Wearing a low-cut gown, the young lady went to the dance with her boyfriend."

3. Keep Your Sentences Brief

Sentences written like 10-word advertisements are hard to read. You cannot get the kind of brevity you want by leaving out the articles (*a, an,* and *the*). You can get brevity by dividing complex ideas into bite-size sentences and by avoiding unnecessary words and phrases and needless repetition and elaboration. Here are some suggestions that will help you to write short, straightforward sentences.

USE VERBS THAT WORK

The verb—the action word—is the most important word in a sentence. It is the power plant that supplies the energy, vitality, and motion in the sentence. So use strong verbs, verbs that really *work* in your sentences.

USE THE ACTIVE VOICE

Sentences written in the basic subject-verb-object pattern are said to be written in the *active voice*. In such sentences someone or something *does* something to the object—there is a forward movement of the idea. In sentences written in the *passive voice*, the subject merely receives the action—it has something done to it by someone or something, and there is no feeling of forward movement of the idea.

The active voice, in general, is preferable to the passive voice because it helps to give writing a sense of energy, vitality, and motion. When we use the passive voice predominantly, our writing doesn't seem to have much life, the actor in the sentences is not allowed to act, and verbs become weak. So don't rob your writing of its power by using the passive voice when you can use the active voice. Nine out of ten sentences will be both shorter (up to 25 percent shorter) and stronger in the active voice.

Let's compare the two voices:

Active: The pilot flew   the aircraft.
        (Actor)   (action) (acted upon)

Passive: The aircraft was flown by the pilot.
        (Acted upon)   (action)   (actor)

Now let's see some typical passive examples:

The committee will be appointed by the principal.
Reports have been received . . .
Provisions will be made by the manager in case of a subway strike.

Aren't these familiar? In most of these we should be emphasizing the actor rather than leaving out or subordinating him or her.

See how much more effective those sentences are when they are written in the active voice.

The principal will appoint the committee.
We have received reports . . .
The manager will make provisions in case of a subway strike.

AVOID USING THE PASSIVE VOICE

The passive voice always takes more words to say what could be said just as well (and probably better) in the active voice. In the passive voice the subject also becomes less personal and may seem less important, and the motion of the sentence grinds to a halt.

There are times, of course, when the passive voice is useful and justified—as when the person or thing doing the action is unknown or unimportant.

When we use the lifeless passive voice indiscriminately, we make our writing weak, ineffective, and dull. Remember that the normal English word order is subject-verb-object. There may be occasions in your writing when you feel that the passive voice is preferable. But should such an occasion arise, think twice before you write; the passive voice rarely improves your style. Before using a passive construction, make certain that you have a specific reason. After using it, check to see that your sentence is not misleading.

TAKE A DIRECT APPROACH

Closely related to passive voice construction is indirect phrasing.

It is requested . . .
It is recommended . . .
It has been brought to the attention of . . .
It is the opinion of . . .

Again this is so familiar to us that we don't even question it. But who requested? Who recommended? Who knows? Who believes? No one knows from reading such sentences!

This indirect way of writing, this use of the passive voice and the indirect phrase, is perhaps the most characteristic feature of the formal style of the past. There are many explanations for it. A psychiatrist might say the writer was afraid to take the responsibility for what he or she is writing or merely passing the buck. The writer may unjustifiably believe this style makes him or her anonymous, or makes him or her sound less dogmatic and authoritarian.

Express your ideas immediately and directly. Unnecessary expressions like *it*, *there is*, and *there are* weaken sentences and delay comprehension. They also tend to place part of the sentence in the passive voice. *It is the recommendation of the sales manager that the report be forwarded immediately* is more directly expressed as *The sales manager recommends that we send the report immediately.*

Change Long Modifiers to Shorter Ones

Mr. Barnes, who is president of the board, will preside.

Mr. Barnes, the board president, will preside.

Vehicles that are defective are . . .

Defective vehicles are . . .

They gave us a month for accomplishment of the task.

They gave us a month to do the job.

Break Up Long Sentences

There is not enough time available for the average executive to do everything that might be done and so it is necessary for him to determine wisely the essentials and do them first, then spend the remaining time on things that are "nice to do."

The average executive lacks time to do everything that might be done. Consequently, he must decide what is essential and do it first. Then he can spend the remaining time on things that are "nice to do."

4. Make Every Word Count

Don't cheat your readers. They are looking for ideas—for meaning—when they read your letter, report, or directive. If they have to read several words that have little to do with the real meaning of a sentence or if they have to read a number of sentences to get just a little meaning, you are cheating them. Much of their time and effort is wasted because they aren't getting full benefit from it. They expected something that you didn't deliver.

MAKE EACH WORD ADVANCE YOUR THOUGHT

Each word in a sentence should advance the thought of that sentence. To leave it out would destroy the meaning you are trying to convey.

"Naturally," you say. "Of course!" But reread the last letter you wrote. Aren't some of your sentences rather wordy? Couldn't you have said the same thing in fewer words? And finally, how many times did you use a whole phrase to say what could have been said in one word, or a whole clause for what could have been expressed in a short phrase? In short, try tightening up a sentence like this:

The reason that prices rose was that the demand was increasing at the same time that the production was decreasing.

Rewritten:

Prices rose because the demand increased while production decreased.

Doesn't our rewrite say the same thing as the original? Yet we have saved the reader some effort by squeezing the unnecessary words out of a wordy sentence.

Now try this one:

Wordy: The following statistics serve to give a good idea of the cost of production.

Improved: The following statistics give a good idea of the production costs.

or

These statistics show production costs.

And this one:

Wordy: I have a production supervisor who likes to talk a great deal.

Improved: I have a talkative production supervisor.

In all of those rewritten sentences we have saved our reader some time. The same thing has been said in fewer words.

Of course you can be *too* concise. If your writing is too brief or terse, it may "sound" rude and abrupt, and you may lose more than you gain. You need, then, to be politely concise. What you are writing, what you are writing about, and whom you are writing for will help you decide just where to draw the line. However, the general rule, make every word count, still stands. Say what you have to say in as few words as clarity *and tact* will allow.

CONSOLIDATE IDEAS

A second way to save the reader's effort is to consolidate ideas whenever possible. Pack as much meaning as possible into each sentence *without making the sentence structure too complicated.*

Each sentence is by definition an idea, a unit of thought. Each time the readers read one of these units they should get as much meaning as possible. It takes just about as much effort to read a sentence with a simple thought as it does to read one with a strong idea or with two or three strong ideas.

There are several things we can do to pack meaning into a sentence. In general, they all have to do with summarizing, combining, and consolidating ideas.

Some people write sentences that are weak and insignificant, both in structure and thought. Ordinarily several such sentences can be summarized and the thought put into one good, mature sentence. For example:

We left Wisconsin the next morning. I remember watching three aircraft. They were F-4s. They were flying very low. I felt sure they were going to crash over a half a dozen times. The F-4 is new to me. I hadn't seen one before.

Rewritten:

When we left Wisconsin the next morning, I remember watching three F-4s, a type of aircraft I had never seen before. They were flying so low that over a half dozen times I felt sure they were going to crash.

When summarizing like this, be sure to emphasize the main action. Notice in the next example how we have kept the main action as our verb and made the other actions subordinate by changing them to verbals.

Poor:　　It was in 1959 that he *retired* from teaching and he *devoted* his time to *writing* his autobiography. (three verbs, one verbal)

Improved:　　In 1959 he *retired* from teaching to *devote* his time to *writing* his autobiography. (one verb, two verbals)

Here is an example similar to ones we might find in a directive:

Poor: The evaluation forms will be picked up from your respective personnel office. You should have these completed by 1700 hours, 18 May. They will be delivered immediately to the security section.

Notice that in the above instructions all of the actions are to be performed by the reader or "you." Now let's put these into one sentence, placing the things to be done in a series and using a single subject.

Improved: Pick up the evaluation forms from your personnel office; complete and deliver them to the security section by 1700 hours, 18 May. (The subject [you] is understood.)

The same thing can be done with subjects or predicates:

Poor: Horror stories shown on television appear to contribute to juvenile delinquency. Comic books with their horror stories seem to have the same effect. Even the reports of criminal activities which appear in our newspapers seem to contribute to juvenile delinquency.

Improved: Television, comic books, and newspapers seem to contribute to juvenile delinquency by emphasizing stories of horror and crime.

There is one more thing we can do to make our sentences better. We can vary their length and complexity. The following paragraphs suggest ways to do this.

5. Vary Your Sentence Patterns

We should, as a general rule, write predominantly short sentences. Similarly, we should keep our sentences simple enough for our readers to understand them easily and quickly.

But most people soon get tired of nothing but simple, straightforward sentences. So, give your reader an occasional change of pace. Vary both the length and the construction of your sentences.

VARY SENTENCE LENGTH

Some writers use nothing but short, choppy sentences ("The road ended in a wrecked village. The lines were up beyond. There was much artillery around.") In the hands of a Hemingway, from whom this example is taken, short sentences can give an effect of purity and simplicity; in the hands of a less skillful writer, choppy sentences are usually only monotonous.

The other extreme, of course, is just as bad. The writer who always writes heavy sentences of 20 to 30 words soon loses the reader. Some great writers use long sentences effectively, but most writers do not.

The readability experts suggest that, for the most effective *communication*, a sentence should rarely exceed 20 words. Their suggestion is a good rule of thumb, but sentence length should vary. And an occasional long sentence is not hard to read if it is followed by shorter ones. A fair goal for most letter-writers is an average of 21 words per sentence, or less. For longer types of writing, such as regulations and manuals, sentences should average 15 words or less. The sentences in opening paragraphs and in short letters may run a little longer than the average.

VARY SENTENCE CONSTRUCTION

Just as important as varied sentence length is variety of construction. Four common sentence categories are simple, compound, complex, and compound-complex.

A *simple sentence* consists of only one main (independent) clause:

Rain came down in torrents.
Rain and hail started falling. (Simple sentence with compound subject)
The storm began and soon grew in intensity. (Simple sentence with compound predicate)

A *compound sentence* has two or more main clauses:

Rain started falling, and all work stopped.
The storm began; all work stopped.
The storm began, the workers found shelter, and all work stopped.

A *complex sentence* has one main clause and at least one subordinate (dependent) clause. (Subordinate clauses are underlined in the following sentences.)

They were just starting their work <u>when the rain started.</u>
<u>Before they had made any progress,</u> the rain started falling.
The storm, <u>which grew rapidly in intensity,</u> stopped all work.

A *compound-complex sentence* has two or more main clauses and at least one subordinate clause. (Subordinate clauses are underlined in the following sentences.)

Rain started falling, and all work stopped <u>before they had made any progress. Although the workers were eager to finish the job,</u> the storm forced them to stop, and they quickly found shelter.

They had made some progress <u>before the storm began,</u> but, <u>when it started,</u> all work stopped.

The names of the categories are really not important except to remind you to vary your sentence construction when you write. But remember that sentence variety is not just a mechanical chore to perform after your draft is complete. Good sentence variety comes naturally as the result of proper coordination and subordination when you write.

For example:

If two or more short sentences have the same subject, combine them into one simple sentence with a compound verb:

The men were hot. They were tired, too. They were also angry.
The men were hot and tired and angry.

If you have two ideas of equal weight or parallel thought, write them as two clauses in a compound sentence.

The day was hot and humid. The men had worked hard.
The men had worked hard, and the day was hot and humid.
The day was hot and humid, but the men had worked hard.

If one idea is more important than others, put it in the main clause of a complex sentence:

Poor: The men were tired, and they had worked hard, and the day was hot.

Better: The men were tired because they had worked hard on a hot day.

    or

Although the day was hot and the men were tired, they worked hard.

If the adverbial modifier is the least important part of a complex sentence, put it first and keep the end position for the more important main clause:

Instead of: The men finished the job in record time, even though the day was hot and humid and they were tired.

Better: Even though the day was hot and humid and the men were tired, they finished the job in record time.

But be careful about having long, involved subordinate clauses come before the main clause. The reader may get lost or confused before getting to your main point or give up before getting to it. Also beware of letting too many modifying words, phrases, or clauses come between the subject and the verb. This is torture for the reader. The subject and the verb are usually the most important elements of a sentence; keep them close together whenever possible.

A Brief Review of English Grammar

Frequent Grammatical Problems

Split Infinitive. By the 17th century English had developed a two-word infinitive—*to go, to run, to talk*, etc. The word *to* was coupled with the verb and stood next to it. Since the Latin infinitive was always treated as one word, scholars decided that the infinitive in English must also be treated as one word. It was considered an error to split these two words by inserting an adverb between them.

But English isn't Latin, so the people went on splitting the infinitive whenever it suited their purpose And we've been doing it ever since.

It isn't necessary to split the infinitive deliberately, of course, but if it sounds better or seems more natural, or will add emphasis, then do so. The following sentence is an example of a permissible split infinitive: "After they had won the baseball trophy, they went to the party to *proudly display* their prize." (*Proudly to display* or *to display proudly* makes the sentence stiff. And *they went proudly to the party to display their prize* changes the original meaning.)

Ending a Sentence with a Preposition. The old "rule" that you should never end a sentence with a preposition was another attempt to force Latin on English, and it also is fading out. Often, to avoid this "error," we have to write a much longer and more awkward sentence.

Which sounds better?

This is a rule up with which I will not put.
This is a rule I won't put up with.

Distinction between "Shall" and "Will." Formal usage required *shall* in the first person and *will* in the second and third person when forming the simple future. For the emphatic future, these were reversed. Today most of us use *will* in all persons for both simple and emphatic future.

"It Is I." This question of which pronoun to use probably causes more uncertainty than any other problem in grammar. We do not change the form of a noun whether we use it as a subject or as an object. But we do have different forms for our pronouns.

For example, *I, you, he, they, we, etc.*, are the nominative forms and are used as subjects. *Me, you, him, them, us, etc.*, are the objective forms. Normally we use the objective form after a verb, but after the *be* verbs (am, is, are, was, will be, etc.) we have traditionally used the nominative form; thus, *it is I* rather than *it is me.*

Usage, however, is divided on this. In informal conversation we often say, "It's me," just as the French do—"C'est moi." The argument for this usage is pretty sound. The predicate is thought of as object territory and it feels strange to us to use the nominative form here. Still, the traditional use of this form has come to be regarded as a sign of the well-educated man. So, until "it is me" has become more widely accepted, we should continue to use "it is I."

Examples of the nominative forms for other pronouns may prove helpful:

It was he (not *It was him*)
This is she (not *This is her*)
Had it been they (not *Had it been them*)

There should be no question about using the objective case of the pronoun after other verbs. "The chairman appointed *him* and *me*," is considered correct, not "The chairman appointed *he* and *I*." But often in trying to avoid this decision we make an even worse error. Instead of the objective form we use the reflective—myself, himself, etc. "He appointed John and myself" is definitely wrong.

"Who" versus "Whom." The pronoun *who* is used for the subject and *whom* is used for the object.

Give the letter to *whoever* answers the door. (not to *whomever . . .*) the pronoun *whoever* is the subject of its clause.
Tell me *whom* you borrowed the money from. (not *who . . .* from)
The pronoun *whomever* is the object of the preposition *from*.

The pronoun *who* used as the subject of a verb is not affected by a parenthetical expression such as *I think, he believes, they say* intervening between the subject and the verb.

He is the person *who* I think is best qualified.
Mr. Jameson is the attorney *who* we suppose will prepare the brief.

Adverbs and Adjectives. We seem to have more trouble with adverbs than with adjectives. A simple guide is this: An *adverb* may modify a verb, another adverb, or an adjective; an *adjective* may modify only a noun or a pronoun.

Our biggest problem comes in confusing adjectives and adverbs. For example, we may use the adjective *good* when we should use the adverb *well*:

Poor: The engines are running *good.*
Proper: The engines are running *well.*

Note: Both *good* and *well* may be used after a linking verb as predicate adjectives. For example: "I feel good" indicates a state of well being; but "I feel well" indicates either that you are not sick or that your ability to use your sense of touch is above average.

Common Errors in Grammar

Most of us do not have too much trouble writing grammatically acceptable sentences. We just habitually follow the basic word order. But sometimes we get careless or we fall into bad habits in our use of this important principle. When we do, we can interfere with the meaning and with the movement of our sentences.

Here are some common grammatical errors which may confuse our reader. They may be so simple that the reader quickly sees the error, revises the sentence in his mind, and gets the proper message. But this is your job, not his. Too often the reader won't catch the error and will get the wrong idea about what you are trying to say.

Misplaced Modifiers

1. Avoid dangling modifiers. When a word or phrase seems to modify another word which it cannot logically modify, we say it has been left dangling. Usually it will be a phrase beginning the sentence. From its position we expect it to modify the subject. But the connection is illogical.

Confusing:	Approaching the flight line from the east side, the operations building can be easily seen. (The operations building obviously does not approach the flight line.)
Improved:	A person approaching the flight line from the east side can easily see the operations building.
Confusing:	To make a climbing turn, the throttle is opened wider.
Improved:	To make a climbing turn, open the throttle wider. (The subject *you* is understood.)

2. Keep your modifiers close to the words they modify. Sometimes we widely separate a modifier from its modified word and end up confusing the reader.

Confusing:	It was impossible to find the book I had been reading in the dark.
Improved:	It was impossible in the dark to find the book I had been reading.
Confusing:	He had marked on the map the places where we were to watch for turns in red ink.
Improved:	He marked on the map in red ink the places where we were to watch for turns.

3. Avoid using "squinting" modifiers that may refer to either of two parts of a sentence. A squinting modifier is so placed in a sentence that it could logically modify either the words that came before it or the words that follow it; it "squints" both ways. This may confuse the reader. He may not realize the ambiguity and misinterpret the intended meaning.

Confusing: Personnel who drive their cars to work *only occasionally* can count on finding a parking space.

Improved: Only *occasionally* can personnel who drive their cars to work count on finding a parking space.

Confusing: The electrician said Wednesday he would repair the light. (Did he make the statement on Wednesday, or did he say that he would repair the light on Wednesday?)

Improved: Wednesday the electrician said he would repair the light.

or

The electrician said that he would repair the light on Wednesday.

By misplacing modifiers we make it easy for the reader to misunderstand the meaning of our sentences, sometimes with dire results. We can eliminate such errors by reading and revising our writing before we release it. Don't confuse your reader or make him do your work. Keep your modifiers close to the words they modify.

Confusing Pronouns and Other Reference Words

1. Make sure that a pronoun agrees in number with the noun it refers to.

Confusing: Though there may be different teacher unions, the policy of *its* delegates should be similar.

Improved: Though there may be different teacher unions, the policy of *their* delegates should be similar.

2. Make sure a pronoun or other reference word has a definite and clearly understood antecedent, We often use words or pronouns such as *which*, the *latter*, the *former, this it*, etc., to refer to something we have previously mentioned. This reference must be clear to the reader.

Confusing: A piece of thread dangled over his belt which was at least 8 inches long.

Improved: A piece of thread which was at least 8 inches long dangled over his belt.

Confusing: The president told the executive he would handle all personnel assignments.

Improved: The president told the executive to handle all personnel assignments.

or

The president told the executive that he, the president, would handle all personnel assignments.

Non-Parallel Structure

Express parallel ideas in words with the same grammatical construction. Nothing sounds quite so disorganized in writing as structure that is not parallel.

Not Parallel: Briefly, the functions of a staff are to advise the general manager, transmit his instructions, and the supervision of the execution of his decisions.

Parallel: Briefly, the functions of a staff are to advise the general manager, transmit his instructions, and supervise the execution of his decisions.

Not Parallel: I have learned three things: that one should not argue about legalisms, never expect miracles, and the impropriety of using a singular verb with a compound subject.

Parallel: I have learned three things: never argue about legalisms, never expect miracles, and never use a singular verb with a compound subject.

Some Basic Grammatical Terms

Parts of Speech

Nouns—names of people, things, qualities, acts, ideas, relationships: General Smith, Texas, aircraft, confusion, running, predestination, grandfather.

Pronouns—words that refer indirectly to people, places, things, etc.: he, she, which, it, someone.

Adjectives—words that point out or indicate a quality of nouns or pronouns: big, lowest, cold, hard.

Prepositions—words that link nouns and pronouns to other words by showing the relationship between them: to, by, between, above, behind, about, of, in, on, from.

Conjunctions—words used to join other words, phrases, and clauses: and, but, however, because, although.

Verbs—words that express action or indicate a state, feeling, or simply existence: go, hate, fly, feel, is.

Adverbs—words that tell how, where, when, or to what degree acts were performed or indicate a degree of quality: slowly, well, today, much, very.

Note: Many of our words can serve as more than one part of speech. Some words may be used as nouns, adjectives, and verbs without any change in spelling: *Drinking* coffee is a popular pastime; He broke the *drinking* glass; the boy is *drinking* a glass of milk. Often they may be both adjectives and adverbs: *better, well, fast.* Ordinarily we add *ly* to words to form adverbs, while adjectives may be formed by adding *able, ly, ing, al, ese, ful, ish, ous, y,* etc. But these endings are not always necessary: *college* (noun); *college boy* (noun used as an adjective to modify the noun *boy*).

Other Grammatical Terms

Subject—a noun or pronoun (or word or phrase used as a noun) which names the actor in a sentence. The term may be used in a broader sense to include all of the words that are related to the actor.

Predicate—the verb with its modifiers and its object or complement.

Predicate complement—a noun completing the meaning of a linking verb and modifying the subject.

Jones is *chief* (noun). He was *pale* (adjective).

Linking verb—a verb with little or no meaning of its own that usually indicates a state of being or condition. It functions chiefly to connect the subject with an adjective or noun in the predicate. The most common linking verb is the verb to be (am, are, is, was, were, had been), but there are others.

He *feels* nervous.
He *acts* old.
He *seems* tired.

Clause—an element which is part of a complex or compound sentence and has a subject, a verb, and often an object. "Nero killed Agrippina" is a clause but is not ordinarily called one because it is the complete sentence. In the compound sentence, "*Nero killed Agrippina,* but *he paid* *the penalty,*" each italicized group of words is an independent clause. In the complex sentence, "*Because he killed Agrippina*, Nero paid the penalty," the italicized clause is made dependent or subordinate by the word *because*; it depends upon the rest of the sentence for the complete meaning.

Phrase—two or more words without a subject and predicate that function as a grammatical unit in a clause or sentence. A phrase may modify another word or may be used as a noun or verb. For example: beside the radiator, approaching the pier, to fly a kite.

Verbals—words made from verbs but used as other parts of speech:

Gerund (a verb used as a noun):

   Swimming was his favorite sport.

Participle (a verb used as an adjective):

   The aircraft *piloted* by Colonel Jones has crashed.

Infinitive (a verb used as a noun, adjective, or adverb):

   To travel is my greatest pleasure. (infinitive used as a noun)
   I've have four days *to spend* at home. (infinitive used as an adjective)
   Bruce was glad to *have joined*. (infinitive used as adverb)

Common Grammar Errors Classified by Part of Speech

CORRECTION

I. Nouns

Incorrect form to express plural number: *He shot two deers.*	He shot two *deer*.
Incorrect form to express masculine or feminine gender: *She was a wizard.*	She was a *witch*.
Incorrect form of the possessive case: *Two boy's heads and two sheeps' heads.*	Two *boys'* heads and two *sheep's* heads.
Use of the objective case for the possessive: *I was sorry to hear of John doing wrong.*	I was sorry to hear of *John's* doing wrong.

II. Pronouns

Pronoun *I* placed incorrectly:
I and my sister will attend the concert.

My *sister* and I will attend the concert.

Use of compound personal pronoun for simple personal pronoun:
Sam and myself will do it.

Sam and *I* will do it.

Incorrect choice of relative pronoun:
I have a dog who barks at night. This is the person which did the wrong. This is the house what Jack built. Columbus, that discovered America, was an Italian.

I have a dog *which* barks at night. This is the person *who* did the wrong. This is the house *which* Jack built. Columbus, *who* discovered America, was an Italian.

Lack of agreement between pronoun and antecedent:
Every one of the pupils lost their books.

Every one of the pupils lost *his* book.

Incorrect case form:
The book is yours or his. I recognize it's cover.

The book is *yours* or *his*. I recognize *its* cover.

Use of nominative case for objective:
Give it to Kate and I. I knew it to be she.

Give it to Kate and *me*. I knew it to be *her*.

Use of objective case for nominative:
Him and me are brothers. Whom do you suppose she is? It was her.

He and *I* are brothers. *Who* do you suppose she is? It was *she*.

Use of objective case for possessive:
There is no chance of me being chosen.

There is no chance of *my* being chosen.

Pleonastic use:
John, he tried, and then Mary, she tried.

John *tried* and then Mary *tried*.

Ambiguous use:
The man told his son to take his coat to the tailor's.

The man told his son to take *his (the man's)* coat to the tailor's.

III. Verbs and Verbals

Use of the indicative mood for the subjunctive:
I wish I was you.

I wish I *were* you.

CORRECTION

Use of the subjunctive mood for the indicative:

If the cavern were of artificial construction, considerable pains had been taken to make it look natural.

If the cavern *was* of artificial construction, considerable pains had been taken to make it look natural.

Use of incorrect form to express tense:

I done it. He seen it. She come late yesterday. I see him last week. The boy has went home. My hands were froze. He teached me all I know. I ain't seen it.

I *did* it. He *saw* it. She *came* late yesterday. I *saw* him last week. The boy *has gone* home. My hands were *frozen*. He *taught* me all I know. I *haven't seen* it.

Error in sequence of tenses:

I meant, when first I came, to have bought all Paris. He did not know that mercury was a metal.

I meant, when first I came, *to buy* all Paris. He did not know that mercury *is* a metal.

Lack of agreement between verb and subject:

Was you glad to see us? Neither he nor she have ever been there. It don't cost much.

Were you glad to see us? Neither he nor she *has* ever been there. It *doesn't* cost much.

Use of incorrect forms of principal parts of certain verbs; e.g., sit and lie:

The hen sets on the eggs. The book lays on the table. It laid there yesterday. It has laid there all week.

The hen *sits* on the eggs. The book *lies* on the table. It *lay* there yesterday. It has *lain* there all week.

Use of adjective participle without modified word:

Coming into the room, a great noise was heard.

Coming into the room, *I* heard a great noise.

IV. Adjectives

Omission of article:

The noun and pronoun are inflected.

The noun and *the* pronoun are inflected.

Use of superfluous article:

I do not like this kind of a story.

I do not like this *kind of* story.

Use of *a* for *an* and *an* for *a*:

This is an universal custom. I should like a apple.

This is *a* universal custom. I should like *an* apple.

CORRECTION

Use of adverb for predicate adjective:
She looks nicely.

She looks *nice.*

Lack of concord between certain adjectives and the words they modify:
I do not like these kind of grapes.

I do not like *this kind* of grapes.

Incorrect forms of comparison:
His ways have become eviler.

His ways have been *more evil.*

Use of comparative form not accompanied by certain necessary words:
He is shorter than any boy in his class.

He is shorter than any *other* boy in his class.

Use of superlative form accompanied by certain superfluous words:
This is of all others the most important.

This is the most important.

Use of double comparative or superlative forms:
She is more kinder than you.

She is *kinder* than you.

Incorrect placing of adjective phrases and clauses:
The mariner shot the bird with an unfeeling heart.

With an unfeeling heart, the mariner shot the bird.

V. Adverbs

Use of adjective for adverb:
She sings real well.

She sings *really* well.

Incorrect use of double negatives:
I cannot go no faster.

I cannot go *any* faster.

Incorrect placing of adverbs and of adverbial phrases and clauses:
I only came yesterday, and I go today.

I came *only* yesterday, and I go today.

VI. Prepositions

Incorrect choice of prepositions:
I walked from the hall in the room. Divide this between the three boys. I was to New York today.

I walked from the hall *into* the room. Divide this *among* the three boys. I was *in* New York today.

Omission of preposition:
She is an example of what a person in good health is capable.

She is an example of what a person in good health is capable *of.*

Use of superfluous preposition:
The book in which the story appears in is mine.

The book in which the story appears is mine.

VII. Conjunctions

Incorrect choice of conjunctions; especially *like* for *as*, and *as* for *whether:*
I cannot write like you do. I don't know as I can go.

I cannot write *as* you do. I don't know *whether* I can go.

Incorrect choice of correlatives:
Neither this or that will do.

Neither this *nor* that will do.

Use of a superfluous conjunction:
I have no doubt but that he will come. This is a fine picture and which all will admire.

I have no doubt *that* he will come. This is a fine picture *which* all will admire.

Incorrect placing of correlatives:
He is neither disposed to sanction bloodshed nor deceit. (Place *neither* before *bloodshed.*)

He is disposed to sanction *neither* bloodshed nor deceit.

Grammar

Following are some directions for and samples of some of the other question types on the SAT Writing Test.

IDENTIFYING ERRORS

> **Directions:** **The following sentences test your knowledge of grammar, usage, diction (choice of words), and idiom.**
>
> **Some sentences are correct.**
> **No sentence contains more than one error.**
>
> **You will find that the error, if there is one, is underlined and lettered. Elements of the sentence that are not underlined will not be changed. In choosing answers, follow the requirements of standard written English.**
>
> **If there is an error, select the <u>one underlined part</u> that must be changed to make the sentence correct and fill in the corresponding oval on your answer sheet.**
>
> **If there is no error, fill in answer oval E.**
>
> **EXAMPLE:**   **SAMPLE ANSWER**
> <u>The other</u> delegates and <u>him</u> <u>immediately</u>
>   A   B   C   Ⓐ ● Ⓒ Ⓓ Ⓔ
> accepted the resolution <u>drafted by</u> the
>   D
> neutral states. <u>No error</u>
>   E

Sample Questions with Answers

1. <u>Even before</u> he became the youngest
    A
player to win the Wimbledon men's <u>singles</u>
                              B
championship, Boris Becker <u>had sensed</u>
                       C
that his life would <u>no longer</u> be the same.
                 D
<u>No error</u>.
 E

2. If any signer of the Constitution <u>was</u> to
                            A
return to life <u>for a day,</u> his opinion <u>of</u> our
            B   C
amendments <u>would be</u> interesting.
           D
<u>No error</u>.
 E

3. The dean <u>of the college</u>, together <u>with</u>
              A   B
some other faculty members, <u>are</u>
                             C
planning a conference for the purpose
of <u>laying</u> down certain regulations.
      D
<u>No error</u>.
   E

4. If one <u>lives</u> in Florida <u>one day</u> and in
        A   B
Iceland the <u>next,</u> he is <u>certain</u> to feel the
          C   D
change in temperature. <u>No error</u>.
                   E

5. <u>Now</u> that the stress of examinations and
  A
interviews <u>are</u> over, we can <u>all</u> <u>relax</u> for a
         B   C D
while. <u>No error</u>.
         E

6. The industrial <u>trend</u> <u>is</u> in the direction of
              A B
   <u>more</u> machines and <u>less</u> people.
    C   D
<u>No error</u>.
   E

7. The American standard of living <u>is</u> still
                           A
<u>higher</u> <u>than</u> <u>most</u> of the <u>other countries</u>
  B   C   D
of the world. <u>No error</u>.
            E

8. <u>At last,</u> <u>late</u> in the afternoon, a long line
   A   B
of flags and colored umbrellas <u>were</u> seen
                          C
moving <u>toward</u> the gate of the palace.
          D
<u>No error</u>.
   E

9. <u>Due to</u> the failure of the air-cooling
   A
system, many in the audience <u>had left</u>
                              B
the meeting <u>before</u> the principal
            C
speaker <u>arrived</u>. <u>No error</u>.
        D   E

10. Psychologists and psychiatrists <u>will tell</u>
                                     A
us that it is of utmost importance that a
<u>disturbed</u> child <u>receive</u> professional
  B   C
attention <u>as soon as</u> possible. <u>No error</u>.
             D   E

11. <u>After we were waiting</u> in line
          A
<u>for three hours,</u>
       B
<u>much to our disgust, the tickets had</u>
                   C
been sold out <u>when</u> we reached the
               D
window. <u>No error</u>.
          E

12. That angry outburst of <u>Father's</u> last night
                      A
was so annoying that it resulted in our
<u>guests</u> <u>packing up</u> and leaving <u>this</u>
  B   C   D
morning. <u>No error</u>.
          E

13. <u>Sharp</u> advances last week in the
   A
wholesale price of beef <u>is</u> a strong
                  B

indication of higher meat <u>costs</u> to
                           C

come, but so far retail prices continue
<u>favorable</u>. <u>No error</u>.
 D   E

14. An acquaintance with the memoirs of
Elizabeth Barrett Browning and Robert
Browning <u>enable</u> us
         A
to appreciate the <u>depth of influence</u> that
                 B
two people of talent can have <u>on</u>
                         C
<u>each other</u>. <u>No error</u>.
  D   E

15. The supervisor <u>was advised</u> to give the
              A
assignment to <u>whomever</u> <u>he believed</u>
           B   C
had a strong sense of responsibility, and
the courage <u>of</u> his conviction. <u>No error</u>.
         D   E

16. If he <u>would have</u> <u>lain</u> quietly as
       A   B
instructed by the doctor, he
<u>might not</u> <u>have had</u> a second heart
  C   D
attack. <u>No error</u>.
       E

17. The founder and, <u>for many years</u>, the
               A
<u>guiding spirit</u> of the "Kenyon Review" is
 B
John Crowe Ransom, <u>who</u> you must
                C
know <u>as</u> an outstanding American critic.
    D
<u>No error</u>.
  E

18. <u>Though</u> you may not <u>agree with</u> the
  A   B
philosophy of Malcolm X, you must
admit that he <u>had</u> tremendous
          C
influence <u>over</u> a great many followers.
         D
<u>No error</u>.
  E

19. There is no objection to <u>him</u> joining
                   A
the party <u>provided</u> he is willing to
         B
<u>fit in with</u> the plans of the group and is
 C
<u>ready and</u> able to do his share of the
 D
work. <u>No error</u>.
     E

20. <u>Ceremonies</u> <u>were opened</u> by a drum and
   A   B
bugle corps of Chinese children parading
<u>up</u> Mott Street <u>in colorfulful uniforms</u>.
 C   D
<u>No error</u>.
  E

21. The reason <u>most</u> Americans <u>don't</u> pay
          A   B
much attention to <u>rising</u> African
               C
nationalism is <u>because</u> they really do not
              D
know modern Africa. <u>No error</u>.
                     E

22. There <u>remains</u> many reasons for the
        A
<u>animosity</u> that <u>exists</u> <u>between</u> the Arab
  B   C   D
countries and Israel. <u>No error</u>.
                   E

23. The Federal Aviation Administration
<u>ordered</u> an emergency inspection
 A
<u>of several</u> Pan American planes
  B
<u>on account of</u> a Pan American Boeing
  C
707 <u>had</u> <u>crashed</u> on Bali, in Indonesia.
      D
<u>No error</u>.
  E

24. A gang <u>of armed thieves</u>, directed by a
        A
young woman, <u>has raided</u> the mansion
            B
of a <u>gold-mining</u> millionaire <u>near Dublin</u>
     C   D
late last night. <u>No error</u>.
           E

25. I <u>had</u> a male <u>chauvinist pig dream</u> that
   A   B
the women of the world <u>rose up</u> and
              C
denounced the <u>women's</u> liberation
        E
movement. <u>No error</u>
      E

IMPROVING SENTENCES

<u>Directions:</u> The following sentences test correctness and effectiveness of expression. In choosing answers, follow the requirements of standard written English; that is, pay attention to grammar, choice of words, sentence construction, and punctuation.

In each of the following sentences, part of the sentence or the entire sentence is underlined. Beneath each sentence you will find five ways of phrasing the underlined part. Choice A repeats the original; the other four are different.

Choose the answer that best expresses the meaning of the original sentence. If you think the original is better than any of the alternatives, choose it; otherwise choose one of the others. Your choice should produce the most effective sentence—clear and precise, without awkwardness or ambiguity.

EXAMPLE: SAMPLE ANSWER

Laura Ingalls Wilder published
her first book
<u>and she was sixty-five years old then</u>.

(A) and she was sixty-five years old then
(B) when she was sixty-five
(C) being age sixty-five years old
(D) upon the reaching of sixty-five years
(E) at the time when she was sixty-five

Sample Questions with Answers

26. <u>Such of his novels as was humorous were</u> successful.

   (A) Such of his novels as was humorous were successful.
   (B) Such of his novels as were humorous were successful.
   (C) His novels such as were humorous were successful.
   (D) His novels were successful and humorous.
   (E) Novels such as his humorous ones were successful.

27. <u>Being that the plane was grounded, we stayed over</u> until the next morning so that we could get the first flight out.

   (A) Being that the plane was grounded, we stayed over
   (B) In view of the fact that the plane was grounded, we stayed over
   (C) Since the plane was grounded, we stayed over
   (D) Because the plane was grounded, we stood over
   (E) On account of the plane being grounded, we stayed over

28. <u>He never has and he never will</u> keep his word.

    (A)   He never has and he never will
    (B)   He has never yet and never will
    (C)   He has not ever and he will not
    (D)   He never has or will
    (E)   He never has kept and he never will

29. The teacher <u>felt badly because she had scolded the bright child</u> who was restless for want of something to do.

    (A)   felt badly because she had scolded the bright child
    (B)   felt badly why she had scolded the bright child
    (C)   felt bad because she had scolded the bright child
    (D)   felt bad by scolding the bright child
    (E)   had felt badly because she scolded the bright child

30. This book <u>does not describe the struggle of the blacks to win their voting rights that I bought</u>.

    (A)   does not describe the struggle of the blacks to win their voting rights that I bought
    (B)   does not describe the black struggle to win their voting rights that I bought
    (C)   does not, although I bought it, describe the struggle of the blacks to win their voting rights
    (D)   which I bought does not describe the struggle to win for blacks their voting rights
    (E)   that I bought does not describe the struggle of the blacks to win their voting rights

31. <u>Barbara cannot help but think</u> that she will win a college scholarship.

    (A)   Barbara cannot help but think
    (B)   Barbara cannot help but to think
    (C)   Barbara cannot help not to think
    (D)   Barbara can help but think
    (E)   Barbara cannot but help thinking

32. In spite of <u>Tom wanting to study</u>, his sister made him wash the dishes.

    (A)   Tom wanting to study
    (B)   the fact that Tom wanted to study
    (C)   Tom's need to study
    (D)   Tom's wanting to study
    (E)   Tom studying

33. The old sea captain <u>told my wife and me</u> many interesting yarns about his many voyages.

    (A)   my wife and me
    (B)   me and my wife
    (C)   my wife and I
    (D)   I and my wife
    (E)   my wife along with me

34. A great many students from several universities <u>are planning to, if the weather is favorable, attend next Saturday's mass rally in Washington.</u>

    (A)   are planning to, if the weather is favorable, attend next Saturday's mass rally in Washington
    (B)   are planning, if the weather is favorable, to attend next Saturday's mass rally in Washington
    (C)   are planning to attend, if the weather is favorable, next Saturday's mass rally in Washington
    (D)   are planning to attend next Saturday's mass rally in Washington, if the weather is favorable
    (E)   are, if the weather is favorable, planning to attend next Saturday's mass rally in Washington

35. Jane's body movements are <u>like those of a dancer</u>.

    (A)   like those of a dancer
    (B)   the same as a dancer
    (C)   like a dancer
    (D)   a dancer's
    (E)   like those of a dancer's

Explanatory Answers

1. Choice E is correct. All underlined parts are correct.

2. Choice A is correct. "If any signer of the Constitution *were* to return to life . . ." The verb in the "if clause" of a present contrary-to-fact conditional statement must have a past subjunctive form (*were*).

3. Choice C is correct. "The dean of the college . . . *is* planning . . ." The subject of the sentence (*dean*) is singular. Therefore, the verb must be singular (*is planning*).

4. Choice E is correct. All underlined parts are correct.

5. Choice B is correct. "Now that the stress . . . *is* over . . ." The subject of the subordinate clause is singular (*stress*). Accordingly, the verb of the clause must be singular (*is*—not *are*). Incidentally, *examinations* and *interviews* are not subjects—they are objects of the preposition *of*.

6. Choice D is correct. ". . . of more machines and *fewer* people." We use *fewer* for persons and things that may be counted. We use *less* for bulk or mass.

7. Choice C or D is correct. ". . . than *that of most* of the other countries of the world." We must have parallelism so that the word *standard* in the main clause of the sentence acts as an antecedent for the pronoun *that* in the subordinate clause. As the original sentence reads, the American standard of living is still higher than the countries themselves. Note: You could also have said, "The American standard of living is still higher than most of the other countries' standard of living of the world." This would also make Choice D is correct.

8. Choice C is correct. ". . . a long line of flags . . . *was* seen . . ." The subject of the sentence is singular (*line*). Therefore, the verb must be singular (*was seen*).

9. Choice A is correct. "*Because* of the failure . . ." Never start a sentence with *Due to*.

10. Choice E is correct. All underlined parts are correct.

11. Choice C is correct. "After we were waiting in line for three hours, the tickets had, *much to our disgust*, been sold out when we reached the window." Avoid squinting constructions—that is, modifiers that are so placed that the reader cannot tell whether they are modifying the words immediately preceding the construction or the words immediately following the construction. That is, as the sentence initially reads, we don't know whether "much to our disgust" modifies "After we were waiting in line for three hours" or modifies "the tickets had been sold out when we reached the window."

12. Choice B is correct. ". . . resulted in our *guests'* packing up . . ." A noun or pronoun immediately preceding a gerund is in the possessive case. Note that the noun *guests* followed by an apostrophe is possessive.

13. Choice B is correct. "Sharp advances . . . are . . ." Since the subject of the

sentence is plural (*advances*), the verb must be plural (*are*).

14. Choice A is correct. "An acquaintance with the memoirs . . . *enables* us . . ." Since the subject of the sentence is singular (*acquaintance*), the verb must be singular (*enables*).

15. Choice B is correct. ". . . to *whoever* . . . had a strong sense . . ." The subject of the subordinate clause is *whoever*, and it takes a nominative form (*whoever*—not *whomever*) since it is a subject. Incidentally, the expression *he believed* is parenthetical, so it has no grammatical relationship with the rest of the sentence.

16. Choice A is correct. "If he *had lain* . . ." The verb in the "if clause" of a past contrary-to-fact conditional statement must take the *had lain* form—not the *would have lain* form.

17. Choice C is correct. ". . . John Crowe Ransom, *whom* you must know as an outstanding American critic." The direct object of the subordinate clause—or of any clause or sentence—must be in the objective case and, accordingly, must take the objective form (*whom*—not *who*).

18. Choice E is correct. All underlined parts are correct.

19. Choice A is correct. "There is no objection to *his* joining . . ." We have here a pronoun that is acting as the subject of the gerund *joining*. As a subject of the gerund, the pronoun must be in the possessive case (*his*).

20. Choice D is correct. ". . . of Chinese children parading *in colorful uniforms* up Mott Street." In the original sentence, *in colorful uniforms* was a misplaced modifier.

21. Choice D is correct. "The reason . . . is *that* . . ." We must say *the reason is that*—not *the reason* is *because*.

22. Choice A is correct. "There *remain* many reasons . . ." The word "There" in this sentence is an expletive or introductory adverb. The subject of the sentence ("reasons") must agree with the verb ("remain") in number.

23. Choice C is correct. ". . . *because* a Pan American Boeing 707 had crashed . . ." The word group *on account of* has the function of a preposition. We need a subordinate conjunction (*because*) here in order to introduce the clause.

24. Choice B is correct. ". . . *raided* the mansion . . ." The past tense (*raided*)—not the present perfect tense (*has raided*)—is necessary because the sentence has a specific past time reference (*last night*).

25. Choice E is correct. All underlined parts are correct.

26. Choice B is correct. Choice A is incorrect because the plural verb ("were") is necessary. The reason for the plural verb is that the subject "as" acts as a relative pronoun whose antecedent is the plural noun "novels." Choice B is correct. Choice C is awkward. Choice D changes the meaning of the original sentence—so does Choice E.

27. Choice C is correct. Choice A is incorrect—never start a sentence with "being that." Choice B is too wordy. Choice D is incorrect because we "stayed"—not "stood." Choice E is incorrect because "on account of" may never be used as a subordinate conjunction.

28. Choice E is correct. Avoid improper ellipsis. Choices A, B, C, and D are incorrect for this reason. The word "kept" must be included since the second part of the sentence uses another form of the verb ("keep").

29. Choice C is correct. Choice A is incorrect because the copulative verb "felt" takes a predicate adjective ("bad")—not an adverb ("badly"). Choice B is incorrect for the same reason. Moreover, we don't say "felt bad why." Choice D is incorrect because the verbal phrase "by scolding" is awkward in this context. Choice E is incorrect because of the use of "badly" and because the past perfect form of the verb ("had felt") is wrong in this time sequence.

30. Choice E is correct. Choices A, B, and C are incorrect because the part of the sentence that deals with the buying of the book is in the wrong position. Choice D is incorrect because the meaning of the original sentence has been changed. According to this choice, others besides blacks have been struggling.

31. Choice A is correct. The other choices are unidiomatic.

32. Choice D is correct. Choice A is incorrect because the possessive form of the noun ("Tom's") must be used to modify the gerund ("wanting"). Choice B is too wordy. Choice C changes the meaning of the original sentence. Choice E is incorrect for the same reason that Choice A is incorrect. Also, Choice E changes the meaning of the original sentence.

33. Choice A is correct. Choice B is incorrect because "wife" should precede "me." Choice C is incorrect because the object form "me" (not the nominative form "I") should be used as the indirect object. Choice D is incorrect for the reasons given above for Choices B and C. Choice E is too roundabout.

34. Choice D is correct. Choices A, B, C, and E are incorrect because of the misplacement of the subordinate clause ("if the weather is favorable").

35. Choice A is correct. Choices B and C are incorrect because of improper ellipsis. The words "those of" are necessary in these choices. Choice D is incorrect because the "body movements" are not "a dancer's." The possessive use of "dancer's" is incorrect in Choice E.

Improving Paragraphs: Revision-in-Context and Passage with Questions

Directions: The following passage is an early draft of an essay. Some parts of the passage need to be rewritten. Read the passage and select the best answers for the questions that follow. Some questions are about particular sentences or parts of sentences and ask you to improve sentence structure and word choice. Other questions refer to parts of the essay or the entire essay and ask you to consider organization and development. In making your decisions, follow the conventions of standard written English.

(1) *In more and more families, both husbands and wives work nowadays and with this there are new problems that result.* (2) *One reason there are so many two-career couples is that the cost of living is very high.* (3) *Another is because women are now more independent.*

(4) *An example of a two-career couple is Mr. and Mrs. Long.* (5) *Mrs. Long is a university professor.* (6) *Her husband works for a large corporation as a personnel counselor.* (7) *They have two children.* (8) *The Longs believe that the number of two-career couples is likely to increase.* (9) *However, society generally still expects a married woman to continue to fulfill the traditional roles of companion, housekeeper, mother, hostess.* (10) *Thus, as the Longs have experienced, conflicts arise in many ways.* (11) *When career opportunities clash, it is difficult for them to decide which career is more important.*

(12) *There are some basic things that can be done to try to solve a couple's problems.* (13) *Partners should discuss issues with each other openly.* (14) *Keep a realistic estimate on how much can be done.* (15) *Each partner must set priorities, make choices, and agree to trade-offs.* (16) *Men and women have to understand each other's feelings and be aware of this problem before they get involved.*

(SENTENCE STRUCTURE)

1. Which of the following is the best revision of the underlined portion of sentence 1 below?

   In more and more families, both husbands and wives work <u>nowadays and with this there are new problems that result</u>.

   (A) nowadays, a situation that is causing new problems
   (B) nowadays and this is what is causing new problems
   (C) nowadays and this makes them have new problems as a result
   (D) nowadays and with it are new problems
   (E) nowadays, they are having new problems

(USAGE)

2. Which of the following is the best revision of the underlined portion of sentence 3 below?

   Another <u>is because women are</u> now more independent.

   (A) is women which are
   (B) reason is that women are
   (C) comes from women being

(D) reason is due to the fact that women are

(E) is caused by the women's being

(SENTENCE COMBINING)

3. Which of the following is the best way to combine sentences 5, 6, and 7?

(A) Mrs. Long, a university professor, and her husband, a personnel counselor for a large corporation, have two children.

(B) As a personnel counselor for a large corporation and as a university professor, Mr. and Mrs. Long have two children.

(C) Having two children are Mr. and Mrs. Long, a personnel counselor for a large corporation and a university professor.

(D) Mrs. Long is a university professor and her husband is a personnel counselor for a large corporation and they have two children.

(E) Mr. and Mrs. Long have two children—he is a personnel counselor for a large corporation and she is a university professor.

(PASSAGE ORGANIZATION)

4. In relation to the passage as a whole, which of the following best describes the writer's intention in the second paragraph?

(A) To summarize contradictory evidence

(B) To propose a solution to a problem

(C) To provide an example

(D) To evaluate opinions set forth in the first paragraph

(E) To convince the reader to alter his or her opinion

(SENTENCE STRUCTURE)

5. In the context of the sentences preceding and following sentence 14, which of the following is the best revision of sentence 14?

(A) You should keep a realistic estimate of how much you can do.

(B) Estimate realistically how much can be done.

(C) Keep estimating realistically about how much can be done.

(D) They should be estimating realistically about how much it is possible for them to do.

(E) They should estimate realistically how much they can do.

Answer Key

1. A, 2. B, 3. A, 4. C, 5. E.

Sample Test with Answers

[1]To enter the perceptual world of whales and dolphins, you would have to change your primary sense from sight to sound. [2]Your brain would process and store sound pictures rather than visual images. [3]Individuals and other creatures would be recognized either by the sounds they made or by the echoes they returned from the sounds you made. [4]Your sense of neighborhood, of where you are, and whom you are with, would be a sound sense. [5]Sound is the primary sense in the life of whales and dolphins. [6]Vision is often difficult or impossible in the dark and murky seas. [7]Many whales and dolphins navigate and hunt at night or below the zone of illuminated water. [8]Vision depends on the presence of light, sounds can be made and used at any time of the day or night, and at all depths. [9]Sounds are infinitely variable: loud to soft, high notes to low notes, short silences to long silences, and many other combinations. [10]Sounds can be stopped abruptly in order to listen to a neighbor in the silence. [11]They can be finitely directed and pinpointed by the listener. [12]And communicating and locating by sound does not require a disruption of daily routines. [13]Whales and dolphins can keep in sound contact simply by blowing bubbles as they exhale.

1. If the passage were split into two paragraphs, the second paragraph should begin with the sentence

    (A) Many whales and dolphins navigate and hunt at night or below the zone of illuminated water.
    (B) Sounds are infinitely variable (etc.).
    (C) Sound is the primary sense in the life of whales and dolphins.
    (D) Your sense of neighborhood, of where you are, and whom you are with, would be a sound sense.

    (E) Vision is often difficult or impossible in the dark and murky seas.

2. What should be done with sentence 8?

    (A) The comma after the word *light* should be omitted and the word *and* inserted.
    (B) A semicolon should be substituted for the comma after *light*.
    (C) After the word *sounds* there should be a comma, then the word *however*, and then another comma.
    (D) The sentence should begin with the words for *instance*.
    (E) The sentence should begin with the word *whereas*.

3. Sentence 11 would be more clear if

    (A) The words *by the speaker* were added after the word *directed*.
    (B) The sentence began with *Sounds* rather than *They*.
    (C) The word *finitely* were used again before *pinpointed*.
    (D) The words *by whales or dolphins* were inserted after *directed*.
    (E) The word *always* followed the word *can*.

4. The last sentence, sentence 13, should be

    (A) omitted
    (B) left as it is
    (C) placed before sentence 12
    (D) expanded to explain that whales and dolphins are mammals and therefore exhale through lungs
    (E) changed to read: *Whales and dolphins can keep in contact with each other through sound simply by blowing bubbles as they exhale.*

Explanatory Answers

1. Choice C is correct. Choice A is incorrect because the sentence is dealing with the limitations in the use of vision in whales and dolphins, and the subject of vision has already been introduced in the previous sentence, sentence 6. Choice B is incorrect for similar reasons: The subject of sound has just been discussed in the previous sentence, and it is logical that this discussion continue. All the sentences before this address themselves to the reader and explain what changes would have to occur in order for us to perceive the world as whales and dolphins do. Sentence 5 turns the discussion to whales and dolphins themselves and their use of sound. (Notice that sentence 1 says ". . . *you* would have to change *your primary sense* . . . ," and sentence 5 says "Sound is the *primary sense* in the life of *whales and dolphins*.") This is the only logical place to begin a second paragraph. Choice D is incorrect because, as it has been stated, sentences 1 through 4 address the reader and therefore belong in one paragraph. Choice E is wrong because, although it is introducing the subject of vision in whales and dolphins for the first time, it is necessary that it follow directly after sentence 5 in order to show that sound is the primary sense *because* vision is restricted in the dark and murky seas.

2. Choice E is correct. As it stands, sentence 8 contains two complete thoughts—one about vision and one about sound, separated only by a comma, which is grammatically incorrect. Although Choice A remedies this situation, it does not make clear that a *comparison* is being made between the uses of vision and hearing. This is also true of Choice B. Choice C makes the comparison clear by the use of the word *however*, but leaves the two thoughts separated only by a comma, and is therefore wrong. Choice D is wrong for two reasons: The sentence is not really giving an example of something which was stated previously, and therefore the words *for instance* do not make sense here; furthermore, the words *for instance* do not make the comparison clear, and so the sentence remains as two separate thoughts with only a comma between them. Choice E remedies the situation completely: The word *whereas* tells us immediately that a comparison is about to be made, and the first part of the sentence ("Whereas vision depends on the presence of light") is now an *incomplete* thought which must be followed by a comma and then the rest of the sentence.

3. Choice A is correct. The sentence as it stands is unclear because it would make it seem that the listener directs as well as pinpoints the sounds, whereas it is the *speaker* who directs them. Therefore Choice A is correct. There is no need for the sentence to begin with the word *sounds;* since sentence 10 began with it, the word *they* in sentence 11 clearly refers to *sounds*. Therefore Choice B does nothing to improve the sentence. Choice C is incorrect because to pinpoint means to locate precisely or exactly, and therefore it would be redundant to insert the word *finitely*. Although Choice D improves the sentence by telling us *who* directs the sounds, Choice A is better because it is the *speaker* who directs the sounds

and the listener who pinpoints them, whether whale or dolphin. Choice E is wrong because it would be assumed by the reader that if sounds *can* be finitely directed and pinpointed, they would be in most cases; to say *always can* would be too extreme.

4. Choice B is correct. Sentence 13 is necessary to show that emitting and listening to sounds do not disrupt the routines of whales and dolphins, stated in sentence 12. To omit the sentence, as Choice A suggests, is incorrect. Choice B is correct; it should be left as it is. Choice C is wrong; sentence 13 explains sentence 12, and therefore needs to follow it, not precede it. Choice D is incorrect because the passage is about the use of sound by whales and dolphins, not about the fact that they are mammals. To go into an explanation of this would be to go into disproportionate detail on this one topic. Choice E is wrong for two reasons: (1) The *with each other* is understood (one has contact *with* something; otherwise it is not *contact*). (2) It also implies that whales keep in contact with dolphins and dolphins with whales, whereas what the author means is that whales and dolphins keep in contact with their own kind. To insert *with each other*, therefore, makes the sentence quite confusing.

THE HARDEST ACTUAL SAT QUESTIONS AND THEIR TOP STRATEGIC SOLUTIONS*

Math

1. In the integer 3,589 the digits are all different and increase from left to right. How many integers between 4,000 and 5,000 have digits that are all different and that increase from left to right?

1. [Strategies 5, 9] Pay attention to exactly what is given. If the digits increase from left to right, you would try all numbers that fit this condition in a *stepwise* fashion.

   Start with $4567 - 5, 6, 7$ shows an increase

   Now try other numbers stepwise:

   4568, 4569, 4578, 4579, 4589, 4678, 4679, 4689, 4789. There are **10** numbers.

2. In triangle PQR, the length of side QR is 12 and the length of side PR is 20. What is the greatest possible integer length of side PQ?

   (A)9 (B)16 (C)25 (D)27 (E)31

2. (E) [Strategy 20] Draw and label sides of the triangle:

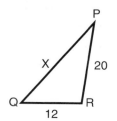

Now ask yourself-what do I know about the sides of a triangle? I know the sum of the lengths of two sides is <u>greater</u> than the length of the third side. So write down <u>all</u> the possibilities: (Don't worry if you feel you are writing down too many possibilities)

(1) $20 + 12 > x$
(2) $12 + x > 20$
(3) $20 + x > 12$

This gives

(1) $32 > x$
(2) $x > 8$
(3) $x > -8$ (which of course is obvious since $x > 0$)

Thus from (1) and (2) we get $32 > x > 8$. So the **greatest** possible **integer** for x is **31**.

3. For all positive integers, x, let $\underline{x}$ be defined to be the sum of the digits of x multiplied by the number of digits of x. For example, $\underline{31} = (3 + 1) \times 2 = 8$. What is the value of $\underline{314}$?

   (A) 12 (B) 16 (C) 18 (D) 24 (E) 36

3. (D) [Strategies 16, 5] Pay attention to exactly what you are asked to find. You are asked to find the <u>sum of the digits</u> multiplied by the <u>number of digits</u>.

   The *sum* of the digits of $314 = 3 + 1 + 4 = 8$. The *number* of digits is 3. So $\underline{314} = 8 \times 3 = $ **24**.

---

* The purpose of this section is to show that even the hardest SAT questions can be answered using simple but important strategies, showing that many students can achieve a top score on the SAT.

4.

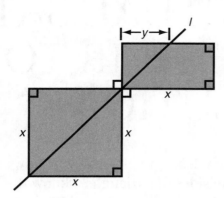

In the figure above, line l passes through two vertices of the square. Which of the following represents the sum of the areas of the shaded regions?

(A) $x^2 + xy$

(B) $x^2 + \sqrt{2}\, xy$

(C) $2x^2 + xy$

(D) $xy + y^2$

(E) $2x^2 - y^2$

4. (A) [Strategy 9] This is tricky. You might think that you don't have enough information. You are tempted to look at just the sides but you have to look at the angles, which will tell you more information about the sides. Note that the line cuts 45 degree angles. Thus since we have a 45-45-90 triangle, the side of the rectangle is y. So the area of the rectangle is xy and since the area of the square is x^2, the areas of both shaded regions is $x^2 + xy$.

See diagram:

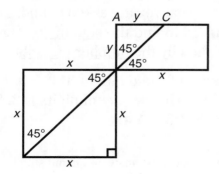

5. Jason uses two different mixtures of windshield washer fluid for his car. In summer the mixture is one part washer fluid to three parts water; in winter the mixture is two parts washer fluid to one part water. How many ounces of washer fluid should Jason add to 24 ounces of the summer mixture in order to produce the winter mixture?

(A) 3

(B) 12

(C) 30

(D) 36

(E) 48

5. (C) [Strategy 7] Let the amount of washer fluid in the summer mixture be f and water be w. The the amount of water in the summer mixture will be $3f$. If the summer mixture is 24 oz., $f + 3f = 24$ and $f = 6$, $w = 3f = 18$. and if I add x oz. of washer fluid to the summer mixture, I get $x + 6$ for f and I have 18 for w. The winter mixture is 2 parts of washer fluid to 1 part of water. So I get:

$$\frac{x+6}{18} = \frac{2}{1}$$

Solving, $x + 6 = 36$ and $x = \mathbf{30}$

6.

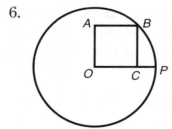

In the figure above, O is the center of the circle, $OABC$ is a square, and $OP = 8$ inches. What is the area of the square, in square inches?

(A) 32

(B) 36

(C) 64

(D) $16\sqrt{2}$

(E) $16\sqrt{3}$

6. (A) [Strategy 20] We make use of the strategy of drawing lines to get more information. In order to find the area of the square we need to find how long a side is. So Draw OB which is just the radius; call it r.

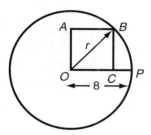

Now r = OP = 8.

Label the side of the square x. To find the side of the square, x, use the Pythagorean theorem:

$x^2 + x^2 = r^2$,

$2x^2 = r^2$

$x^2 = r^2/2$ so the area is just $8^2/2 = \textbf{32}$.

7. HOURS OF TELEVISION VIEWING IN A WEEK

Hours per Child	Number of Children
6	1
9	4
11	2
14	3
18	5

The table above shows the numbers of hours of television viewing by 15 children last week. What is the median number of hours of viewing per child?

(A) 9

(B) 11

(C) 12

(D) 13

(E) 14

7. (E) [Strategy 5] The median is the middle term of a set of numbers. Like if you have 1,2,4,7,9 the median is 4. So in the question, we have the numbers:

6	9 9 9 9	11 11
(1 child)	(4 children)	(2 children)

14 14 14   18 18 18 18 18
(3 children)   (5 children)

The median (middle number) is **14**

8. If $(x + y)(x^2 - y^2) = 0$, which of the following must be true?

(A) $x = y$

(B) $x = -y$

(C) $x^2 = y^2$

(D) $x^2 = -y^2$

(E) $x^3 = y^3$

8. (C) [Strategy 13] Here's a question where you really have to decide what to do first. You should factor $x^2 - y^2 = (x + y)(x - y)$ and then get $(x + y)(x + y)(x - y) = 0$

Now you should realize that there are three possibilities for this to be true:

(1) $x + y = 0$ only

(2) $x - y = 0$ only

(3) $x + y = 0$ and $x - y = 0$

If (1) is true then $x = -y$
If (2) is true then $x = +y$
If (3) is true then $x = -y$ and $x = +y$

Notice that in either of the three cases, **$x^2 = y^2$.**

9. The output at a factory was 40 chairs per hour for the first 3 hours of an 8-hour shift. The output then increased to 60 chairs per hour for the remainder of the 8-hour shift. What was the average (arithmetic mean) number of chairs produced per hour during this shift?

9. **52.5** [Strategy 12] We write: 40 chairs/hr X 3 hours = 120 chairs

60 chairs/hr $\times$ 5 = 300 chairs

So $\dfrac{420 \text{ (the total chairs)}}{8 \text{ (total hours)}}$

420/8 = **52.5**

10. The Friends of the Library meet on the third Sunday of every month. What is the latest possible day of the month that this meeting could take place?

(A) The 20th
(B) The 21st
(C) The 22nd
(D) The 23rd
(E) The 24th

10. (B) [Strategy 5] You need to use a trial and error type of strategy. Draw a calendr and try the first Sunday as the 1st of the month and let's see what we get.

Sun	Mon	Tues	Wed	Thurs	Fri	Sat
1						
8						
15						

Now let's try Mon as the 1st:

Sun	Mon	Tues	Wed	Thurs	Fri	Sat
	1					
7	8					
14	15					
21						

Try Tues as the first:

Sun	Mon	Tues	Wed	Thurs	Fri	Sat
		1				
6	7	8				
13						
20						

You can see that when Monday is the 1st of the month, the third Sunday is the **21**, and that's the latest day of the month that the meeting could take place.

11.

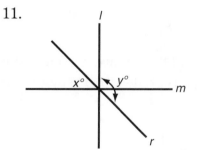

Note: Figure not drawn to scale.

In the figure above, lines l, m, and r intersect in a point. If $l \perp m$ and $y = 110$, what is the value of x?

(A) 55
(B) 45
(C) 40
(D) 35
(E) 20

11. (E) [Strategy 20] Immediately try to bring the x closer to the 110. Use vertical angles.

See diagram:

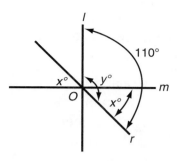

∡ *m*O*r* = *x*.
Since ∡ O*m* = 90, we have 90 + *x* = 110,
and *x* = **20**

12.

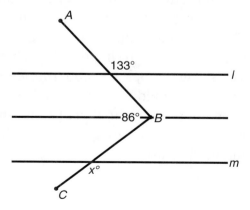

In the figure above, *l* ∥ *m* and segments $\overline{AB}$ and $\overline{BC}$ intersect at point *B*. What is the value of *x*?

12. **141** [Strategy 20] Use the strategy of drawing lines and moving the variables to get a better picture of things.

Draw parallel line CB

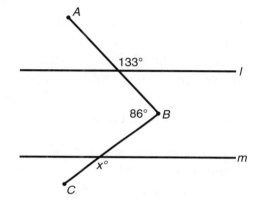

Now we have to get *x* closer to B and find the supplement of the angle 133 using parallel lines and angles facts.

We draw the angles using the fact of angles of parallel lines and that the sum of the angles of a straight line is 180.

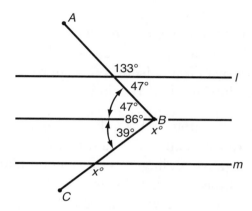

We get *x* + 39 = 180
x = **141**

Sentence Completions

1. Feeling —— by a voting process that ultimately led to their votes being invalidated, these citizens —— their discontent by way of a lawsuit.

    (A) heartened . . . voiced
    (B) emboldened . . . denied
    (C) compromised . . . garnered
    (D) disenfranchised . . . registered
    (E) intrigued . . . revoked

1. (D) [Strategy 3] Look at feelings of words in blanks. The first blank denotes a negative feeling and the second blank must have a word like *expressed, showed,* etc. So what word in the first blank choice is negative? It is Choice C and D. Choice D is more negative, so I would choose D.

2. Peregrine falcons are among the avian world's great ——, sometimes migrating as much as 18,000 miles each year.

    (A) mercenaries
    (B) itinerants
    (C) charlatans
    (D) recidivists
    (E) provincials

2. (B) [Strategy 16] Look at key words here and something that also stands out. *18,000* stands out and *migrating* is a key word. So look for a word that has lots of movement. Note Choice B: itinerants. You can associate *itinerants* with *itinerary* which has to do with travel (*migrating*). So I'd choose B.

3. Though Judd is typically —— and reserved in social gatherings, at last

night's reception he spoke and acted with uncharacteristic ——.

    (A) loquacious . . . alacrity
    (B) querulous . . . languor
    (C) disaffected . . . resentment
    (D) diplomatic . . . decorum
    (E) diffident . . . aplomb

3. (E) [Strategy 5] Here is a situation where you may not know most or any of the words in the choices. In this case, if you can figure out the meaning of just one word on a choice and it sounds like it may fit, choose that choice. Note that "diffident" sounds like it may be an opposite of "confident." And the opposite of the word "confident" does fit in the first blank. So I would choose Choice E.

4. It seemed rather —— that in a society of supersophisticated ——, we often suffer from a shortage of listeners.

    (A) unfortunate . . . technology
    (B) incongruous . . . communication
    (C) relevant . . . intellectuals
    (D) presumptuous . . . dilitantes
    (E) peculiar . . . polititians

4. (B) [Strategy 5 and Vocabulary Strategy 3] The word *"incongruous"* means "lacking in agreement." You can figure this word out from "in"—"not" and "congruous" from "congruent" as in "congruent triangles"—"same triangles." So where there is "supersophisticated *communication,*" we wouldn't expect to have a shortage of people who don't listen. And thus it would seem *incongruous* that this would be the case.

Writing

Directions: For questions 1 and 3, choose the part A, B, C, or D hat has the error, or choose E if ther is no error. For Questions 2, 4, and 5, replace the underlined part with the choice that makes the sentence correct.

1. <u>Until</u> the train stopped at the station,
   A
neither the engineer nor the conductor
<u>were</u> aware <u>that one</u> of the
 B   C
passengers <u>had become</u> ill. <u>No error</u>
        D   E

1. (B) Neither the engineer nor the conductor *was* . . . If it stated "the engineer and the conductor, it would be "the engineer and the conductor *were.*

2. Dr. Seuss, whose 44 books have sold more than 500 million copies, <u>have made him</u> probably the best-selling children's author in history.

    (A) have made him
    (B) making him
    (C) and was thereby
    (D) is
    (E) are

2. (D) We are talking about Dr. Suess, before the comma. So Choice D would be correct. *Dr. Seuss is*, not *Dr. Seuss have made him*.

3. The atmosphere <u>at</u> the Wimbledon
            A
tennis tournament is <u>far more</u> sedate and
               B
traditional <u>than the tournament</u> <u>we saw</u>.
         C   D
<u>No error</u>
  E

3. (C) We are talking about *atmosphere* here(not the *tournament*). So <u>than the tournament</u> should be changed to <u>than the atmosphere of the tournament</u>.

4. At the beginning of the new school year, the administration announced <u>that all students' backpacks must be kept in their lockers while attending classes</u>.

    (A) that all students' backpacks must be kept in their lockers while attending classes
    (B) that all students attending classes, they must keep their backpacks in their lockers
    (C) that all students must keep their backpacks in their lockers while attending classes
    (D) that, while attending classes, all backpacks must be kept in students' lockers
    (E) that, while they attend classes, all their backpacks must be kept in students' lockers

4. (C) The way the sentence reads, it seems that the students' backpacks are attending classes. Choice C clarifies that.

5. Meteorites are of great interest to <u>astrophysicists, since this is how they obtain information</u> about the chemical composition of early solar systems.

    (A) astrophysicists, since this is how they obtain information
    (B) astrophysicists, who obtain from them information
    (C) astrophysicists because information is obtained by them

(D) astrophysicists; they obtain information this way

(E) astrophysicists, which is how they obtain information

5. (B) *Meteorites* is not how astrophysicists obtain information. We need to clarify this, so choice B is correct.

THE SHORTEST SAT TEST— 16 QUESTIONS TO APPROXIMATE YOUR SAT SCORE AND THE EXACT STRATEGIES YOU NEED TO IMPROVE YOUR SCORE

Although it shouldn't take you more than 40 seconds to answer each verbal (Critical Reading) and writing question and 1 minute to answer each math question, you may take this test untimed and still get a fairly accurate prediction.

Note: The PSAT score is approximately calculated by dividing the SAT score by 10 and is used for National Merit Scholarships.

The top schools require SAT scores above 1800. Following is a test that can determine if you have the goods—and it won't take you more than 15 minutes.

Verbal (Critical Reading)

Allow 7 minutes for this part.

Sentence Completions

Fill in the blank(s) with the appropriate choice:

1. The instructor displayed extreme stubbornness; although he _____ the logic of the student's argument, he _____ to acknowledge her conclusion as correct.

    (A) accepted . . . refused
    (B) concluded . . . consented
    (C) denounced . . . declined
    (D) asserted . . . acceded
    (E) rejected . . . preferred

2. In spite of the _____ of his presentation, many people were _____ with the speaker's concepts and ideas.

    (A) interest . . . enthralled
    (B) power . . . taken
    (C) intensity . . . shocked
    (D) greatness . . . gratified
    (E) strength . . . bored

3. Richard Wagner was frequently intolerant; moreover, his strange behavior caused most of his acquaintances to _____ the composer whenever possible.

    (A) contradict
    (B) interrogate
    (C) shun
    (D) revere
    (E) tolerate

Reading Comprehension

Read the following passage. Then answer the questions:

1 Sometimes the meaning of glowing water is ominous. Off the Pacific Coast of North America, it may mean that the sea is filled with a minute plant that contains a poison
5 of strange and terrible virulence. About four days after this minute plant comes to alter the coastal plankton, some of the fishes and shellfish in the vicinity become toxic. This is because in their normal
10 feeding, they have strained the poisonous plankton out of the water.

4. Fish and shellfish become toxic when they

    (A) swim in poisonous water
    (B) feed on poisonous plants or animals
    (C) change their feeding habits
    (D) give off a strange glow
    (E) take strychnine into their systems

5. In the context of the passage, the word *virulence* in line 5 means

    (A) strangeness
    (B) color
    (C) calamity
    (D) potency
    (E) powerful odor

6. The paragraph preceding the one in the passage most probably discussed the

    (A) phenomena of the Pacific coastline
    (B) poisons that affect man
    (C) toxic plants in the sea
    (D) characteristics of plankton
    (E) phenomena of the sea

7. It can be assumed that "plankton" in line 7 are

    (A) fish and shellfish
    (B) small plants or animals
    (C) sand deposits
    (D) land parasites
    (E) glacier or rock formations

Math

Allow 7 minutes for this part.

Answer the following questions:

1. If $2x + 3y = 4$ and $y = 2$, find the value of x.

   (A) $+2$
   (B) $+1$
   (C) 0
   (D) -1
   (E) -2

2. Where $a \neq 1$, $(a^7 - a^6)/(a - 1) =$

   (A) $a/(a - 1)$
   (B) $1/(a - 1)$
   (C) $a^6 - a^5$
   (D) a^5
   (E) a^6

3. Sarah is twice as old as John. Six years ago Sarah was four times as old as John was then. In years, how old is John now?

   (A) 3
   (B) 9
   (C) 18
   (D) 20
   (E) Cannot be determined

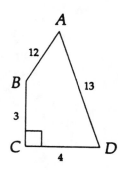

(Note: Figure is not drawn to scale.)

4. The area of the above figure *ABCD*

   (A) is 36
   (B) is 108
   (C) is 156
   (D) is 1872
   (E) Cannot be determined

In the following questions you must find an answer without referring to choices:

5. If $x + y = 7$ and $xy = 4$, then find the value of $x^2 + y^2$.

6. If $y + 2q = 15$, $q + 2p = 5$ and $p + 2y = 7$, then find the value of $p + q + y$.

7. On a street with 25 houses, 10 houses have *fewer than 6 rooms*, 10 houses have *more than 7 rooms*, and 4 houses have *more than 8 rooms*. What is the total number of houses on the street that are either 6-, 7-, or 8-room houses?

Writing

Allow 1 minute for this part.

Indentifying Sentence Errors:

Which part (A, B, C, or D) in the sentence below is incorrect? Choose E if there is no error.

If any signer of the Constitution (A) *was* to return to life (B) *for a day*, his opinion (C) *of* our amendments (D) *would be* interesting.

Improving Sentences:

Which choice correctly replaces the sentence below?

He never has and never will keep his word.

    (A) He never has and never will keep his word.
    (B) He has never yet and never will keep his word.
    (C) He has not ever and will not keep his word.
    (D) He never has or will keep his word.
    (E) He never has kept and he never will keep his word.

Answers

Verbal (Critical Reading)

1. A
2. E
3. C
4. B
5. D
6. E
7. B

Math

1. D
2. E
3. B
4. A
5. 41
6. 9
7. 11

Writing

1. A
2. E

What You Did Wrong, Explanatory Answers and Scoring, Strategies, and Basic Skills Needed to Improve

Now go to the website www.sourcebookscollege.com/gruberquiz and record your answers in the grid given on the site. Even though you may have gotten a wrong answer, you may have come close to the answer or done part of it correctly. The computer will assess your patterns and give you:

1. Your approximate SAT score.

2. Why you got the questions wrong, what you should use to get a question right, and a detailed explanation of the best way you should answer the question.

3. The strategy and basic skill you need to use for each type of question.

SAT PRACTICE TEST

Answer Sheet for Practice Test
SECTION 1

Begin your essay on this page. If you need more space, continue on the next page. Do not write outside of the essay box.

Continue on the next page if necessary.

Continuation of ESSAY Section 1 from previous page. Write below only if you need more space.

Start with number 1 for each new section. If a section has fewer questions than answer spaces, leave the extra answer spaces blank. Be sure to erase any errors or stray marks completely.

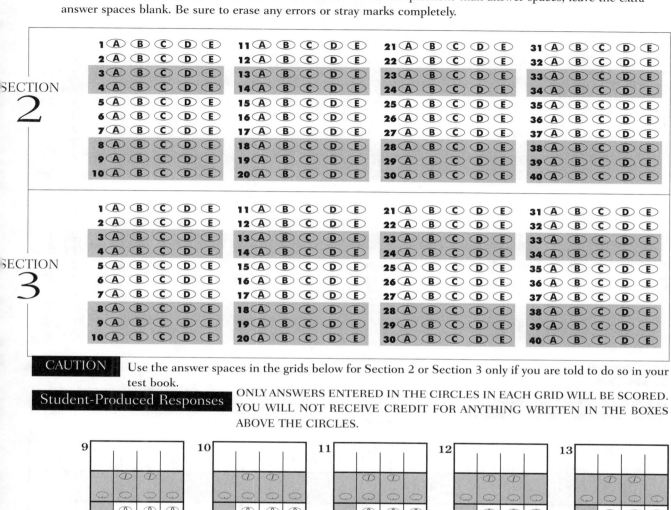

CAUTION   Use the answer spaces in the grids below for Section 2 or Section 3 only if you are told to do so in your test book.

Student-Produced Responses   ONLY ANSWERS ENTERED IN THE CIRCLES IN EACH GRID WILL BE SCORED. YOU WILL NOT RECEIVE CREDIT FOR ANYTHING WRITTEN IN THE BOXES ABOVE THE CIRCLES.

Start with number 1 for each new section. If a section has fewer questions than answer spaces, leave the extra answer spaces blank. Be sure to erase any errors or stray marks completely.

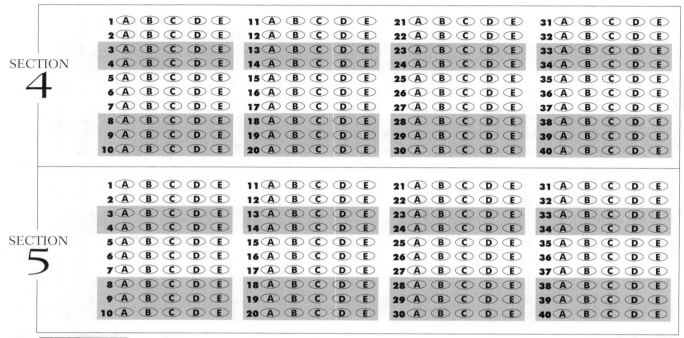

SECTION
4

SECTION
5

CAUTION Use the answer spaces in the grids below for Section 4 or Section 5 only if you are told to do so in your test book.

Student-Produced Responses ONLY ANSWERS ENTERED IN THE CIRCLES IN EACH GRID WILL BE SCORED. YOU WILL NOT RECEIVE CREDIT FOR ANYTHING WRITTEN IN THE BOXES ABOVE THE CIRCLES.

Start with number 1 for each new section. If a section has fewer questions than answer spaces, leave the extra answer spaces blank. Be sure to erase any errors or stray marks completely.

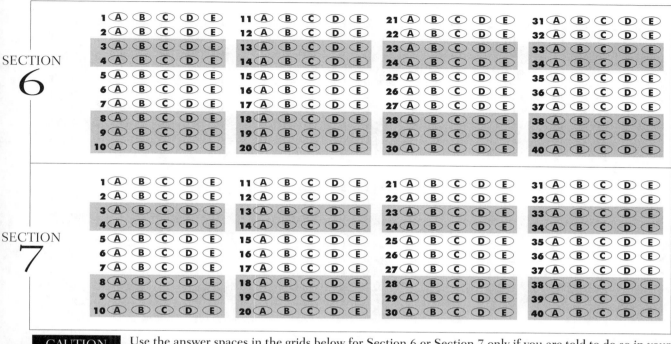

SECTION
6

SECTION
7

CAUTION Use the answer spaces in the grids below for Section 6 or Section 7 only if you are told to do so in your test book.

Student-Produced Responses ONLY ANSWERS ENTERED IN THE CIRCLES IN EACH GRID WILL BE SCORED. YOU WILL NOT RECEIVE CREDIT FOR ANYTHING WRITTEN IN THE BOXES ABOVE THE CIRCLES.

Start with number 1 for each new section. If a section has fewer questions than answer spaces, leave the extra answer spaces blank. Be sure to erase any errors or stray marks completely.

SECTION 8

1 Ⓐ Ⓑ Ⓒ Ⓓ Ⓔ	11 Ⓐ Ⓑ Ⓒ Ⓓ Ⓔ	21 Ⓐ Ⓑ Ⓒ Ⓓ Ⓔ	31 Ⓐ Ⓑ Ⓒ Ⓓ Ⓔ
2 Ⓐ Ⓑ Ⓒ Ⓓ Ⓔ	12 Ⓐ Ⓑ Ⓒ Ⓓ Ⓔ	22 Ⓐ Ⓑ Ⓒ Ⓓ Ⓔ	32 Ⓐ Ⓑ Ⓒ Ⓓ Ⓔ
3 Ⓐ Ⓑ Ⓒ Ⓓ Ⓔ	13 Ⓐ Ⓑ Ⓒ Ⓓ Ⓔ	23 Ⓐ Ⓑ Ⓒ Ⓓ Ⓔ	33 Ⓐ Ⓑ Ⓒ Ⓓ Ⓔ
4 Ⓐ Ⓑ Ⓒ Ⓓ Ⓔ	14 Ⓐ Ⓑ Ⓒ Ⓓ Ⓔ	24 Ⓐ Ⓑ Ⓒ Ⓓ Ⓔ	34 Ⓐ Ⓑ Ⓒ Ⓓ Ⓔ
5 Ⓐ Ⓑ Ⓒ Ⓓ Ⓔ	15 Ⓐ Ⓑ Ⓒ Ⓓ Ⓔ	25 Ⓐ Ⓑ Ⓒ Ⓓ Ⓔ	35 Ⓐ Ⓑ Ⓒ Ⓓ Ⓔ
6 Ⓐ Ⓑ Ⓒ Ⓓ Ⓔ	16 Ⓐ Ⓑ Ⓒ Ⓓ Ⓔ	26 Ⓐ Ⓑ Ⓒ Ⓓ Ⓔ	36 Ⓐ Ⓑ Ⓒ Ⓓ Ⓔ
7 Ⓐ Ⓑ Ⓒ Ⓓ Ⓔ	17 Ⓐ Ⓑ Ⓒ Ⓓ Ⓔ	27 Ⓐ Ⓑ Ⓒ Ⓓ Ⓔ	37 Ⓐ Ⓑ Ⓒ Ⓓ Ⓔ
8 Ⓐ Ⓑ Ⓒ Ⓓ Ⓔ	18 Ⓐ Ⓑ Ⓒ Ⓓ Ⓔ	28 Ⓐ Ⓑ Ⓒ Ⓓ Ⓔ	38 Ⓐ Ⓑ Ⓒ Ⓓ Ⓔ
9 Ⓐ Ⓑ Ⓒ Ⓓ Ⓔ	19 Ⓐ Ⓑ Ⓒ Ⓓ Ⓔ	29 Ⓐ Ⓑ Ⓒ Ⓓ Ⓔ	39 Ⓐ Ⓑ Ⓒ Ⓓ Ⓔ
10 Ⓐ Ⓑ Ⓒ Ⓓ Ⓔ	20 Ⓐ Ⓑ Ⓒ Ⓓ Ⓔ	30 Ⓐ Ⓑ Ⓒ Ⓓ Ⓔ	40 Ⓐ Ⓑ Ⓒ Ⓓ Ⓔ

SECTION 9

1 Ⓐ Ⓑ Ⓒ Ⓓ Ⓔ	11 Ⓐ Ⓑ Ⓒ Ⓓ Ⓔ	21 Ⓐ Ⓑ Ⓒ Ⓓ Ⓔ	31 Ⓐ Ⓑ Ⓒ Ⓓ Ⓔ
2 Ⓐ Ⓑ Ⓒ Ⓓ Ⓔ	12 Ⓐ Ⓑ Ⓒ Ⓓ Ⓔ	22 Ⓐ Ⓑ Ⓒ Ⓓ Ⓔ	32 Ⓐ Ⓑ Ⓒ Ⓓ Ⓔ
3 Ⓐ Ⓑ Ⓒ Ⓓ Ⓔ	13 Ⓐ Ⓑ Ⓒ Ⓓ Ⓔ	23 Ⓐ Ⓑ Ⓒ Ⓓ Ⓔ	33 Ⓐ Ⓑ Ⓒ Ⓓ Ⓔ
4 Ⓐ Ⓑ Ⓒ Ⓓ Ⓔ	14 Ⓐ Ⓑ Ⓒ Ⓓ Ⓔ	24 Ⓐ Ⓑ Ⓒ Ⓓ Ⓔ	34 Ⓐ Ⓑ Ⓒ Ⓓ Ⓔ
5 Ⓐ Ⓑ Ⓒ Ⓓ Ⓔ	15 Ⓐ Ⓑ Ⓒ Ⓓ Ⓔ	25 Ⓐ Ⓑ Ⓒ Ⓓ Ⓔ	35 Ⓐ Ⓑ Ⓒ Ⓓ Ⓔ
6 Ⓐ Ⓑ Ⓒ Ⓓ Ⓔ	16 Ⓐ Ⓑ Ⓒ Ⓓ Ⓔ	26 Ⓐ Ⓑ Ⓒ Ⓓ Ⓔ	36 Ⓐ Ⓑ Ⓒ Ⓓ Ⓔ
7 Ⓐ Ⓑ Ⓒ Ⓓ Ⓔ	17 Ⓐ Ⓑ Ⓒ Ⓓ Ⓔ	27 Ⓐ Ⓑ Ⓒ Ⓓ Ⓔ	37 Ⓐ Ⓑ Ⓒ Ⓓ Ⓔ
8 Ⓐ Ⓑ Ⓒ Ⓓ Ⓔ	18 Ⓐ Ⓑ Ⓒ Ⓓ Ⓔ	28 Ⓐ Ⓑ Ⓒ Ⓓ Ⓔ	38 Ⓐ Ⓑ Ⓒ Ⓓ Ⓔ
9 Ⓐ Ⓑ Ⓒ Ⓓ Ⓔ	19 Ⓐ Ⓑ Ⓒ Ⓓ Ⓔ	29 Ⓐ Ⓑ Ⓒ Ⓓ Ⓔ	39 Ⓐ Ⓑ Ⓒ Ⓓ Ⓔ
10 Ⓐ Ⓑ Ⓒ Ⓓ Ⓔ	20 Ⓐ Ⓑ Ⓒ Ⓓ Ⓔ	30 Ⓐ Ⓑ Ⓒ Ⓓ Ⓔ	40 Ⓐ Ⓑ Ⓒ Ⓓ Ⓔ

SECTION 10

1 Ⓐ Ⓑ Ⓒ Ⓓ Ⓔ	11 Ⓐ Ⓑ Ⓒ Ⓓ Ⓔ	21 Ⓐ Ⓑ Ⓒ Ⓓ Ⓔ	31 Ⓐ Ⓑ Ⓒ Ⓓ Ⓔ
2 Ⓐ Ⓑ Ⓒ Ⓓ Ⓔ	12 Ⓐ Ⓑ Ⓒ Ⓓ Ⓔ	22 Ⓐ Ⓑ Ⓒ Ⓓ Ⓔ	32 Ⓐ Ⓑ Ⓒ Ⓓ Ⓔ
3 Ⓐ Ⓑ Ⓒ Ⓓ Ⓔ	13 Ⓐ Ⓑ Ⓒ Ⓓ Ⓔ	23 Ⓐ Ⓑ Ⓒ Ⓓ Ⓔ	33 Ⓐ Ⓑ Ⓒ Ⓓ Ⓔ
4 Ⓐ Ⓑ Ⓒ Ⓓ Ⓔ	14 Ⓐ Ⓑ Ⓒ Ⓓ Ⓔ	24 Ⓐ Ⓑ Ⓒ Ⓓ Ⓔ	34 Ⓐ Ⓑ Ⓒ Ⓓ Ⓔ
5 Ⓐ Ⓑ Ⓒ Ⓓ Ⓔ	15 Ⓐ Ⓑ Ⓒ Ⓓ Ⓔ	25 Ⓐ Ⓑ Ⓒ Ⓓ Ⓔ	35 Ⓐ Ⓑ Ⓒ Ⓓ Ⓔ
6 Ⓐ Ⓑ Ⓒ Ⓓ Ⓔ	16 Ⓐ Ⓑ Ⓒ Ⓓ Ⓔ	26 Ⓐ Ⓑ Ⓒ Ⓓ Ⓔ	36 Ⓐ Ⓑ Ⓒ Ⓓ Ⓔ
7 Ⓐ Ⓑ Ⓒ Ⓓ Ⓔ	17 Ⓐ Ⓑ Ⓒ Ⓓ Ⓔ	27 Ⓐ Ⓑ Ⓒ Ⓓ Ⓔ	37 Ⓐ Ⓑ Ⓒ Ⓓ Ⓔ
8 Ⓐ Ⓑ Ⓒ Ⓓ Ⓔ	18 Ⓐ Ⓑ Ⓒ Ⓓ Ⓔ	28 Ⓐ Ⓑ Ⓒ Ⓓ Ⓔ	38 Ⓐ Ⓑ Ⓒ Ⓓ Ⓔ
9 Ⓐ Ⓑ Ⓒ Ⓓ Ⓔ	19 Ⓐ Ⓑ Ⓒ Ⓓ Ⓔ	29 Ⓐ Ⓑ Ⓒ Ⓓ Ⓔ	39 Ⓐ Ⓑ Ⓒ Ⓓ Ⓔ
10 Ⓐ Ⓑ Ⓒ Ⓓ Ⓔ	20 Ⓐ Ⓑ Ⓒ Ⓓ Ⓔ	30 Ⓐ Ⓑ Ⓒ Ⓓ Ⓔ	40 Ⓐ Ⓑ Ⓒ Ⓓ Ⓔ

SAT Practice Test
SECTION 1

Time: 25 Minutes—Turn to page 207 of your answer sheet to write your ESSAY.

The purpose of the essay is to have you show how well you can express and develop your ideas. You should develop your point of view, logically and clearly present your ideas, and use language accurately.

You should write your essay on the lines provided on your answer sheet. You should not write on any other paper. You will have enough space if you write on every line and if you keep your handwriting to a reasonable size. Make sure that your handwriting is legible to other readers.

You will have 25 minutes to write an essay on the assignment below. *Do not write on any other topic. If you do so, you will receive a score of 0.*

Think carefully about the issue presented in the following excerpt and the assignment below.

"One of the main purposes of education is to get students excited about the 'process' behind problem solving instead of rushing into an answer and just concentrating on the final result. Often students can extract something from a problem that leads to the answer. Students can relax and think more clearly when they concentrate on the game or the wonderful process, if you will, thinking."
—Adapted from G. Gruber, "A Superlative Guide to the Hows and Wise," *Omni Magazine*

Assignment: Do you agree with the above quote? In many cases is the problem solver concerned just about getting an answer, and not about concentrating on the "process" to get the answer? Do you agree that by not having faith in the process, he or she often does not arrive at the solution? In answering these questions, describe in your own experience why you agree or disagree and what rewards are lost or gained when you just concentrate on an answer without being aware of or interested in the process in arriving at the answer.

DO NOT WRITE YOUR ESSAY IN YOUR TEST BOOK. You will receive credit only for what you write on your answer sheet.

BEGIN WRITING YOUR ESSAY ON PAGE 207 OF THE ANSWER SHEET.

If you finish before time is called, you may check your work on this section only.
Do not turn to any other section in the test.

SECTION 2

Time: 25 Minutes—Turn to Section 2 (page 209) of your answer sheet to answer the questions in this section.
   20 Questions

Directions: For this section, solve each problem and decide which is the best of the choices given. Fill in the corresponding circle on the answer sheet. You may use any available space for scratchwork.

Notes:

1. The use of a calculator is permitted.
2. All numbers used are real numbers.
3. Figures that accompany problems in this test are intended to provide information useful in solving the problems. They are drawn as accurately as possible EXCEPT when it is stated in a specific problem that the figure is not drawn to scale. All figures lie in a plane unless otherwise indicated.
4. Unless otherwise specified, the domain of any function f is assumed to be the set of all real numbers x for which $f(x)$ is a real number.

REFERENCE INFORMATION

       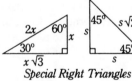

$A = \pi r^2$ $A = lw$ $A = \frac{1}{2}bh$ $V = lwh$ $V = \pi r^2h$ $c^2 = a^2 + b^2$ *Special Right Triangles*
$C = 2\pi r$

The number of degrees of arc in a circle is 360.
The sum of the measures in degrees of the angles of a triangle is 180.

$$\begin{array}{r} 59\triangle \\ -293 \\ \hline \square 97 \end{array}$$

1. In the subtraction problem above, what digit is represented by the $\square$?

   (A) 0
   (B) 1
   (C) 2
   (D) 3
   (E) 4

2. If $\dfrac{a-b}{b} = \dfrac{1}{2}$, find $\dfrac{a}{b}$.

   (A) $\dfrac{9}{2}$

   (B) $\dfrac{7}{2}$

   (C) $\dfrac{5}{2}$

   (D) $\dfrac{1}{2}$

   (E) $\dfrac{3}{2}$

GO ON TO THE NEXT PAGE

Number of pounds of force	Height object is raised
3	6 feet
6	12 feet
9	18 feet

3. In a certain pulley system, the height an object is raised is equal to a constant c times the number of pounds of force exerted. The table above shows some pounds of force and the corresponding height raised. If a particular object is raised 15 feet, how many pounds of force were exerted?

(A) $3\frac{3}{4}$

(B) 7

(C) $7\frac{1}{2}$

(D) 8

(E) 11

4. If $\frac{y}{3}$, $\frac{y}{4}$ and $\frac{y}{7}$ represent integers, then y could be

(A) 42
(B) 56
(C) 70
(D) 84
(E) 126

5. The above line is marked with 12 points. The distance between any 2 adjacent points is 3 units. Find the total number of points that are more than 19 units away from point P.

(A) 2
(B) 3
(C) 4
(D) 5
(E) 6

6. Given $(a + 2, a - 2) = [a]$ for all integers a, $(6, 2) =$

(A) [3]
(B) [4]
(C) [5]
(D) [6]
(E) [8]

GO ON TO THE NEXT PAGE

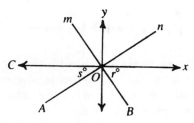

Note: Figure is not drawn to scale.

7. If $m \perp n$ in the figure above and COx is a straight line, find the value of $r + s$.

(A) 180
(B) 135
(C) 110
(D) 90
(E) The answer cannot be determined from the information given.

9. One out of 4 students at Ridge High School studies German. If there are 2,800 students at the school, how many students do *not* study German?

(A) 2,500
(B) 2,100
(C) 1,800
(D) 1,000
(E) 700

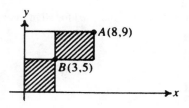

8. Points A and B have coordinates as shown in the figure above. Find the combined area of the two shaded rectangles.

(A) 20
(B) 26
(C) 32
(D) 35
(E) 87

10. The cost of a drive-in movie is $\$y$ per vehicle. A group of friends in a van shared the admission cost by paying \$0.40 each. If 6 more friends had gone along, everyone would have paid only \$0.25 each. What is the value of $\$y$?

(A) \$4
(B) \$6
(C) \$8
(D) \$10
(E) \$12

GO ON TO THE NEXT PAGE

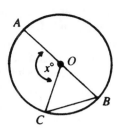

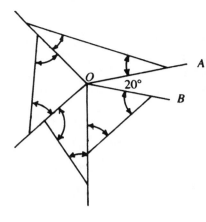

11. If *AB* is a diameter of circle *O* in the figure above, and *CB* = *OB*, then $\dfrac{x}{6}$ =

(A) 60
(B) 30
(C) 20
(D) 10
(E) 5

13. If $\angle AOB = 20°$ in the figure above and *O* is a common vertex of the four triangles, find the sum of the measures of the marked angles in the triangles.

(A) 380
(B) 560
(C) 740
(D) 760
(E) 920

12. A certain store is selling an $80 radio for $64. If a different radio had a list price of $200 and was discounted at $1\frac{1}{2}$ times the percent discount on the $80 model, what would its selling price be?

(A) $90
(B) $105
(C) $120
(D) $140
(E) $160

14. Some integers in set X are odd.

If the statement above is true, which of the following must also be true?

(A) If an integer is odd, it is in set X.
(B) If an integer is even, it is in set X.
(C) All integers in set X are odd.
(D) All integers in set X are even.
(E) Not all integers in set X are even.

GO ON TO THE NEXT PAGE

15. If $|y + 3| < 3$, then

(A) $0 > y > -6$
(B) $y > 3$
(C) $3 > y > 0$
(D) $y = -1$
(E) $y = -2$

17. A certain printer can print at the rate of 80 characters per second, and there is an average (arithmetic mean) of 2,400 characters per page. If the printer continued to print at this rate, how many *minutes* would it take to print an *M*-page report?

(A) $\dfrac{M}{30}$

(B) $\dfrac{M}{60}$

(C) $\dfrac{M}{2}$

(D) $\dfrac{2}{M}$

(E) $\dfrac{60}{M}$

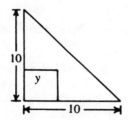

16. In the figure above, the area of the square is equal to $\dfrac{1}{5}$ the area of the triangle. Find the value of y, the side of the square.

(A) 2
(B) 4
(C) 5
(D) $2\sqrt{5}$
(E) $\sqrt{10}$

18. A certain satellite passed over Washington, D.C., at midnight on Friday. If the satellite completes an orbit every 5 hours, when is the next day that it will pass over Washington, D.C., at midnight?

(A) Monday
(B) Wednesday
(C) Friday
(D) Saturday
(E) Sunday

GO ON TO THE NEXT PAGE

19. The price of a car is reduced by 30 percent. The resulting price is reduced 40 percent. The two reductions are equal to one reduction of

(A) 28%
(B) 42%
(C) 50%
(D) 58%
(E) 70%

20. In the figure above, the circle is inscribed in the equilateral triangle. If the diameter of the circle is 2, what is the sum of the shaded area?

(A) $3\sqrt{3} - \pi$
(B) $3\sqrt{3} - 4\pi$
(C) $3\sqrt{3} - \dfrac{3\pi}{2}$
(D) $6\sqrt{3} - \dfrac{3\pi}{2}$
(E) $108 - \pi$

STOP
If you finish before time is called, you may check your work on this section only.
Do not turn to any other section in the test.

Take a 5 minute break
before starting section 3

SECTION 3

Time: 25 Minutes—Turn to Section 3 (page 209) of your answer sheet to answer the questions in this section.
20 Questions

Directions: For this section, solve each problem and decide which is the best of the choices given. Fill in the corresponding circle on the answer sheet. You may use any available space for scratchwork.

Notes:

1. The use of a calculator is permitted.
2. All numbers used are real numbers.
3. Figures that accompany problems in this test are intended to provide information useful in solving the problems. They are drawn as accurately as possible EXCEPT when it is stated in a specific problem that the figure is not drawn to scale. All figures lie in a plane unless otherwise indicated.
4. Unless otherwise specified, the domain of any function f is assumed to be the set of all real numbers x for which $f(x)$ is a real number.

REFERENCE INFORMATION

      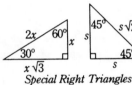

$A = \pi r^2$ $A = lw$ $A = \frac{1}{2}bh$ $V = lwh$ $V = \pi r^2 h$ $c^2 = a^2 + b^2$ *Special Right Triangles*
$C = 2\pi r$

The number of degrees of arc in a circle is 360.
The sum of the measures in degrees of the angles of a triangle is 180.

1. After giving $5 to Greg, David has $25. Greg now has $\frac{1}{5}$ as much as David does. How much did Greg start with?

    (A) $0
    (B) $5
    (C) $7
    (D) $10
    (E) $15

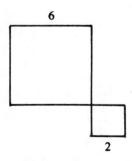

2. The figure above shows two squares with sides as shown. What is the ratio of the perimeter of the larger square to that of the smaller?

    (A) 3 : 2
    (B) 2 : 1
    (C) 3 : 1
    (D) 6 : 1
    (E) 9 : 1

GO ON TO THE NEXT PAGE

3. A car travels 1,056 feet in 12 seconds. In feet per second, what is the average speed of the car?

(A) 98.0
(B) 78.8
(C) 85.8
(D) 84.0
(E) 88.0

5. $2(w)(x)(-y) - 2(-w)(-x)(y) =$

(A) 0
(B) $-4wxy$
(C) $4wxy$
(D) $-4w^2x^2y^2$
(E) $2w^2x^2y^2$

4. If $2z + 1 + 2 + 2z + 3 + 2z = 3 + 1 + 2$, then $z + 4 =$

(A) 1
(B) 4
(C) 5
(D) 6
(E) 10

6. What is an expression for 5 times the sum of the square of x and the square of y?

(A) $5(x^2 + y^2)$
(B) $5x^2 + y^2$
(C) $5(x + y)^2$
(D) $5x^2 + y$
(E) $5(2x + 2y)$

GO ON TO THE NEXT PAGE

7. If p and q are positive integers, x and y are negative integers, and if $p > q$ and $x > y$, which of the following must be less than zero?

   I. $q - p$
  II. qy
 III. $p + x$

(A) I only
(B) III only
(C) I and II only
(D) II and III only
(E) I, II, and III

8. If $a = 1$, $b = -2$ and $c = -2$, find the value of

$$\frac{b^2 c}{(a - c)^2}$$

(A) $-\dfrac{8}{9}$

(B) $-\dfrac{2}{3}$

(C) $\dfrac{8}{9}$

(D) 8

(E) 9

9. If $y = 28j$, where j is any integer, then $\dfrac{y}{2}$ will always be

(A) even
(B) odd
(C) positive
(D) negative
(E) less than $\dfrac{y}{3}$

10. If $3a + 4b = 4a - 4b = 21$, find the value of a.

(A) 3
(B) 6
(C) 21
(D) 42
(E) The answer cannot be determined from the information given.

GO ON TO THE NEXT PAGE

11. If N is a positive integer, which of the following does *not* have to be a divisor of the sum of N, $6N$, and $9N$?

(A) 1
(B) 2
(C) 4
(D) 9
(E) 16

13. If $p + pq$ is 4 times $p - pq$, which of the following has exactly one value? ($pq \neq 0$)

(A) p
(B) q
(C) pq
(D) $p + pq$
(E) $p - pq$

12. If $x = 3a - 18$ and $5y = 3a + 7$, then find $5y - x$.

(A) -11
(B) 11
(C) 18
(D) 25
(E) $6a - 11$

14. If $2 + \dfrac{1}{z} = 0$, then what is the value of $9 + 9z$?

(A) $-\dfrac{9}{2}$

(B) $-\dfrac{1}{2}$

(C) 0

(D) $\dfrac{9}{2}$

(E) The answer cannot be determined from the information given.

GO ON TO THE NEXT PAGE

15. How many times does the graph of $y = x^2$ intersect the graph of $y = x$?

(A) 0
(B) 1
(C) 2
(D) 3
(E) 4

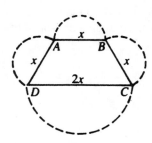

17. The quadrilateral $ABCD$ is a trapezoid with $x = 4$. The diameter of each semicircle is a side of the trapezoid. What is the sum of the lengths of the 4 dotted semicircles?

(A) 8π
(B) 10π
(C) 12π
(D) 14π
(E) 20π

16. Let $wx = y$, where $wxy \neq 0$.

If both x and y are multiplied by 6, then w is

(A) multiplied by $\dfrac{1}{36}$

(B) multiplied by $\dfrac{1}{6}$

(C) multiplied by 1
(D) multiplied by 6
(E) multiplied by 36

18. $\dfrac{7x}{144}$ yards and $\dfrac{5y}{12}$ feet together equal how many inches?

(A) $\dfrac{7x}{12} + \dfrac{5y}{4}$

(B) $\dfrac{7x}{12} + 5y$

(C) $\dfrac{7x}{4} + 5y$

(D) $\dfrac{7x}{4} + 60y$

(E) $7x + \dfrac{5}{4}y$

GO ON TO THE NEXT PAGE

19. If $x < 0$ and $y < 0$, which of the following must always be positive?

  I. $x \times y$
  II. $x + y$
  III. $x - y$

  (A) I only
  (B) I and II only
  (C) I and III only
  (D) II and III only
  (E) I, II, and III

20. Given that $a + 3b = 11$ and a and b are positive integers, what is the largest possible value of a?

  (A) 4
  (B) 6
  (C) 7
  (D) 8
  (E) 10

STOP

If you finish before time is called, you may check your work on this section only.
Do not turn to any other section in the test.

SECTION 4

Time: 25 Minutes—Turn to Section 4 (page 210) of your answer sheet to answer the questions in this section.
24 Questions

Directions: For each question in this section, select the best answer from among the choices given and fill in the corresponding circle on the answer sheet.

Each sentence below has one or two blanks, each blank indicating that something has been omitted. Beneath the sentence are five words or sets of words labeled A through E. Choose the word or set of words that, when inserted in the sentence, best fits the meaning of the sentence as a whole.

Example:

Hoping to _____ the dispute, negotiators proposed a compromise that they felt would be _____ to both labor and management.

(A) enforce . . useful
(B) end . . divisive
(C) overcome . . unattractive
(D) extend . . satisfactory
(E) resolve . . acceptable

Ⓐ Ⓑ Ⓒ Ⓓ ●

1. Athens was ruled not by kings and emperors as was common among other _____ at the time, but by a citizenry, which _____ fully in the affairs of the city.

   (A) committees . . cooperated
   (B) tribes . . engaged
   (C) cities . . revolutionized
   (D) populations . . applied
   (E) societies . . participated

2. Fossils are _____ in rock formations that were once soft and have _____ with the passage of time.

   (A) abolished . . corresponded
   (B) interactive . . communicated
   (C) preserved . . hardened
   (D) created . . revived
   (E) discounted . . deteriorated

3. The social-cultural trends of the 1960s _____ not only the relative affluence of the postwar period but also the coming to maturity of a generation that was a product of that _____.

   (A) dominated . . movement
   (B) reflected . . prosperity
   (C) accentuated . . depression
   (D) cautioned . . decade
   (E) accepted . . revolution

4. Rotation of crops helps to _____ soil fertility and soil usefulness for a long period of time.

   (A) conserve
   (B) disperse
   (C) employ
   (D) research
   (E) shorten

5. Some illnesses, such as malaria, which have been virtually eliminated in the United States, are still _____ in many places abroad.

   (A) discussed
   (B) prevalent
   (C) scarce
   (D) unknown
   (E) hospitalized

6. With lack of _____ , almost anyone can develop the disease we call alcoholism, just as any of us can contract pneumonia by _____ exposing ourselves to its causes.

   (A) advice . . carefully
   (B) control . . foolishly
   (C) opportunity . . knowingly
   (D) sympathy . . fortunately
   (E) conscience . . happily

GO ON TO THE NEXT PAGE ⇨

7. Use of air conditioners and other electrical apparatus had to be _____ that summer because of the _____ of the generating system.

(A) postulated . . reaction
(B) curtailed . . inefficiency
(C) implemented . . residuals
(D) augmented . . responsiveness
(E) manipulated . . intensity

8. The Bavarians consider beer their national beverage, yet at the same time they do not view it as a drink but rather as _____ bread—a staple food.

(A) fresh
(B) liquid
(C) stale
(D) bitter
(E) costly

GO ON TO THE NEXT PAGE

Each passage below is followed by questions based on its content. Answer the questions on the basis of what is stated or implied in each passage and in any introductory material that may be provided.

Questions 9–10 are based on the following passage.

1   Despite the many categories of the historian, there are only two ages of man. The first age, the age from the beginnings of recorded time to the present, is the age of the cave man. It is the age of war. It is today. The second age, still
5 only a prospect, is the age of civilized man. The test of civilized man will be represented by his ability to use his inventiveness for his own good by substituting world law for world anarchy. That second age is still within the reach of the individual in our time. It is not a part-time job, how-
10 ever. It calls for total awareness, total commitment.

9.   The title below that best expresses the ideas of this passage is:

    (A) The Historian at Work
    (B) The Dangers of All-out War
    (C) The Power of World Anarchy
    (D) Mankind on the Threshold
    (E) The Decline of Civilization

10.   The author's attitude toward the possibility of man's reaching an age of civilization is one of

    (A) limited hope
    (B) complete despair
    (C) marked uncertainty
    (D) complacency
    (E) anger

Questions 11–12 are based on the following passage.

1   Readers in the past seem to have been more patient than the readers of today. There were few diversions, and they had more time to read novels of a length that seems to us now inordinate. It may be that they were not irritated
5 by the digressions and irrelevances that interrupted the narration. But some of the novels that suffer from these defects are among the greatest that have ever been written. It is deplorable that on this account they should be less and less read.

11.   The title below that best expresses the ideas of this passage is:

    (A) Defects of Today's Novels
    (B) Novel Reading Then and Now
    (C) The Great Novel
    (D) The Impatient Reader of Novels
    (E) Decline in Education

12.   The author implies that

    (A) authors of the past did not use narration to any extent
    (B) great novels are usually long
    (C) digressions and irrelevances are characteristic of modern novels
    (D) readers of the past were more capable
    (E) people today have more pastimes than formerly

GO ON TO THE NEXT PAGE

Questions 13–24 are based on the following passage.

This passage describes the relationship between age and income throughout various periods of American history and the effects this trend will have on the various population groups in the future.

The relationship between age and income is only casually appreciated by recent theories on the purported redistribution of income. It is known, of course, that the average person's income begins to decline after he is fifty-five years
5 of age, and that it declines sharply after sixty-five. For example as early as in 1957, 58 percent of the spending units headed by persons sixty-five years and older earned less than $2,000. The relationship between old age and low income has often been considered a reflection of sociologi-
10 cal rather than economic factors—and therefore not to be included in any study of the economy. Actually, the character of the relationship is too integrated to be dissected. However, its significance is mounting with the increase in the number of older persons. The lowest-income groups
15 include a heavy concentration of older persons—in 1957, one-third of all spending units in the $0–$2,000 class were headed by persons sixty-five years and older; in 1948, it was 28 percent.

But in economic planning and social policy, it must be
20 remembered that, with the same income, the sixty-five-or-more spending unit will not spend less or need less than the younger spending unit, even though the pressure to save is greater than on the young. The functional ethos of our economy dictates that the comparatively unproductive old-
25 age population should consume in accordance with their output rather than their requirements. Most social scientists have accepted these values; they have assumed that the minimum economic needs of the aged should be lower than those of the younger family. But it is precisely at
30 retirement that personal requirements and the new demands of leisure call for an even larger income if this period is to be something more enjoyable than a wait for death.

The relationship between age and income is seen most clearly in the unionized blue-collar worker. Except for lay-
35 offs, which his seniority minimizes, and wage increments for higher productivity, awarded in many industries, his income range is determined by his occupation. But within that income range, the deciding factor is the man's age. After forty-five, the average worker who loses his job has
40 more difficulty in finding a new one. Despite his seniority, the older worker is likely to be downgraded to a lower-paying job when he can no longer maintain the pace set by younger men. This is especially true of unskilled and semi-skilled workers.

45 The early and lower income period of a person's working life, during which he acquires his basic vocational skills, is most pronounced for the skilled, managerial, or professional worker. Then, between the ages of twenty-five and fifty, the average worker receives his peak earnings.
50 Meanwhile, his family expenses rise, there are children to support and basic household durables to obtain. Although

his family's income may rise substantially until he is somewhere between thirty-five and forty-five, per capita consumption may drop at the same time. For the growing,
55 working-class family, limited in income by the very nature of the breadwinner's occupation, the economic consequences of this parallel rise in age, income, and obligations are especially pressing. Many in the low-income classes are just as vulnerable to poverty during middle age, when they
60 have a substantially larger income, as in old age. As family obligations finally do begin declining, so does income. Consequently, most members of these classes never have an adequate income.

Thus we see that, for a time, increasing age means
65 increasing income, and therefore a probable boost in income-tenth position. Although there are no extensive data in the matter, it can be confidently asserted that the higher income-tenths have a much greater representation of spending units headed by persons aged thirty-five to fifty-
70 five than do the lower income-tenths. This is demonstrably the case among the richest 5 percent of the consumer units. The real question is: To what extent does distribution of income-tenths within a certain age group deviate from distribution of income-tenths generally? Although information
75 is not as complete as might be desired, there is more than enough to make contingent generalizations. Detailed data exist on income distribution by tenths and by age for 1935–36 and 1948, and on income-size distribution by age for the postwar years. They disclose sharp income inequal-
80 ities within every age group (although more moderate in the eighteen-to-twenty-five category)—inequalities that closely parallel the overall national income pattern. The implication is clear: A spending unit's income-tenth position *within his age category* varies much less, if at all, and is
85 determined primarily by his occupation.

In other words, in America, the legendary land of economic opportunity where any man can work his way to the top, there is only slight income mobility outside the natural age cycle of rising, then falling income. Since most
90 of the sixty-five-and-over age group falls into the low-income brackets and constitutes the largest segment of the $0–$2,000 income class, it is of obvious importance in analyzing future poverty in the United States to examine the growth trends of this group. The sixty-five-and-over
95 population composed 4.0 percent of the total population in 1900, 5.3 percent in 1930, 8.4 percent in 1955, and will reach an estimated 10.8 percent in 2010. Between 1900 and 2010, the total national population is expected to increase 276 percent, but those from ages forty-five through sixty-
100 four are expected to increase 416 percent, and those sixty-five and over are expected to increase 672 percent. Between 1990 and 2010, the population aged eighteen to twenty-five is also expected to grow far more rapidly than the middle-aged population. With the more rapid expansion of these
105 two low-income groups, the young and the old, in the years immediately ahead, an increase in the extent of poverty is probable.

GO ON TO THE NEXT PAGE

13. According to the passage, most social scientists erroneously assume that

   (A) personal expenses increase with the age of the spending unit
   (B) the needs of the younger spending unit are greater than those of the aged
   (C) the relationship between old age and low income is an economic and not a sociological problem
   (D) members of the old-age population should consume in accordance with their requirements
   (E) leisure living requires increased income

14. The word "appreciated" in line 2 most nearly means

   (A) had artistic interest
   (B) increased in value
   (C) had curiosity
   (D) had gratitude
   (E) understood

15. It can be inferred that in the 35–55 age category

   (A) income-tenth positions vary greatly
   (B) income-tenth positions vary very little
   (C) earning potential does not resemble the overall national income pattern
   (D) occupations have little bearing on the income-tenth position
   (E) there is great mobility between income-tenth positions

16. The author believes which of the following?

   I. The aged will continue to increase as a percentage of the total population.
   II. Income inequalities decrease with increasing age.
   III. Managerial and professional workers have greater income mobility than blue-collar workers.

   (A) I only
   (B) II only
   (C) III only
   (D) I and II only
   (E) I and III only

17. In the passage the term "functional ethos" in line 23 means

   (A) national group
   (B) ethnic influence
   (C) prevailing ideology
   (D) biased opinion
   (E) practical ethics

18. The article states that the old-age population

   (A) has increased because of longer life expectancy
   (B) exceeds all but the 18–25 age group in growth rate
   (C) is well represented among the higher income-tenths
   (D) is increasing as a percentage of the low income-tenths
   (E) has its greatest numbers among the middle income group

19. According to the author, aside from the natural age cycle, economic opportunity in America is greatly limited by

   I. occupation
   II. income inequality within every group
   III. class

   (A) I only
   (B) II only
   (C) III only
   (D) I and III only
   (E) I and II only

20. The word "ethos" in line 23 most nearly means

   (A) the character of a group of people
   (B) economic–sociological ramifications
   (C) the productivity of all age groups
   (D) the management of large corporations
   (E) the social scientists who deal with the economy

21. According to the passage, the older, unionized blue-collar workers are

   (A) assured constant salary until retirement
   (B) given preference over new workers because of seniority
   (C) likely to receive downgraded salary
   (D) more susceptible to layoff after 40
   (E) encouraged to move to slower-paced but equal-paying jobs

GO ON TO THE NEXT PAGE

22. The article states that the average worker finds that

(A) as family obligations begin escalating, income begins to decline
(B) he reaches economic stability at middle age because of the parallel rise in age, obligations, and income
(C) he earns least while he is acquiring vocational skills
(D) he reaches peak earning power between the ages of 40 and 65
(E) his wage gains coincide with the decline of family needs

23. It can be inferred that one could most accurately predict a person's income from

(A) his age
(B) his natural age cycle
(C) his occupation
(D) his occupation and age
(E) his seniority position

24. Which lines in the passage illustrate the author's sarcasm?

(A) lines 19–23
(B) lines 45–48
(C) lines 64–66
(D) lines 86–89
(E) lines 104–107

STOP

If you finish before time is called, you may check your work on this section only.
Do not turn to any other section in the test.

Take a 1 minute break

before starting section 5

SECTION 5

Time: 25 Minutes—Turn to Section 5 (page 210) of your answer sheet to answer the questions in this section.
35 Questions

Directions: For each question in this section, select the best answer from among the choices given and fill in the corresponding circle on the answer sheet.

The following sentences test correctness and effectiveness of expression. Part of each sentence or the entire sentence is underlined; beneath each sentence are five ways of phrasing the underlined material. Choice A repeats the original phrasing; the other four choices are different. If you think the original phrasing produces a better sentence than any of the alternatives, select choice A; if not, select one of the other choices.

In making your selection, follow the requirements of standard written English; that is, pay attention to grammar, choice of words, sentence construction, and punctuation. Your selection should result in the most effective sentence—clear and precise, without awkwardness or ambiguity.

EXAMPLE:

Laura Ingalls Wilder published her first book and she was sixty-five years old then.

(A) and she was sixty-five years old then
(B) when she was sixty-five
(C) at age sixty-five years old
(D) upon the reaching of sixty-five years
(E) at the time when she was sixty-five

1. Joe couldn't wait for his return to his home after being in the army for two years.

    (A) Joe couldn't wait for his return to his home
    (B) There was a strong desire on Joe's part to return home
    (C) Joe was eager to return home
    (D) Joe wanted home badly
    (E) Joe arranged to return home

2. Trash, filth, and muck are clogging the streets of the city and that's not all, the sidewalks are full of garbage.

    (A) that's not all, the sidewalks are full of garbage
    (B) another thing: garbage is all over the sidewalks
    (C) the garbage cans haven't been emptied for days
    (D) in addition, garbage is lying all over the sidewalks
    (E) what's more, the sidewalks have garbage that is lying all over them

3. Tired and discouraged by the problems of the day, Myra decided to have a good dinner, and then lie down for an hour, and then go dancing.

    (A) Myra decided to have a good dinner, and then lie down for an hour, and then go dancing.
    (B) Myra decided to have a good dinner, lying down for an hour, and then dancing.
    (C) Myra decided to have a good dinner, lie down for an hour, and then dancing.
    (D) Myra decided to have a good dinner, lay down for an hour, and then dance.
    (E) Myra decided to have a good dinner, lie down for an hour, and then go dancing.

4. I am not certain in respect to which courses to take.

    (A) in respect to which courses
    (B) about which courses
    (C) which courses
    (D) as to the choice of which courses
    (E) for which courses I am

5. The people of the besieged village had no doubt that the end was drawing near.

    (A) that the end was drawing near
    (B) about the nearness of the end
    (C) it was clear that the end was near
    (D) concerning the end's being near
    (E) that all would die

6. There isn't a single man among us <u>who is skilled in the art of administering first-aid</u>.

    (A) who is skilled in the art of administering first-aid
    (B) who knows how to administer first-aid
    (C) who knows the administration of first-aid
    (D) who is a first-aid man
    (E) who administers first-aid

7. This is the hole <u>that was squeezed through by the mouse</u>.

    (A) that was squeezed through by the mouse
    (B) that the mouse was seen to squeeze through
    (C) the mouse squeezed through it
    (D) that the mouse squeezed through
    (E) like what the mouse squeezed through

8. <u>She soundly feel asleep</u> after having finished the novel.

    (A) She soundly feel asleep
    (B) She decided to sleep
    (C) She went on to her sleep
    (D) She fell to sleep
    (E) She fell fast asleep

9. This is one restaurant I won't patronize because <u>I was served a fried egg by the waitress that was rotten</u>.

    (A) I was served a fried egg by the waitress that was rotten
    (B) I was served by the waitress a fried egg that was rotten
    (C) a fried egg was served to me by the waitress that was rotten
    (D) the waitress served me a fried egg that was rotten
    (E) a rotten fried egg was served to me by the waitress

10. Watching the familiar story unfold on the screen, he was glad <u>that he read the book with such painstaking attention to detail</u>.

    (A) that he read the book with such painstaking attention to detail
    (B) that he had read the book with such painstaking attention to detail
    (C) that he read the book with such attention to particulars
    (D) that he read the book with such intense effort
    (E) that he paid so much attention to the plot of the book

11. If anyone requested tea instead of coffee, <u>it was a simple matter to serve it to them</u> from the teapot at the rear of the table.

    (A) it was a simple matter to serve it to them
    (B) it was easy to serve them
    (C) it was a simple matter to serve them
    (D) it was a simple matter to serve it to him
    (E) he could serve himself

GO ON TO THE NEXT PAGE

The following sentences test your ability to recognize grammar and usage errors. Each sentence contains either a single error or no error at all. No sentence contains more than one error. The error, if there is one, is underlined and lettered. If the sentence contains an error, select the one underlined part that must be changed to make the sentence correct. If the sentence is correct, select choice E. In choosing answers, follow the requirements of standard written English.

EXAMPLE:

The <u>other</u> delegates and <u>him</u> <u>immediately</u>
    A   B   C
accepted the resolution <u>drafted by</u>
                       D
the neutral states. <u>No error.</u>
                   E

12. <u>Since</u> we first started high school, there <u>has been</u>
    A   B
    great competition for grades <u>between</u> him and <u>I</u>.
                             C   D
    <u>No error.</u>
      E

13. Many people in the suburbs <u>scarcely</u> know <u>about</u>
                             A   B
    the transportation problems <u>that</u> city dwellers
                            C
    experience <u>every day</u>. <u>No error.</u>
                D   E

14. The subject of the evening editorial was <u>us</u>
                                     A
    instructors <u>who have refused</u> to cross the picket
              B   C
    lines of the <u>striking</u> food service workers.
                 D
    <u>No error.</u>
      E

15. After the contestants <u>had completed</u> their speeches,
                   A
    I knew that the prize would go to <u>he</u> <u>whom</u>
                                B   C
    the audience had given a <u>standing</u> ovation.
                      D
    <u>No error.</u>
      E

16. Falsely accused of a <u>triple-murder</u> and <u>imprisoned</u>
                      A   B
    for 19 years, Ruben (Hurricane) Carter, a former
    boxer, was <u>freed</u> when a Federal judge declared
               C
    <u>him</u> guiltless. <u>No error.</u>
     D   E

17. Your math instructor would have been <u>happy</u> to
                                  A
    give you a makeup examination if you <u>would have</u>
                                  B
    gone to him and <u>explained</u> that your parents were
                  C
    <u>hospitalized</u>. <u>No error.</u>
       D   E

18. The <u>child</u> <u>asking</u> a difficult question was perhaps
         A   B
    more shocking to the speaker <u>than</u> to the <u>child's</u>
                         C   D
    parents. <u>No error.</u>
          E

19. <u>Now</u> that the pressure of <u>selling</u> the house and
    A   B
    packing our belongings is <u>over</u>, we can <u>look forward</u>
                     C   D
    to moving to our new home in California.
    <u>No error.</u>
      E

20. My grandmother <u>leads</u> a more active life <u>than</u>
                 A   B
    many other retirees <u>who</u> are younger than <u>her</u>.
                   C   D
    <u>No error.</u>
      E

21. I appreciate <u>your</u> offering <u>to change</u> my flat tire,
              A   B
    but I would <u>rather</u> have you drive me to my meeting
              C
    <u>so that</u> I will be on time. <u>No error.</u>
      D   E

22. The novelists <u>who</u> readers <u>choose</u> <u>as</u> their
                 A   B   C
    favorites are not always the <u>most</u> skilled writers.
                           D
    <u>No error.</u>
      E

GO ON TO THE NEXT PAGE

23. The problem of <u>how to deal</u> with all the
         A
    <u>mosquitoes</u> <u>disturb</u> many <u>residents</u> of the Tropics.
      B   C   D
    <u>No error</u>.
      E

24. The <u>family's</u> only son <u>could of</u> <u>gone</u> to college, but
        A   B   C
    he decided to join the army after he graduated

    <u>from</u> high school. <u>No error</u>.
      D   E

25. <u>Yesterday</u> at the race track many <u>persons</u> were
      A   B
    <u>fearful of</u> betting on the horse <u>who</u> had fallen in the
      C   D
    last race. <u>No error</u>.
            E

26. If someone wants to buy <u>all</u> the antiques <u>that</u> I have
               A   B
    for the rummage sale, <u>then</u> <u>they</u> should make me
                 C   D
    a reasonable offer. <u>No error</u>.
            E

27. The man <u>who</u> Mexican authorities believe <u>to be</u>
          A   B
    the country's number 1 drug <u>trafficker</u> <u>has been</u>
                      C   D
    <u>arrested</u> in a Pacific resort area. <u>No error</u>.
      D   E

28. <u>While</u> her mother was inside the house <u>talking</u> on
      A   B
    the phone, the child fell <u>off of</u> the <u>unscreened</u>
                    C   D
    porch. <u>No error</u>.
         E

29. The racehorse ran <u>swifter</u> in <u>today's</u> race than he
             A   B
    <u>ran</u> in his practice sessions <u>last week</u>. <u>No error</u>.
      C   D   E

GO ON TO THE NEXT PAGE

Directions: The following passage is an early draft of an essay. Some parts of the passage need to be rewritten.

Read the passage and select the best answers for the questions that follow. Some questions are about particular sentences or parts of sentences and ask you to improve sentence structure or word choice. Other questions ask you to consider organization and development. In choosing answers, follow the requirements of standard written English.

Questions 30–35 refer to the following passage.

¹Lampe-Pigeon is the charming name for a tall kerosene lamp, over nine and one-half inches in height, created more than 100 years ago for use in the wine caves of France. ²Its diminutive size makes it suitable for being used on a mantel, as a center-piece in lieu of candles, or even bracketed as a wall sconce. ³The brass lamp, which contains within it a glass globe, is still being handmade by the same company, though one is more likely to see it in a French home these days than in a cave. ⁴And, of course, it would be a handy source of light in the event of a power failure. ⁵Other antique-type lamps have been manu-factured and they do not have the elegance or simplicity of the Lampe-Pigeon. ⁶Many people prefer more modern lamps especially those of the halogen variety.

30. What should be done with sentence 3?

(A) It should end after the word <u>company</u>.
(B) It should remain as it is.
(C) It should be placed after sentence 4.
(D) It should follow sentence 1.
(E) It should introduce the passage.

31. Sentence 1 would be more logical if it read, <u>Lampe-Pigeon is the charming name for</u>

(A) <u>a tall kerosene lamp, measuring nine and one-half inches, created</u>. . . .
(B) <u>a kerosene lamp, although nine and one-half inches tall, created</u>. . . .
(C) <u>a nine-and-one-half-inch-tall kerosene lamp, created</u>. . . .
(D) <u>a tall nine-and-one-half inch kerosene lamp, created</u>. . . .
(E) <u>a kerosene lamp, of a height of nine and one-half inches, created</u>. . . .

32. The phrase <u>for being used</u> in sentence 2 should be

(A) changed to <u>for use</u>.
(B) left as it is.
(C) changed to <u>for one to use it</u>.
(D) changed to <u>to being used</u>.
(E) changed to <u>as a piece used on a mantel</u>.

33. Sentence 3 would read more smoothly were it to begin

(A) The glass globed brass lamp. . . .
(B) The brass lamp with a glass globe. . . .
(C) The glass globe, found in the brass lamp. . . . .
(D) as it does now.
(E) The brass lamp, inside of which is a glass globe. . . .

34. What should be done with sentence 6?

(A) It should be left as it is.
(B) It should be deleted from the paragraph.
(C) It should be placed before sentence 5.
(D) It should be placed before sentence 4.
(E) It should be placed before sentence 3.

35. In sentence 5,

(A) <u>manufactured</u> should be changed to produced.
(B) <u>Lampe-Pigeon</u> should be changed to lamp in question.
(C) <u>elegance or simplicity</u> should be changed to <u>modernization</u>.
(D) <u>and</u> should be changed to <u>but</u>.
(E) The sentence should remain as it is.

STOP

If you finish before time is called, you may check your work on this section only.
Do not turn to any other section in the test.

SECTION 6

REFERENCE INFORMATION

$A = \pi r^2$ $A = lw$ $A = \frac{1}{2}bh$ $V = lwh$ $V = \pi r^2 h$ $c^2 = a^2 + b^2$ *Special Right Triangles*
$C = 2\pi r$

The number of degrees of arc in a circle is 360.
The sum of the measures in degrees of the angles of a triangle is 180.

---

1. In the equation $5\sqrt{x} + 14 = 20$, the value of x is

   (A) $\sqrt{6/5}$
   (B) $34^2/25^2$
   (C) $6 - \sqrt{5}$
   (D) $6/5$
   (E) $36/25$

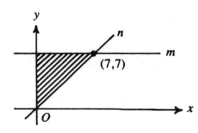

2. In the figure above, m is parallel to the x-axis. All of the following points lie in the shaded area EXCEPT

   (A) $(4,3)$
   (B) $(1,2)$
   (C) $(5,6)$
   (D) $(4,5)$
   (E) $(2,5)$

GO ON TO THE NEXT PAGE ⟩

3. At Lincoln County High School, 36 students are taking either calculus or physics or both, and 10 students are taking both calculus and physics. If there are 31 students in the calculus class, how many students are in the physics class?

(A) 14
(B) 15
(C) 16
(D) 17
(E) 18

4. Mr. Simmons stated that if $a^2 > b^2$ where a and b are real, then it follows that $a > b$. Mr. Simmons' statement would be refuted if $(a, b) =$

(A) (2,3)
(B) (3,2)
(C) (4, −2)
(D) (−4, −2)
(E) (−2, −3)

5. Which of the following is always true for real numbers a, b, and c?

 I. $\sqrt{a+b} = \sqrt{a} + \sqrt{b}$
 II. $a^2 + b^2 = (a+b)^2$
 III. $a^b + a^c = a^{(b+c)}$

(A) I only
(B) II only
(C) III only
(D) I, II, III
(E) neither I, II or III

Question 6 refers to the following:

$$R = \{x : 1 \geqq x \geqq -1\}$$
$$S = \{x : x \geqq 1\}$$

6. The number of elements that is (are) common to both R and S is (are)

(A) 0
(B) 1
(C) 2
(D) 3
(E) infinite

GO ON TO THE NEXT PAGE

7. Two lines in a plane are represented by $y = x - 1$ and $2x + 5y = 9$. The coordinates of the point at which the lines intersect are

(A) (2,1)
(B) (1,2)
(C) (2,5)
(D) (5,2)
(E) (3,5)

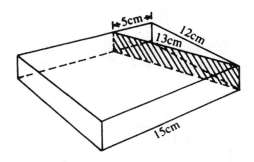

8. The rectangular box above has a rectangular dividing wall inside, as shown. The dividing wall has an area of 39 cm^2. What is the volume of the larger compartment?

(A) 90 cm^3
(B) 180 cm^3
(C) 360 cm^3
(D) 450 cm^3
(E) 540 cm^3

GO ON TO THE NEXT PAGE

Directions: For Student-Produced Response questions 9–18, use the grids at the bottom of the answer sheet page on which you have answered questions 1–8.

Each of the remaining 10 questions requires you to solve the problem and enter your answer by marking the circles in the special grid, as shown in the examples below. You may use any available space for scratchwork.

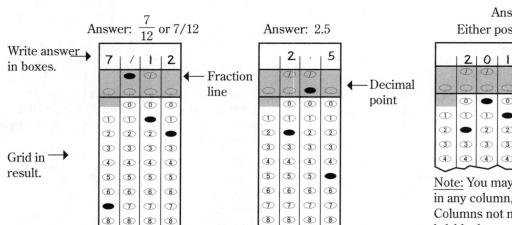

Answer: $\frac{7}{12}$ or 7/12

Answer: 2.5

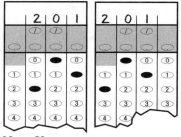

Answer: 201
Either position is correct.

Write answer in boxes.

← Fraction line

← Decimal point

Grid in result.

Note: You may start your answers in any column, space permitting. Columns not needed should be left blank.

- Mark no more than one oval in any column.

- Because the answer sheet will be machine-scored, **you will receive credit only if the ovals are filled in correctly.**

- Although not required, it is suggested that you write your answer in the boxes at the top of the columns to help you fill in the ovals accurately.

- Some problems may have more than one correct answer. In such cases, grid only one answer.

- No question has a negative answer.

- **Mixed numbers** such as $2\frac{1}{2}$ must be gridded as 2.5 or 5/2. (If $\boxed{2\ |\ 1\ /\ 2}$ is gridded, it will be interpreted as $\frac{21}{2}$, not $2\frac{1}{2}$.)

- Decimal Accuracy: If you obtain a decimal answer, **enter the most accurate value the grid will accommodate.** For example, if you obtain an answer such as 0.6666 … , you should record the result as .666 or .667. **Less accurate values such as .66 or .67 are not acceptable.**

Acceptable ways to grid $\frac{2}{3}$ = .6666 …

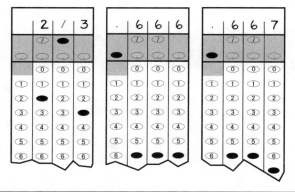

9. $\left(\frac{1}{2} - \frac{1}{3}\right) + \left(\frac{1}{3} - \frac{1}{4}\right) + \left(\frac{1}{4} - \frac{1}{5}\right) + \left(\frac{1}{5} - \frac{1}{6}\right) + \left(\frac{1}{6} - \frac{1}{7}\right) + \left(\frac{1}{7} - \frac{1}{8}\right) + \left(\frac{1}{8} - \frac{1}{9}\right)$ is equal to what value?

10. If the first two elements of a number series are 1 and 2, and if each succeeding term is found by multiplying the two terms immediately preceding it, what is the fifth element of the series?

GO ON TO THE NEXT PAGE

11. If p is $\frac{3}{5}$ of m and if q is $\frac{9}{10}$ of m, then, when $q \neq 0$, the ratio $\frac{p}{q}$ is equal to what value?

12. If the average (arithmetic mean) of 40, 40, 40, and z is 45, then find the value of z.

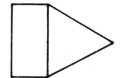

13. In the figure above, the perimeter of the equilateral triangle is 39 and the area of the rectangle is 65. What is the perimeter of the rectangle?

Game	Darrin	Tom
1	69	43
2	59	60
3	72	55
4	70	68
5	78	73
Totals	348	299

14. Darrin and Tom played five games of darts. The table above lists the scores for each of the games. By how many points was Tom behind Darrin at the end of the first four games?

15. A box contains 17 slips of paper. Each is labeled with a different integer from 1 to 17 inclusive. If 5 even-numbered slips of paper are removed, what fraction of the remaining slips of paper are even numbered?

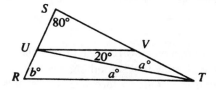

Note: Figure is not drawn to scale.

16. In $\triangle RST$ above $UV \parallel RT$. Find b.

17. Rose has earned \$44 in 8 days. If she continues to earn at the same daily rate, in how many *more* days will her total earnings be \$99?

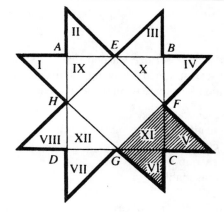

18. The areas of triangles I, II, III, IV, V, VI, VII, VIII, IX, X, XI, XII are the same. If the region outlined by the heavy line has area = 256 and the area of square *ABCD* is 128, determine the shaded area.

STOP

If you finish before time is called, you may check your work on this section only.
Do not turn to any other section in the test.

Take a 5 minute break

before starting section 7

SECTION 7

Time: 25 Minutes—Turn to Section 7 (page 211) of your answer sheet to answer the questions in this section.
24 Questions

Directions: For each question in this section, select the best answer from among the choices given and fill in the corresponding circle on the answer sheet.

Each sentence below has one or two blanks, each blank indicating that something has been omitted. Beneath the sentence are five words or sets of words labeled A through E. Choose the word or set of words that, when inserted in the sentence, best fits the meaning of the sentence as a whole.

Example:

Hoping to _____ the dispute, negotiators proposed a compromise that they felt would be _____ to both labor and management.

(A) enforce . . useful
(B) end . . divisive
(C) overcome . . unattractive
(D) extend . . satisfactory
(E) resolve . . acceptable

Ⓐ Ⓑ Ⓒ Ⓓ ●

---

1. The Forest Service warned that the spring forest fire season was in full swing and urged that _____ caution be exercised in wooded areas.

   (A) moderate
   (B) scant
   (C) customary
   (D) extreme
   (E) reasonable

2. The Classical age of Greek art ended with the defeat of Athens by Sparta; the _____ effect of the long war was the weakening and _____ of the Greek spirit.

   (A) cumulative . . corrosion
   (B) immediate . . storing
   (C) imagined . . cooperation
   (D) delayed . . rebuilding
   (E) intuitive . . cancelation

3. Mary, bored by even the briefest periods of idleness, was _____ switching from one activity to another.

   (A) hesitantly
   (B) lazily
   (C) slowly
   (D) surprisingly
   (E) continually

4. The bee _____ the nectar from the different flowers and then _____ the liquid into honey.

   (A) consumes . . conforms
   (B) observes . . pours
   (C) rejects . . solidifies
   (D) crushes . . injects
   (E) extracts . . converts

5. The plan turned out to be _____ because it would have required more financial backing than was available.

   (A) intractable
   (B) chaotic
   (C) irreversible
   (D) untenable
   (E) superfluous

GO ON TO THE NEXT PAGE →

The passages below are followed by questions based on their content; questions following a pair of related passages may also be based on the relationship between the paired passages. Answer the questions on the basis of what is stated or implied in the passages and in any introductory material that may be provided.

Questions 6–9 are based on the following passages.

Passage 1

1   All the arts contain some preposterous fiction, but the theatre is the most preposterous of all. Imagine asking us to believe that we are in Venice in the sixteenth century, and that Mr. Billington is a Moor, and that he is about to sti-
5   fle the much admired Miss Huckaby with a pillow; and imagine trying to make us believe that people ever talked in blank verse—more than that: that people were ever so marvelously articulate. The theatre is a lily that inexplicably arises from a jungle of weedy falsities. Yet it is precisely
10   from the tension produced by all this absurdity that it is able to create such poetry, power, enchantment and truth.

Passage 2

     The theater is a venue for the most realistic and direct fiction ever imagined. So many of the contemporary plays make us realize how we are living our lives and perhaps
15   how we should change them. From these "reality shows" we can feel all the poverty, despair, and unfairness in our world which then affords us the opportunity for change for the better.

6. Which statement best illustrates the author's meaning when he says, "The theatre is a lily that inexplicably arises from a jungle of weedy falsities"?

    (A) The theatre is the "flower" among the arts.
    (B) The theatre helps to raise public taste to a higher level.
    (C) The theatre can create an illusion of truth from improbable situations.
    (D) The theatre has overcome the unsavory reputation of earlier periods.
    (E) In the theatre, real acting talent can be developed from unpromising material.

7. The author's feeling toward contemporary plays is that they

    (A) have no value for the spectator
    (B) can be appreciated by everyone
    (C) elicit the negative aspects of life
    (D) have a long-lasting effect on us
    (E) do not deal with poetry or truth

8. The two passages are similar in that

    (A) both describe specific examples from specific plays
    (B) both are completely objective in their respective arguments
    (C) both authors of them believe that they depict the accuracy of the particular time
    (D) both authors show the same intensity and passion in their argument
    (E) both show that something positive can come out of something negative

9. Which of the following is true?

    (A) One author would not disagree with the other's premise.
    (B) The author of Paragraph 1 despises all characters in 16th century plays.
    (C) The author of Paragraph 1 believes that people in the 16th century were very articulate.
    (D) Analogies to objects and places is a literary device used in only one passage.
    (E) The author of Paragraph 2 believes that the theater compromises reality.

GO ON TO THE NEXT PAGE

Questions 10–15 are based on the following passage.

The following passage deals with adjustment to one's surroundings and the terms and theory associated with such adjustment.

As in the case of so many words used by the biologist and physiologist, the word *acclimatization* is hard to define. With increase in knowledge and understanding, meanings of words change. Originally the term *acclimatization* was
5 taken to mean only the ability of human beings or animals or plants to accustom themselves to new and strange climatic conditions, primarily altered temperature. A person or a wolf moves to a hot climate and is uncomfortable there, but after a time is better able to withstand the heat. But aside
10 from temperature, there are other aspects of climate. A person or an animal may become adjusted to living at higher altitudes than those it was originally accustomed to. At really high altitudes, such as aviators may be exposed to, the low atmospheric pressure becomes a factor of primary importance
15 In changing to a new environment, a person may, therefore, meet new conditions of temperature or pressure, and in addition may have to contend with different chemical surroundings. On high mountains, the amount of oxygen in the atmosphere may be relatively small; in crowded cities, a
20 person may become exposed to relatively high concentrations of carbon dioxide or even carbon monoxide, and in various areas may be exposed to conditions in which the water content of the atmosphere is extremely high or extremely low. Thus in the case of humans, animals, and even
25 plants, the concept of acclimatization includes the phenomena of increased toleration of high or low temperature, of altered pressure, and of changes in the chemical environment.

Let us define acclimatization, therefore, as the process
30 in which an organism or a part of an organism becomes inured to an environment which is normally unsuitable to it or lethal for it. By and large, acclimatization is a relatively slow process. The term should not be taken to include relatively rapid adjustments such as our sense organs are con-
35 stantly making. This type of adjustment is commonly referred to by physiologists as "adaptation." Thus our touch sense soon becomes accustomed to the pressure of our clothes and we do not feel them; we soon fail to hear the ticking of a clock; obnoxious orders after a time fail to make
40 much impression on us, and our eyes in strong light rapidly become insensitive.

The fundamental fact about acclimatization is that all animals and plants have some capacity to adjust themselves to changes in their environment. This is one of the most
45 remarkable characteristics of living organisms, a characteristic for which it is extremely difficult to find explanations.

10. According to the reading selection, all animals and plants

(A) have an ability for acclimatization.
(B) can adjust to only one change in the environment at a time.
(C) are successful in adjusting themselves to changes in their environments.
(D) can adjust to natural changes in the environment but not to artificially induced changes.
(E) that have once acclimatized themselves to an environmental change can acclimatize themselves more rapidly to subsequent changes.

11. It can be inferred from the reading selection that

(A) every change in the environment requires acclimatization by living things.
(B) plants and animals are more alike than they are different.
(C) biologists and physiologists study essentially the same things.
(D) the explanation of acclimatization is specific to each plant and animal.
(E) as science develops, the connotation of terms may change.

12. According to the reading selection, acclimatization

(A) is similar to adaptation.
(B) is more important today than it formerly was.
(C) involves positive as well as negative adjustment.
(D) may be involved with a part of an organism but not with the whole organism.
(E) is more difficult to explain with the more complex present-day environment than formerly.

13. By inference from the reading selection, which one of the following would *not* require the process of acclimatization?

(A) an ocean fish placed in a lake
(B) a skin diver making a deep dive
(C) an airplane pilot making a high-altitude flight
(D) a person going from daylight into a darkened room
(E) a businessman moving from Denver, Colorado, to New Orleans, Louisiana

GO ON TO THE NEXT PAGE

14. The word "inured" in line 31 most likely means

(A) exposed
(B) accustomed
(C) attracted
(D) associated
(E) in love with

15. According to the passage, a major distinction between acclimatization and adaptation is that acclimatization

(A) is more important than adaptation.
(B) is relatively slow and adaptation is relatively rapid.
(C) applies to adjustments while adaptation does not apply to adjustments.
(D) applies to terrestrial animals and adaptation to aquatic animals.
(E) is applicable to all animals and plants and adaptation only to higher animals and man.

GO ON TO THE NEXT PAGE

Questions 16–24 are based on the following passage.

The following passage is about the Chinese Empire, the forces that kept the Empire together, its culture, and its philosophy.

First of all, it is important to note that the old China was an empire rather than a state. To the Chinese and their rulers, the word *China* did not exist and to them it would have been meaningless. They sometimes used a term which
5   we translate as "the Middle Kingdom." To them there could be only one legitimate ruler for all civilized mankind. All others were rightly subordinate to him and should acknowledge his suzerainty. From this standpoint, there could not, as in Europe, be diplomatic relations between equal states, each of
10 them sovereign. When, in the nineteenth century, Europeans insisted upon intercourse with China on the basis of equality, the Chinese were at first amused and then scandalized and indignant. Centuries of training had bred in them the conviction that all other rulers should be tributary to the Son of
15 Heaven.

The tie which bound this world-embracing empire together, so the Chinese were taught to believe, was as much cultural as political. As there could be only one legitimate ruler to whom all mankind must be subject, so there could be
20 only one culture that fully deserved to be called civilized. Other cultures might have worth, but ultimately they were more or less barbarous. There could be only one civilization, and that was the civilization of the Middle Kingdom. Beginning with the Han, the ideal of civilization was held to
25 be Confucian. The Confucian interpretation of civilization was adopted and inculcated as the norm. Others might be tolerated, but if they seriously threatened the Confucian institutions and foundations of society they were to be curbed and, perhaps, exterminated as a threat to the highest
30 values.

Since the bond of the Empire was cultural and since the Empire should include all civilized mankind, racial distinctions were not so marked as in most other parts of the world. The Chinese did not have so strong a sense of being of
35 different blood from non-Chinese as twentieth-century conceptions of race and nation later led them to develop. They were proud of being "the sons of Han" or "the men of T'ang," but if a people fully adopted Chinese culture no great distinction was perceived between them and those who earlier had
40 been governed by that culture.

This helps to account for the comparative contentment of Chinese under alien rulers. If, as was usually the case, these invading conquerors adopted the culture of their subjects and governed through the accustomed machinery and
45 by traditional Confucian principles, they were accepted as legitimate Emperors. Few of the non-Chinese dynasties completely made this identification. This probably in part accounts for such restiveness as the Chinese showed under their rule. For instance, so long as they were dominant, the
50 Manchus, while they accepted much of the Chinese culture and prided themselves on being experts in it and posed as its patrons, never completely abandoned their distinctive ancestral ways.

The fact that the tie was cultural rather than racial
55 helps to account for the remarkable homogeneity of the Chinese. Many different ethnic strains have gone to make up the people whom we call the Chinese. Presumably in the Chou and probably, earlier, in the Shang, the bearers of Chinese culture were not a single race. As Chinese culture
60 moved southward it encountered differing cultures and, almost certainly, divergent stocks. The many invaders from the north and west brought in more variety. In contrast with India, where caste and religion have tended to keep apart the racial strata, in China assimilation made great progress.
65 That assimilation has not been complete. Today the discerning observer can notice differences even among those who are Chinese in language and customs, and in many parts of China Proper there are groups who preserve not only their racial but also their linguistic and cultural identity. Still,
70 nowhere else on the globe is there so numerous a people who are so nearly homogeneous as are the Chinese.

This homogeneity is due not merely to a common cultural tie, but also to the particular kind of culture which constitutes that tie. Something in the Chinese tradition rec-
75 ognized as civilized those who conformed to certain ethical standards and social customs. It was the fitting into Confucian patterns of conduct and of family and community life rather than blood kinship or ancestry which labeled one as civilized and as Chinese.

16. The force that kept the Chinese Empire together was largely

(A) religious
(B) military
(C) economic
(D) a fear of invasion from the north and west
(E) the combination of a political and a cultural bond

17. The reason China resisted having diplomatic relations with European nations was that

(A) for centuries the Chinese had believed that their nation must be supreme among all other countries
(B) the Chinese saw nothing of value in European culture
(C) China was afraid of European military power
(D) such relations were against the teachings of the Son of Heaven
(E) the danger of disease was ever present when foreigners arrived

GO ON TO THE NEXT PAGE

18. Confucianism stresses, above all,

 (A) image worship
 (B) recognition of moral values
 (C) division of church and state
 (D) acceptance of foreigners
 (E) separation of social classes

19. Han and T'ang were Chinese

 (A) philosophers
 (B) holidays
 (C) dynasties
 (D) generals
 (E) religions

20. If the unifying force in the Chinese empire had been racial, it is likely that

 (A) China would have never become great
 (B) China would be engaged in constant warfare
 (C) China would have become a highly industrialized nation
 (D) there would have been increasing discontent under foreign rulers
 (E) China would have greatly expanded its influence

21. A problem of contemporary India that does not trouble China is

 (A) overpopulation
 (B) the persistence of the caste system
 (C) a lack of modern industrial development
 (D) a scarcity of universities
 (E) a low standard of living

22. The Manchus encountered some dissatisfaction within the empire because

 (A) of their tyrannical rule
 (B) they retained some of their original cultural practices
 (C) they were of a distinctly foreign race
 (D) of the heavy taxes they levied
 (E) they rejected totally Chinese culture

23. The Chinese are basically a homogeneous people because

 (A) different races were able to assimilate to a great degree
 (B) there has always been only one race in China
 (C) the other races came to look like the Chinese because of geographical factors
 (D) all other races were forcibly kept out of China
 (E) of their antipathy toward intermarriage

24. The word "restiveness" in line 48 means

 (A) authority
 (B) happiness
 (C) impatience
 (D) hyperactivity
 (E) quietude

STOP

If you finish before time is called, you may check your work on this section only.
Do not turn to any other section in the test.

SECTION 8

Time: 20 Minutes—Turn to Section 8 (page 212) of your answer sheet to answer the questions in this section.
16 Questions

Directions: For this section, solve each problem and decide which is the best of the choices given. Fill in the corresponding circle on the answer sheet. You may use any available space for scratchwork.

Notes:

1. The use of a calculator is permitted.
2. All numbers used are real numbers.
3. Figures that accompany problems in this test are intended to provide information useful in solving the problems. They are drawn as accurately as possible EXCEPT when it is stated in a specific problem that the figure is not drawn to scale. All figures lie in a plane unless otherwise indicated.
4. Unless otherwise specified, the domain of any function f is assumed to be the set of all real numbers x for which $f(x)$ is a real number.

REFERENCE INFORMATION

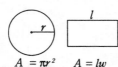   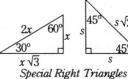

$A = \pi r^2$ $A = lw$ $A = \frac{1}{2}bh$ $V = lwh$ $V = \pi r^2 h$ $c^2 = a^2 + b^2$ *Special Right Triangles*
$C = 2\pi r$

The number of degrees of arc in a circle is 360.
The sum of the measures in degrees of the angles of a triangle is 180.

1. Johnny buys a frying pan and two coffee mugs for $27. Joanna buys the same-priced frying pan and one of the same-priced coffee mugs for $23. How much does one of those frying pans cost?

   (A) $4
   (B) $7
   (C) $19
   (D) $20
   (E) $21

2. A rectangular floor 8 feet long and 6 feet wide is to be completely covered with tiles. Each tile is a square with a perimeter of 2 feet. What is the least number of such tiles necessary to cover the floor?

   (A) 7
   (B) 12
   (C) 24
   (D) 48
   (E) 192

GO ON TO THE NEXT PAGE

3. If 9 and 12 each divide Q without remainder, which of the following must Q divide without remainder?

(A) 1
(B) 3
(C) 36
(D) 72
(E) The answer cannot be determined from the given information.

5. Given three segments of length x, $11 - x$, and $x - 4$, respectively, which of the following indicates the set of all numbers x such that the 3 segments could be the lengths of the sides of a triangle?

(A) $x > 4$
(B) $x < 11$
(C) $0 < x < 7$
(D) $5 < x < 15$
(E) $5 < x < 7$

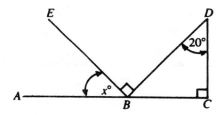

4. In the figure above, $DC \perp AC$, $EB \perp DB$, and AC is a line segment. What is the value of x?

(A) 15
(B) 20
(C) 30
(D) 80
(E) 160

6. Given three integers a, b, and 4. If their average (arithmetic mean) is 6, which of the following could *not* be the value of the product ab?

(A) 13
(B) 14
(C) 40
(D) 48
(E) 49

GO ON TO THE NEXT PAGE

7. If $mn \neq 0$, then $\dfrac{1}{n^2}\left(\dfrac{m^5 n^3}{m^3}\right)^2 =$

(A) mn^4
(B) $m^4 n^2$
(C) $m^4 n^3$
(D) $m^4 n^4$
(E) $m^4 n^5$

Question 9 refers to the figure above, where W, X, Y, and Z are four distinct digits from 0 to 9, inclusive, and $W + X + Y = 5Z$.

9. Under the given conditions, all of the following could be values of Z EXCEPT

(A) 1
(B) 2
(C) 3
(D) 4
(E) 5

8. The probability that only two people in a room of three people are male is

(A) $\dfrac{3}{8}$

(B) $\dfrac{1}{4}$

(C) $\dfrac{2}{5}$

(D) $\dfrac{2}{3}$

(E) $\dfrac{5}{6}$

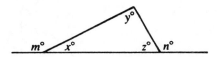

10. In the figure above, $m + n =$

(A) 90
(B) 180
(C) $180 + y$
(D) $90 + x + y + z$
(E) $2(x + y + z)$

GO ON TO THE NEXT PAGE

11. The volume of a cube is less than 25, and the length of one of its edges is a positive integer. What is the largest possible value for the total area of the six faces?

(A) 1
(B) 6
(C) 24
(D) 54
(E) 150

A   B   C   D   E   F   G
├──┼──┼──┼──┼──┼──┤

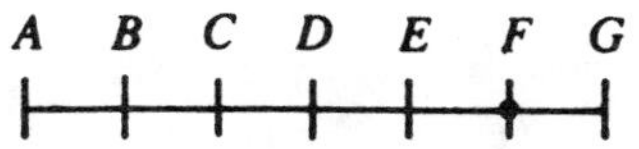

13. *AG* is divided into six equal segments in the figure above. A circle, not visible, with center *F* and radius $\frac{1}{5}$ the length of *AG*, will intersect *AG* between

(A) *F* and *G*
(B) *E* and *F*
(C) *D* and *E*
(D) *C* and *D*
(E) *A* and *B*

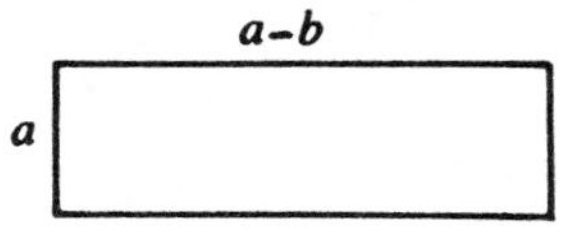

12. The ratio of smokers to nonsmokers on a particular flight was 2 : 3. Smoking passengers represented five more than $\frac{1}{3}$ of all the passengers aboard. How many passengers were on that flight?

(A) 15
(B) 25
(C) 30
(D) 45
(E) 75

a−b

a ▭

14. The figure above is a rectangle having width *a* and length $a - b$. Find its perimeter in terms of *a* and *b*.

(A) $a^2 - ab$
(B) $4a - 2b$
(C) $4a - b$
(D) $2a - 2b$
(E) $2a - b$

GO ON TO THE NEXT PAGE ⟩

$$AB$$
$$+BA$$
$$\overline{CDC}$$

15. If each of the four letters in the sum above represents a *different* digit, which of the following *cannot* be a value of *A*?

(A) 6
(B) 5
(C) 4
(D) 3
(E) 2

16. If for real x, y, $f(x) = x^2 + x$ and $g(y) = y^2$, then $f[g(-1)] =$

(A) 2
(B) -2
(C) 4
(D) -4
(E) -8

STOP

If you finish before time is called, you may check your work on this section only.
Do not turn to any other section in the test.

SECTION 9

Time: 20 Minutes—Turn to Section 9 (page 212) of your answer sheet to answer the questions in this section.
   19 Questions

Directions: For each question in this section, select the best answer from among the choices given and fill in the corresponding circle on the answer sheet.

Each sentence below has one or two blanks, each blank indicating that something has been omitted. Beneath the sentence are five words or sets of words labeled A through E. Choose the word or set of words that, when inserted in the sentence, best fits the meaning of the sentence as a whole.

Example:

Hoping to _____ the dispute, negotiators proposed a compromise that they felt would be _____ to both labor and management.

(A) enforce . . useful
(B) end . . divisive
(C) overcome . . unattractive
(D) extend . . satisfactory
(E) resolve . . acceptable

Ⓐ Ⓑ Ⓒ Ⓓ ●

1. Joining _____ momentum for reform in intercollegiate sports, university presidents have called for swift steps to correct imbalances between classwork and _____ .

(A) a maximum . . studies
(B) a rational . . awards
(C) an increasing . . athletics
(D) an exceptional . . professors
(E) a futile . . contests

2. Thinking nothing can be done, many victims of arthritis ignore or delay _____ countermeasures, thus aggravating the problem.

(A) tardy
(B) injurious
(C) characteristic
(D) weird
(E) effective

3. A strange and _____ fate seemed to keep him helpless and unhappy, despite occasional interludes of _____ .

(A) malevolent . . conflict
(B) bizarre . . disenchantment
(C) virulent . . tension
(D) ineluctable . . serenity
(E) intriguing . . inactivity

4. Samuel Clemens chose the _____ Mark Twain as a result of his knowledge of riverboat piloting.

(A) protagonist
(B) pseudonym
(C) mountebank
(D) hallucination
(E) misanthrope

5. For years a vocalist of spirituals, Marian Anderson was finally recognized as _____ singer when the Metropolitan Opera House engaged her.

(A) a versatile
(B) an unusual
(C) an attractive
(D) a cooperative
(E) a mediocre

6. Leonardo da Vinci _____ the law of gravity two centuries before Newton and also made the first complete _____ charts of the human body.

(A) examined . . colorful
(B) anticipated . . anatomical
(C) avoided . . meaningful
(D) realized . . explanatory
(E) suspected . . mural

GO ON TO THE NEXT PAGE

The two passages below are followed by questions based on their content and on the relationship between the two passages. Answer the questions on the basis of what is <u>stated</u> or <u>implied</u> in the passages and in any introductory material that may be provided.

Questions 7–19 are based on the following passages.

The following two passages describe two views of the make-up and character of an artist.

Passage 1

The special quality which makes an artist of any worth might be defined, indeed, as an extraordinary capacity for irritation, a pathological sensitiveness to environmental pricks and stings. He differs from the rest of us mainly
5 because he reacts sharply and in an uncommon manner to phenomena which leave the rest of us unmoved, or, at most, merely annoy us vaguely. He is, in brief, a more delicate fellow than we are, and hence less fitted to prosper and enjoy himself under the conditions of life which he and we must
10 face alike. Therefore, he takes to artistic endeavor, which is at once a criticism of life and an attempt to escape from life.

So much for the theory of it. The more the facts are studied, the more they bear it out. In those fields of art, at all events, which concern themselves with ideas as well as with
15 sensations, it is almost impossible to find any trace of an artist who was not actively hostile to his environment, and thus an indifferent patriot. From Dante to Tolstoy and from Shakespeare to Mark Twain the story is ever the same. Names suggest themselves instantly: Goethe, Heine, Shelley,
20 Byron, Thackeray, Balzac, Rabelais, Cervantes, Swift, Dostoevsky, Carlyle, Moliere, Pope—all bitter critics of their time and nation, most of them piously hated by the contemporary 100 percenters, some of them actually fugitives from rage and reprisal.
25 Dante put all of the patriotic Italians of his day into Hell, and showed them boiling, roasting and writhing on hooks. Cervantes drew such a devastating picture of the Spain that he lived in that it ruined the Spaniards. Shakespeare made his heroes foreigners and his clowns Englishmen.
30 Goethe was in favor of Napoleon. Rabelais, a citizen of Christendom rather than of France, raised a cackle against it that Christendom is still trying in vain to suppress. Swift, having finished the Irish and then the English, proceeded to finish the whole human race. The exceptions are few and far
35 between, and not many of them will bear examination. So far as I know, the only eminent writer in English history who was also a 100% Englishman, absolutely beyond suspicion, was Samuel Johnson. But was Johnson actually an artist? If he was, then a kazoo-player is a musician. He employed the
40 materials of one of the arts, to wit, words, but his use of them was mechanical, not artistic. If Johnson were alive today, he would be a United States Senator, or a university president. He left such wounds upon English prose that it was a century recovering from them.

Passage 2

45 For the ease and pleasure of treading the old road, accepting the fashions, the education, the religion of society, he takes the cross of making his own, and, of course, the self-accusation, the faint heart, the frequent uncertainty and loss of time, which are the nettles and tangling vines in the way
50 of the self-relying and self-directed, and the state of virtual hostility in which he seems to stand to society, and especially to educated society. For all this loss and scorn, what offset? The artist is to find consolation in exercising the highest functions of human nature. The artist is one who
55 raises himself from private consideration and breathes and lives on public and illustrious thoughts. The artist is the world's eye. He is the world's heart. He is to resist the vulgar prosperity that retrogrades ever to barbarism, by preserving and communicating heroic sentiments, noble biographies,
60 melodious verse, and the conclusions of history. Whatsoever oracles the human heart, in all emergencies, in all solemn hours, has uttered as its commentary on the world of actions—these he shall receive and impart. And whatsoever new verdict Reason from her inviolable seat pronounces on
65 the passing men and women and events of today—this he shall hear and promulgate.

These being his functions, it becomes the artist to feel all confidence in himself, and to defer never to the popular cry. He and he only knows the world. The world of any
70 moment is the merest appearance. Some great decorum, some fetish of a government, some ephemeral trade, or war, or man, is cried up by half mankind and cried down by the other half, as if all depended on this particular up or down. The odds are that the whole question is not worth the
75 poorest thought which the scholar has lost in listening to the controversy. Let her not quit her belief that a popgun is a popgun, though the ancient and honorable of the earth affirm it to be the crack of doom. In silence, in steadiness, in severe abstraction, let him hold by himself; add observation
80 to observation, patient of neglect, patient of reproach, and bide his own time—happy enough if he can satisfy himself alone that this day he has seen something truly. Success treads on every right step. For the instinct is sure, that prompts him to tell his brother what he thinks. The artist then
85 learns that in going down into the secrets of his own mind he has descended into the secrets of all minds. He learns that the artist who has mastered any law in his private thoughts is master to that extent of all translated. The poet, in utter solitude remembering his spontaneous thoughts and record-
90 ing them, is found to have recorded that which men in crowded cities find true for them also. The orator distrusts at

GO ON TO THE NEXT PAGE

first the fitness of his frank confessions, his want of knowledge of the persons he addresses, until he finds that he is the complement of his hearers—that they drink his words because he fulfills for them their own nature; the deeper he dives into his privatest, secretest presentiment, to his wonder he finds this is the most acceptable, most public, and universally true. The people delight in it; the better part of every man feels. This is my music; this is myself.

95

7. Which of the following quotations is related most closely to the principal idea of Passage 1?

(A) "All nature is but art unknown to thee,
    All chance, direction which thou canst not see."
(B) "When to her share some human errors fall,
    Look on her face and you'll forget them all."
(C) "All human things are subject to decay,
    And, when fate summons, monarchs must obey."
(D) "A little learning is a dangerous thing, Drink deep or taste not the Pierian spring."
(E) "Great wits are sure to madness near allied,
    And thin partitions do their bounds divide."

8. The author of Passage 1 seems to regard the artist as

(A) the best representative of his time
(B) an unnecessary threat to the social order
(C) one who creates out of discontent
(D) one who truly knows how to enjoy life
(E) one who is touched with genius

9. It can be inferred that the author of Passage 1 believes that United States Senators and university presidents

(A) must be treated with respect because of their position
(B) are to be held in low esteem
(C) are generally appreciative of the great literary classics
(D) have native writing ability
(E) have the qualities of the artist

10. All of the following ideas about artists are mentioned in Passage 1 *except* that

(A) they are irritated by their surroundings
(B) they are escapists from reality
(C) they are lovers of beauty
(D) they are hated by their contemporaries
(E) they are critical of their times

11. Which of the following best describes Passage 1 author's attitude toward artists?

(A) sharply critical
(B) sincerely sympathetic
(C) deeply resentful
(D) mildly annoyed
(E) completely delighted

12. It is a frequent criticism of the artist that he lives by himself, in an "ivory tower," remote from the problems and business of the world. Which of these below constitutes the best refutation by the writer of Passage 2 to the criticism here noted?

(A) The world's concerns being ephemeral, the artist does well to renounce them and the world.
(B) The artist lives in the past to interpret the present.
(C) The artist at his truest is the spokesman of the people.
(D) The artist is not concerned with the world's doings because he is not selfish and therefore not engrossed in matters of importance to himself and neighbors.
(E) The artist's academic researches of today are the businessman's practical products of tomorrow.

13. The artist's road is rough, according to Passage 2. Which of these is the artist's greatest difficulty?

(A) The artist must renounce religion.
(B) The artist must pioneer new approaches.
(C) The artist must express scorn for and hostility to society.
(D) The artist is uncertain of his course.
(E) There is a pleasure in the main-traveled roads in education, religion, and all social fashions.

14. When the writer of Passage 2 speaks of the "world's eye" and the "world's heart" he means

(A) the same thing
(B) culture and conscience
(C) culture and wisdom
(D) a scanning of all the world's geography and a deep sympathy for every living thing
(E) mind and love

GO ON TO THE NEXT PAGE ⟹

15. By the phrase "nettles and tangling vines" (line 49) the author probably refers to

   (A) "self-accusation" and "loss of time"
   (B) "faint heart" and "self-accusation"
   (C) "the slings and arrows of outrageous fortune"
   (D) a general term for the difficulties of a scholar's life
   (E) "self-accusation" and "uncertainty"

16. The various ideas in Passage 2 are best summarized in which of these groups?

   I.   truth versus society
        the artist and books
        the world and the artist
   II. the ease of living traditionally
        the glory of an artist's life
        true knowledge versus trivia
   III. the hardships of the scholar
        the artist's functions
        the artist's justifications for disregarding the world's business

   (A) I and III together
   (B) I only
   (C) III only
   (D) I, II, and III together
   (E) I and II together

17. "seems to stand" (line 51) means

   (A) is
   (B) ends probably in becoming
   (C) gives the false impression of being
   (D) is seen to be
   (E) the quicksands of time

18. The difference between the description of the artist in Passage 1 as compared with the artist in Passage 2 is that

   (A) one is loyal to his fellow men and women whereas the other is opposed to his or her environment
   (B) one is sensitive to his or her environment whereas the other is apathetic
   (C) one has political aspirations; the other does not
   (D) one has deep knowledge; the other has superficial knowledge
   (E) one could be proficient in a field other than art; the other could create only in his or her present field

19. Which of the following describes statements that refer to the *same* one artist (either the one in Passage 1 *or* the one in Passage 2)?

   I.   This artist's thoughts are also the spectator's thoughts.
        This artist lives modestly and not luxuriously.
   II. This artist admires foreigners over his own countrymen.
        This artist reacts to many things that most people would be neutral to.
   III. This artist is happy to be at his best.
        This artist accepts society.

   (A) I only
   (B) II only
   (C) III only
   (D) I and III only
   (E) I, II, and III

STOP

If you finish before time is called, you may check your work on this section only.

Do not turn to any other section in the test.

SECTION 10

Time: 10 Minutes—Turn to Section 10 (page 212) of your answer sheet to answer the questions in this section.
   14 Questions

Directions: For each question in this section, select the best answer from among the choices given and fill in the corresponding circle on the answer sheet.

The following sentences test correctness and effectiveness of expression. Part of each sentence or the entire sentence is underlined; beneath each sentence are five ways of phrasing the underlined material. Choice A repeats the original phrasing; the other four choices are different. If you think the original phrasing produces a better sentence than any of the alternatives, select choice A; if not, select one of the other choices.

In making your selection, follow the requirements of standard written English; that is, pay attention to grammar, choice of words, sentence construction, and punctuation. Your selection should result in the most effective sentence—clear and precise, without awkwardness or ambiguity.

EXAMPLE:

Laura Ingalls Wilder published her first book and she was sixty-five years old then.

(A) and she was sixty-five years old then
(B) when she was sixty-five
(C) at age sixty-five years old
(D) upon the reaching of sixty-five years
(E) at the time when she was sixty-five

1. He bought some bread, butter, cheese and decided not to eat them until the evening.

(A) some bread, butter, cheese and decided
(B) some bread, butter, cheese and then decided
(C) a little bread, butter, cheese and decided
(D) some bread, butter, cheese, deciding
(E) some bread, butter, and cheese and decided

2. The things the children liked best were swimming in the river and to watch the horses being groomed by the trainer.

(A) swimming in the river and to watch the horses being groomed by the trainer
(B) swimming in the river and to watch the trainer grooming the horses
(C) that they liked to swim in the river and watch the horses being groomed by the trainer
(D) swimming in the river and watching the horses being groomed by the trainer
(E) to swim in the river and watching the horses being groomed by the trainer

3. If an individual wishes to specialize in electrical engineering, they should take courses in trigonometry and calculus.

(A) they should take courses in trigonometry and calculus
(B) trigonometry and calculus is what he should take courses in
(C) trigonometry and calculus are what they should take courses in
(D) he should take courses in trigonometry and calculus
(E) take courses in trigonometry and calculus

4. If the dog will not eat its food, put it through the meat grinder once more.

(A) eat its food, put it through
(B) eat it's food, put it through
(C) eat its food, you should put it through
(D) eat food, put it through
(E) eat its food, put the food through

5. The bank agreed to lend Garcia the money, which made him very happy.

(A) Garcia the money, which made
(B) Garcia the money, a decision which made
(C) Garcia the money; this made
(D) Garcia the money, this making
(E) the money to Garcia and found

6. Miami's daytime attire is <u>less formal than New York</u>.

   (A) less formal than New York
   (B) less formal then that in New York
   (C) less formal than that in New York
   (D) less formal than in New York
   (E) less formal than the daytime attire we see in New York

7. <u>As the fisherman explained that he wanted to hire a guide and row</u> upstream in order to catch game fish.

   (A) As the fisherman explained that he wanted to hire a guide and row
   (B) The reason was as the fisherman explained that he wanted to hire a guide and row
   (C) As the fisherman explained that he wanted to hire a guide and to row
   (D) The fisherman explained that he wanted to hire a guide and row
   (E) The fisherman explaining that he wanted to hire a guide and row

8. The speaker was praised <u>for his organization, choice of subject, and because he was brief</u>.

   (A) for his organization, choice of subject, and because he was brief
   (B) for his organization, his choice of subject and the speech having brevity
   (C) on account of his organization and his choice of subject and the brevity of his speech
   (D) for the organization of his speech, for his choice of subject, and because he was brief
   (E) for his organization, his choice of subject, and his brevity

9. <u>The fact that Charles did not receive a college scholarship</u> disappointed his parents.

   (A) The fact that Charles did not receive a college scholarship
   (B) Because Charles did not receive a college scholarship was the reason he
   (C) Being that Charles did not receive a college scholarship
   (D) Charles not receiving a college scholarship
   (E) Charles did not receive a college scholarship

10. The porch of a famous home collapsed during a party last week, <u>which injured 23 people</u>.

    (A) which injured 23 people
    (B) causing 23 people to be injured
    (C) injuring 23 people
    (D) damaging 23 people
    (E) resulting in 23 people being injured

11. Jack's favorite summer supper includes barbecued chicken, grilled corn on the cob, sliced tomatoes, <u>and he likes green salad</u>.

    (A) and he likes green salad
    (B) in addition to green salad
    (C) adding green salad
    (D) including green salad
    (E) and green salad

12. I want the <u>best price</u> I can get for my car.

    (A) best price
    (B) most highest price
    (C) price which is the best
    (D) most best price
    (E) premium price

13. The injured man was taken to the hospital, <u>where he was treated for facial lacerations and released</u>.

    (A) where he was treated for facial lacerations and released
    (B) where he was treated and released for facial lacerations
    (C) where his facial lacerations were treated and he was released from the hospital
    (D) where his treatment was for facial lacerations and he was released from the hospital
    (E) where he received facial lacerations treatment and was released

14. The wife of the new leader is tough, single-minded, and <u>tries to be independent</u>.

    (A) tries to be independent
    (B) acting independent
    (C) independent
    (D) an independent person
    (E) an independent

STOP

If you finish before time is called, you may check your work on this section only.
Do not turn to any other section in the test.

How Did You Do on This Test?

Step 1.   Go to the Answer Key on pages 260–262.

Step 2.   For your "raw score," calculate it using the directions on pages 263–264.

Step 3.   Get your "scaled score" for the test by referring to the Raw Score/Scaled Score Conversion Tables on pages 265–267.

THERE'S ALWAYS ROOM FOR IMPROVEMENT!

Answer Keys

Math

Section 2	
	Correct Answer
1	C
2	E
3	C
4	D
5	D
6	B
7	D
8	D
9	B
10	A
11	C
12	D
13	A
14	E
15	A
16	E
17	C
18	B
19	D
20	A

Number correct

Number incorrect

Section 3	
	Correct Answer
1	A
2	C
3	E
4	B
5	B
6	A
7	C
8	A
9	A
10	B
11	D
12	D
13	B
14	D
15	C
16	C
17	B
18	C
19	A
20	D

Number correct

Number incorrect

Section 6	
	Correct Answer
1	E
2	A
3	B
4	D
5	E
6	B
7	A
8	D

Number correct

Number incorrect

Student-Produced Response Questions

9	7/18 or .388 or .389
10	8
11	2/3 or .667 or .666
12	60
13	36
14	44
15	1/4 or .25
16	60
17	10
18	48

Number correct

Number incorrect

Section 8	
	Correct Answer
1	C
2	E
3	E
4	B
5	E
6	B
7	D
8	A
9	E
10	C
11	C
12	E
13	C
14	B
15	E
16	A

Number correct

Number incorrect

Critical Reading and Writing

Critical Reading

Section 4			Section 7			Section 9	
	Correct Answer			Correct Answer			Correct Answer
1	E		1	D		1	C
2	C		2	A		2	E
3	B		3	E		3	D
4	A		4	E		4	B
5	B		5	D		5	A
6	B		6	C		6	B
7	B		7	C		7	E
8	B		8	E		8	C
9	D		9	D		9	B
10	A		10	A		10	C
11	B		11	E		11	B
12	E		12	A		12	C
13	B		13	D		13	B
14	E		14	B		14	C
15	A		15	B		15	E
16	E		16	E		16	C
17	C		17	A		17	C
18	D		18	B		18	A
19	D		19	C		19	E
20	A		20	D			
21	C		21	B			
22	C		22	B			
23	C		23	A			
24	D		24	C			

Number correct   Number correct   Number correct

Number incorrect   Number incorrect   Number incorrect

Writing

Section 1

_____

Essay score

Section 5			Section 10		
	Correct Answer			Correct Answer	
1	C		1	E	
2	D		2	D	
3	E		3	D	
4	B		4	E	
5	A		5	B	
6	B		6	C	
7	D		7	D	
8	E		8	E	
9	D		9	A	
10	B		10	C	
11	D		11	E	
12	D		12	A	
13	E		13	A	
14	A		14	C	
15	B				
16	E				
17	B				
18	A				
19	E				
20	D				
21	E				
22	A				
23	C				
24	B				
25	D				
26	D				
27	A				
28	C				
29	A				
30	D				
31	C				
32	A				
33	B				
34	B				
35	D				

Section 10:

_____

Number correct

_____

Number incorrect

Section 5:

_____

Number correct

_____

Number incorrect

Scoring the SAT Practice Test

Check your responses with the correct answers on the previous pages. Fill in the blanks below and do the calculations to get your math, critical reading, and writing raw scores. Use the table to find your math, critical reading, and writing scaled scores.

Get Your Math Score

How many math questions did you get **right?**

Section 2: Questions 1–20   _____

Section 6: Questions 1–18   +   _____

Section 8: Questions 1–16   +   _____

          Total   =   _____ **(A)**

How many multiple-choice math questions did you get **wrong?**

Section 2: Questions 1–20   _____

Section 6: Questions 1–8   +   _____

Section 8: Questions 1–16   +   _____

          Total   =   _____ **(B)**

          $\times\ 0.25$ =   _____

        A − B   =   _____

                Math Raw Score

Round the math raw score to the nearest whole number.

_____

Use the Score Conversion Table to find your math scaled score.

_____

Get Your Critical Reading Score

How many critical reading questions did you get **right?**

Section 4: Questions 1–24   _____

Section 7: Questions 1–24   +   _____

Section 9: Questions 1–19   +   _____

          Total   =   _____ **(A)**

How many critical reading questions did you get **wrong?**

Section 4: Questions 1–24   _____

Section 7: Questions 1–24   +   _____

Section 9: Questions 1–19   +   _____

          Total   =   _____ **(B)**

          $\times\ 0.25$ =   _____

        A − B   =   _____

         Critical Reading Raw Score

Round the critical reading raw score to the nearest whole number.

_____

Use the Score Conversion Table to find your critical reading scaled score.

_____

Get Your Writing Score

How many multiple-choice writing questions did you get **right?**

Section 5: Questions 1–35   _____

Section 10: Questions 1–14   +   _____

         Total   =   _____ **(A)**

How many multiple-choice questions did you get **wrong?**

Section 5: Questions 1–35   _____

Section 10: Questions 1–14   +   _____

         Total   =   _____ **(B)**

         $\times 0.25$ =   _____

         A − B   =   _____

               Writing Raw Score

Round the writing raw score to the nearest whole number.

_____

Use the Score Conversion Table to find your writing multiple-choice scaled score.

_____

Estimate your essay score using the Essay Scoring Guide.

_____

Use the SAT Score Conversion Table for Writing Composite to find your writing scaled score. You will need your Writing Raw Score and your Essay Score to use this table.

_____

SAT Score Conversion Table

Raw Score	Critical Reading Scaled Score	Math Scaled Score	Writing Multiple-Choice Scaled Score*	Raw Score	Critical Reading Scaled Score	Math Scaled Score	Writing Multiple-Choice Scaled Score
67	800			31	510	550	60
66	800			30	510	540	58
65	790			29	500	530	57
64	770			28	490	520	56
63	750			27	490	520	55
62	740			26	480	510	54
61	730			25	480	500	53
60	720			24	470	490	52
59	700			23	460	480	51
58	690			22	460	480	50
57	690			21	450	470	49
56	680			20	440	460	48
55	670			19	440	450	47
54	660	800		18	430	450	46
53	650	790		17	420	440	45
52	650	760		16	420	430	44
51	640	740		15	410	420	44
50	630	720		14	400	410	43
49	620	710	80	13	400	410	42
48	620	700	80	12	390	400	41
47	610	680	80	11	380	390	40
46	600	670	79	10	370	380	39
45	600	660	78	9	360	370	38
44	590	650	76	8	350	360	38
43	590	640	74	7	340	350	37
42	580	630	73	6	330	340	36
41	570	630	71	5	320	330	35
40	570	620	70	4	310	320	34
39	560	610	69	3	300	310	32
38	550	600	67	2	280	290	31
37	550	590	66	1	270	280	30
36	540	580	65	0	250	260	28
35	540	580	64	−1	230	240	27
34	530	570	63	−2	210	220	25
33	520	560	62	−3	200	200	23
32	520	550	61	−4	200	200	20
				and below			

This table is for use only with the test in this book.

*The Writing multiple-choice score is reported on a 20–80 scale. Use the SAT Score Conversion Table for Writing Composite for the total writing scaled score.

SAT Score Conversion Table for Writing Composite

Writing Multiple-Choice Raw Score	Essay Raw Score						
	0	1	2	3	4	5	6
−12	200	200	200	210	240	270	300
−11	200	200	200	210	240	270	300
−10	200	200	200	210	240	270	300
−9	200	200	200	210	240	270	300
−8	200	200	200	210	240	270	300
−7	200	200	200	210	240	270	300
−6	200	200	200	210	240	270	300
−5	200	200	200	210	240	270	300
−4	200	200	200	230	270	300	330
−3	200	210	230	250	290	320	350
−2	200	230	250	280	310	340	370
−1	210	240	260	290	320	360	380
0	230	260	280	300	340	370	400
1	240	270	290	320	350	380	410
2	250	280	300	330	360	390	420
3	260	290	310	340	370	400	430
4	270	300	320	350	380	410	440
5	280	310	330	360	390	420	450
6	290	320	340	360	400	430	460
7	290	330	340	370	410	440	470
8	300	330	350	380	410	450	470
9	310	340	360	390	420	450	480
10	320	350	370	390	430	460	490
11	320	360	370	400	440	470	500
12	330	360	380	410	440	470	500
13	340	370	390	420	450	480	510
14	350	380	390	420	460	490	520
15	350	380	400	430	460	500	530
16	360	390	410	440	470	500	530
17	370	400	420	440	480	510	540
18	380	410	420	450	490	520	550
19	380	410	430	460	490	530	560
20	390	420	440	470	500	530	560
21	400	430	450	480	510	540	570
22	410	440	460	480	520	550	580
23	420	450	470	490	530	560	590
24	420	460	470	500	540	570	600
25	430	460	480	510	540	580	610

Writing Multiple-Choice Raw Score	Essay Raw Score						
	0	1	2	3	4	5	6
26	440	470	490	520	550	590	610
27	450	480	500	530	560	590	620
28	460	490	510	540	570	600	630
29	470	500	520	550	580	610	640
30	480	510	530	560	590	620	650
31	490	520	540	560	600	630	660
32	500	530	550	570	610	640	670
33	510	540	550	580	620	650	680
34	510	550	560	590	630	660	690
35	520	560	570	600	640	670	700
36	530	560	580	610	650	680	710
37	540	570	590	620	660	690	720
38	550	580	600	630	670	700	730
39	560	600	610	640	680	710	740
40	580	610	620	650	690	720	750
41	590	620	640	660	700	730	760
42	600	630	650	680	710	740	770
43	610	640	660	690	720	750	780
44	620	660	670	700	740	770	800
45	640	670	690	720	750	780	800
46	650	690	700	730	770	800	800
47	670	700	720	750	780	800	800
48	680	720	730	760	800	800	800
49	680	720	730	760	800	800	800

Chart for Self-Appraisal
Based on the Practice Test You Have Just Taken

The Self-Appraisal Chart below tells you quickly where your SAT strengths and weaknesses lie. Check or circle the appropriate box in accordance with the number of your correct answers for each area of the Practice Test you have just taken.

	Writing (Multiple-choice)	Sentence Completions	Reading Comprehension	Math Questions*
EXCELLENT	42–49	16–19	40–48	44–54
GOOD	37–41	13–15	35–39	32–43
FAIR	31–36	9–12	26–34	27–31
POOR	20–30	5–8	17–25	16–26
VERY POOR	0–19	0–4	0–16	0–15

* Sections 2, 6, 8 only.

Note: In our tests, we have chosen to have Section 3 as the experimental section. We have also chosen it to be a math section since we felt that students may need more practice in the math area than in the verbal area. Note that on the actual SAT you will take, the order of the sections can vary and you will not know which one is experimental, so it is wise to answer all sections and not to leave any section out.

SAT Verbal and Math Score/Percentile Conversion Table

Critical Reading and Writing

SAT scaled verbal score	Percentile rank
800	99.7+
790	99.5
740–780	99
700–730	97
670–690	95
640–660	91
610–630	85
580–600	77
550–570	68
510–540	57
480–500	46
440–470	32
410–430	21
380–400	13
340–370	6
300–330	2
230–290	1
200–220	0–0.5

Math

SAT scaled math score	Percentile rank
800	99.5+
770–790	99.5
720–760	99
670–710	97
640–660	94
610–630	89
590–600	84
560–580	77
530–550	68
510–520	59
480–500	48
450–470	37
430–440	26
390–420	16
350–380	8
310–340	2
210–300	0.5
200	0

Section 1: Essay

The following are guidelines
for scoring the essay.

The SAT Scoring Guide

Score of 6	Score of 5	Score of 4
An essay in this category is *outstanding,* demonstrating *clear and consistent mastery,* although it may have a few minor errors. A typical essay	An essay in this category is *effective,* demonstrating *reasonably consistent mastery,* although it will have occasional errors or lapses in quality. A typical essay	An essay in this category is *competent,* demonstrating *adequate mastery,* although it will have lapses in quality. A typical essay
• effectively and insightfully develops a point of view on the issue and demonstrates outstanding critical thinking, using clearly appropriate examples, reasons, and other evidence to support its position	• effectively develops a point of view on the issue and demonstrates strong critical thinking, generally using appropriate examples, reasons, and other evidence to support its position	• develops a point of view on the issue and demonstrates competent critical thinking, using adequate examples, reasons, and other evidence to support its position
• is well organized and clearly focused, demonstrating clear coherence and smooth progression of ideas	• is well organized and focused, demonstrating coherence and progression of ideas	• is generally organized and focused, demonstrating some coherence and progression of ideas
• exhibits skillful use of language, using a varied, accurate, and apt vocabulary	• exhibits facility in the use of language, using appropriate vocabulary	• exhibits adequate but inconsistent facility in the use of language, using generally appropriate vocabulary
• demonstrates meaningful variety in sentence structure	• demonstrates variety in sentence structure	• demonstrates some variety in sentence structure
• is free of most errors in grammar, usage, and mechanics	• is generally free of most errors in grammar, usage, and mechanics	• has some errors in grammar, usage, and mechanics
Score of 3	**Score of 2**	**Score of 1**
An essay in this category is *inadequate,* but demonstrates *developing mastery,* and is marked by ONE OR MORE of the following weaknesses:	An essay in this category is *seriously limited,* demonstrating *little mastery,* and is flawed by ONE OR MORE of the following weaknesses:	An essay in this category is *fundamentally lacking,* demonstrating *very little* or *no mastery,* and is severely flawed by ONE OR MORE of the following weaknesses:
• develops a point of view on the issue, demonstrating some critical thinking, but may do so inconsistently or use inadequate examples, reasons, or other evidence to support its position	• develops a point of view on the issue that is vague or seriously limited, demonstrating weak critical thinking, providing inappropriate or insufficient examples, reasons, or other evidence to support its position	• develops no viable point of view on the issue, or provides little or no evidence to support its position
• is limited in its organization or focus, or may demonstrate some lapses in coherence or progression of ideas	• is poorly organized and/or focused, or demonstrates serious problems with coherence or progression of ideas	• is disorganized or unfocused, resulting in a disjointed or incoherent essay
• displays developing facility in the use of language, but sometimes uses weak vocabulary or inappropriate word choice	• displays very little facility in the use of language, using very limited vocabulary or incorrect word choice	• displays fundamental errors in vocabulary
• lacks variety or demonstrates problems in sentence structure	• demonstrates frequent problems in sentence structure	• demonstrates severe flaws in sentence structure
• contains an accumulation of errors in grammar, usage, and mechanics	• contains errors in grammar, usage, and mechanics so serious that meaning is somewhat obscured	• contains pervasive errors in grammar, usage, or mechanics that persistently interfere with meaning

Essays not written on the essay assignment sheet will receive a score of zero.

Explanatory Answers for Practice Test

Section 2: Math

As you read these solutions, do the following if you answered the Math question incorrectly:

When a specific Strategy is referred to in the solution, study that strategy, which you will find in Regular Math Strategies (beginning on page 77).

1. Choice C is correct.

Given:

$$
\begin{array}{r}
59\Delta \\
- \ 293 \\
\hline \square 97
\end{array} \qquad \boxed{1}
$$

(Use Strategy: Use the given information effectively.)

From $\boxed{1}$ we see that $\Delta - 3 = 7$ $\qquad \boxed{2}$

From $\boxed{2}$ we get $\Delta = 10$ $\qquad \boxed{3}$

From $\boxed{1}$ and $\boxed{3}$ we get $\Delta = 0$ in $\boxed{1}$ and we had to borrow to get 10. Thus, we have

$$
\begin{array}{r}
8 \\
5\cancel{9}0 \\
- \ 293 \\
\hline \square 97
\end{array} \qquad \boxed{4}
$$

Calculating $\boxed{4}$, we get

$$
\begin{array}{r}
8 \\
5\cancel{9}0 \\
- \ 293 \\
\hline 297
\end{array}
$$

We see that the digit represented by the $\square$ is 2.

2. Choice E is correct.

Given: $\dfrac{a - b}{b} = \dfrac{1}{2}$ $\qquad \boxed{1}$

(Use Strategy: Find unknowns by multiplication.)

Multiply $\boxed{1}$ by $2b$. We have

$$
2b\left(\frac{a - b}{b}\right) = \left(\frac{1}{2}\right)2b
$$

$$
2(a - b) = b
$$

$$
2a - 2b = b
$$

$$
2a = 3b \qquad \boxed{2}
$$

(Use Strategy: Find unknowns by division.)

Dividing $\boxed{2}$ by $2b$, we get

$$
\frac{2a}{2b} = \frac{3b}{2b}
$$

$$
\frac{a}{b} = \frac{3}{2}
$$

3. Choice C is correct.

Number of pounds of force	Height object is raised
3	6 feet
6	12 feet
9	18 feet

1

(Use Strategy: Translate from words to algebra.)

We are given that:

height raised = c (force exerted)   2

Substituting 1 into 2, we get

$$6 = c(3)$$
$$2 = c$$ 3

Given: Height object is raised = 15 feet   4

Substituting 3 and 4 into 2, we have

$$15 = 2 \text{ (force exerted)}$$
$$7\frac{1}{2} = \text{force exerted}$$

4. Choice D is correct.

Given: $\frac{y}{3}, \frac{y}{4}, \frac{y}{7}$ are integers.   1

(Use Strategy: Use the given information effectively.)

If all items in 1 are integers, then 3, 4, and 7 divide y evenly (zero remainder). y must be a common multiple of 3, 4, and 7. Multiplying 3, 4, and 7 we get 84.

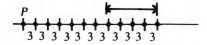

5. Choice D is correct. **(Use Strategy: Use new definitions carefully.)**

We are told that the points are each 3 units apart, as indicated above. We are looking for all those points that are more than 19 units away from point P. By checking the diagram we find 5 such points (marked with arrow in diagram).

6. Choice B is correct.

Given: 1

$(a + 2, a - 2) = [a]$ for all integers a.   2

We need to find (6,2)

(Use Strategy: Use new definitions carefully.)

Using 1 and 2 we have

$$a + 2 = 6 \qquad \text{and} \qquad a - 2 = 2$$
$$a = 4 \qquad\qquad\qquad a = 4 \qquad 3$$

Using 1, 2, and 3, we get

$$(6,2) = [4]$$

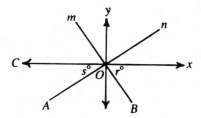

7. Choice D is correct.

Given: $m \perp n$ 1

From 1 we know that $\angle AOB$ is a right angle.

Thus $\angle AOB = 90°$ 2

From the diagram, we see that $\angle COx$ is a straight angle.
Thus $\angle COx = 180°$ 3

(Use Strategy: The whole equals the sum of its parts.)

We know that $\angle COA + \angle AOB + \angle BOx = \angle COx$ 4

Given: $\angle COA = s°$ 5

$\angle BOx = r°$ 6

Substituting 2, 3, 5, and 6 into 4, we get

$$s + 90 + r = 180$$
$$s + r = 90$$
$$r + s = 90$$

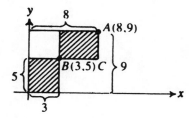

8. Choice D is correct. **(Use Strategy: Use the given information effectively.)**

From the given coordinates, we can find certain distances, as marked above.

Using these distances we find:

$$BC = 8 - 3 = 5 \qquad \boxed{1}$$

$$AC = 9 - 5 = 4 \qquad \boxed{2}$$

We know that Area of a rectangle = length $\times$ width $\qquad \boxed{3}$

Using the diagram and $\boxed{3}$ we have

$$\text{Area of lower rectangle} = 5 \times 3 = 15 \qquad \boxed{4}$$

Substituting $\boxed{1}$ and $\boxed{2}$ into $\boxed{3}$, we get

$$\text{Area of upper rectangle} = 5 \times 4 = 20 \qquad \boxed{5}$$

(Use Strategy: Find unknowns by addition.)

Adding $\boxed{4}$ and $\boxed{5}$ together, we get

$$\text{Total area} = 15 + 20 = 35$$

9. Choice B is correct.

Given: Total number of students = 2,800 $\qquad \boxed{1}$

(Use Strategy: Translate from words to algebra.)

$$\text{Number of German students} = \frac{1}{4} \times 2,800$$
$$= \frac{2,800}{4}$$
$$= 700 \qquad \boxed{2}$$

(Use Strategy: Find unknown by subtraction.)

Subtracting $\boxed{2}$ from $\boxed{1}$ we get

Number of students
not studying German =
$$2,800 - 700 =$$
$$2,100$$

10. Choice A is correct. **(Use Strategy: Translate from words to algebra.)**

Given:
cost per vehicle = \$y $\qquad \boxed{1}$

Let x = number of students paying \$0.40 $\qquad \boxed{2}$

Then $x + 6$ = number of students paying \$0.25 $\boxed{3}$

Using $\boxed{1}$, $\boxed{2}$, and $\boxed{3}$,

We are told that: $x(\$0.40) = \$y \qquad \boxed{4}$

$$(x + 6)(\$0.25) = \$y \qquad \boxed{5}$$

From $\boxed{4}$ and $\boxed{5}$ we get

$$x(\$0.40) = (x + 6)(\$0.25)$$
$$.40x = .25x + 1.50$$
$$.15x = 1.50$$
$$x = 10 \qquad \boxed{6}$$

Substitute $\boxed{6}$ into $\boxed{4}$. We have

$$10(\$0.40) = \$y$$
$$\$4.00 = y$$
$$\$4 = y$$

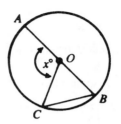

11. Choice C is correct.

Given: AB is a diameter $\qquad \boxed{1}$

O is the center of the circle $\qquad \boxed{2}$

$CB = OB \qquad \boxed{3}$

Using $\boxed{2}$, we know that OB and OC are radii $\boxed{4}$

From $\boxed{4}$ we get that $OB = OC$. $\qquad \boxed{5}$

Using $\boxed{3}$ and $\boxed{5}$ together, we have

$$OB = OC = CB \qquad \boxed{6}$$

(Use Strategy: Remember the equilateral triangle.)

From $\boxed{6}$, we have $\triangle OBC$ is equilateral $\qquad \boxed{7}$

From $\boxed{7}$, we get that $\angle B = \angle C =$

$\angle COB = 60° \qquad \boxed{8}$

From $\boxed{1}$, we get $\angle AOB$ is straight angle. $\boxed{9}$

From $\boxed{9}$, we have $\angle AOB = 180° \qquad \boxed{10}$

(Use Strategy: The whole equals the sum of its parts.)

From the diagram we see that:

$$\angle AOC + \angle COB = \angle AOB \qquad \boxed{11}$$

Given: $\angle AOC = x° \qquad \boxed{12}$

Substituting $\boxed{8}$, $\boxed{10}$, and $\boxed{12}$ into $\boxed{11}$, we get

$$x + 60 = 180$$
$$x = 120 \qquad \boxed{13}$$

(Use Strategy: Find unknowns by division.)

Divide $\boxed{13}$ by 6. We have

$$\frac{x}{6} = \frac{120}{6}$$
$$\frac{x}{6} = 20$$

12. Choice D is correct.

Given: Selling price of radio = $64 $\boxed{1}$

Regular price of radio = $80 $\boxed{2}$

(Use Strategy: Remember how to find percent discount.)

$$\text{Percent discount} = \frac{\text{Amount off}}{\text{original price}} \times 100 \qquad \boxed{3}$$

Subtracting $\boxed{1}$ from $\boxed{2}$, we get

Amount off = $80 − $64 = $16 $\boxed{4}$

Substituting $\boxed{2}$ and $\boxed{4}$ into $\boxed{3}$, we have

$$\text{Percent discount} = \frac{\$16}{\$80} \times 100$$
$$= \frac{\$16 \times 100}{\$80} \qquad \boxed{5}$$

(Use Strategy: Factor and reduce.)

$$\text{Percent discount} = \frac{\cancel{\$16} \times \cancel{5} \times 20}{\cancel{\$16} \times \cancel{5}}$$

Percent discount = 20 $\boxed{6}$

Given: Regular price of different radio = $200 $\boxed{7}$

New percent discount
$$= 1\frac{1}{2} \times \text{Other radio's percent discount} \qquad \boxed{8}$$

Using $\boxed{6}$ and $\boxed{8}$, we have

$$\text{New percent discount} = 1\frac{1}{2} \times 20 =$$
$$= \frac{3}{2} \times 20$$
$$= 30 \qquad \boxed{9}$$

(Use Strategy: Remember how to find percent of a number.)

We know percent of a number =
percent × number. $\boxed{10}$

Substituting $\boxed{7}$ and $\boxed{9}$ into $\boxed{10}$, we have

$$\text{Amount of discount} = 30\% \times \$200$$
$$= \frac{30}{100} \times \$200$$

Amount of discount = $60 $\boxed{11}$

(Use Strategy: Find unknowns by subtraction.)

Subtracting $\boxed{11}$ from $\boxed{7}$, we have

Selling price of different radio
= $200 − $60
= $140

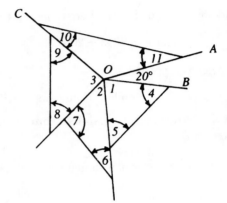

13. Choice A is correct.

Given: $\angle AOB = 20°$ $\boxed{1}$

(Use Strategy: The whole equals the sum of its parts.)

We know that the sum of the angles
of a triangle = 180° $\boxed{2}$

For each of the four triangles, applying $\boxed{2}$ yields:

$$\angle 8 + \angle 9 + \angle 3 = 180 \qquad \boxed{3}$$

$$\angle 6 + \angle 7 + \angle 2 = 180 \qquad \boxed{4}$$

$$\angle 4 + \angle 5 + \angle 1 = 180 \qquad \boxed{5}$$

$$\angle 10 + \angle 11 + \angle COA = 180 \qquad \boxed{6}$$

We know that the sum of all the angles about a point
= 360° $\boxed{7}$

Applying $\boxed{7}$ to point O, we have

$$\angle 1 + \angle 2 + \angle 3 + \angle COA + \angle AOB = 360° \qquad \boxed{8}$$

Substituting $\boxed{1}$ into $\boxed{8}$, we get

$$\angle 1 + \angle 2 + \angle 3 + \angle COA + 20 = 360$$
$$\angle 1 + \angle 2 + \angle 3 + \angle COA = 340 \qquad \boxed{9}$$

(Use Strategy: Find unknowns by addition.)

Adding $\boxed{3}$, $\boxed{4}$, $\boxed{5}$, and $\boxed{6}$, we have

$$\angle 4 + \angle 5 + \angle 6 + \angle 7 + \angle 8 + \angle 9 + \angle 10 +$$
$$\angle 11 + \angle 1 + \angle 2 + \angle 3 + \angle COA = 720° \qquad \boxed{10}$$

(Use Strategy: Find unknowns by subtraction.)

Subtracting $\boxed{9}$ from $\boxed{10}$, we get

$$\angle 4 + \angle 5 + \angle 6 + \angle 7 + \angle 8 +$$
$$\angle 9 + \angle 10 + \angle 11 = 380° \qquad \boxed{11}$$

Thus, the sum of the marked angles = 380°

14. Choice E is correct.

(Use Strategy: When all choices must be tested, start with choice E.) If some of the integers in the set are odd, then not all are even. Note the other choices are not correct. For (D), all integers cannot be even since some are odd. For (C), since *some* integers are odd we cannot imply that all integers are odd. For (B), if an integer is even, it may not be in set X. Similarly for (A) if an integer is odd, it may not be in set X.

15. Choice A is correct. Since the absolute value of $y + 3$ must be less than 3, y must be less than 0 but greater than -6.

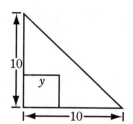

16. Choice E is correct.

We know that Area of a triangle

$$= \frac{1}{2} \times \text{base} \times \text{height} \qquad \boxed{1}$$

Use the diagram, and substituting into $\boxed{1}$, we get

$$\text{Area of triangle} = \frac{1}{2} \times 10 \times 10$$
$$= 50 \qquad \boxed{2}$$

(Use Strategy: Translate from words to algebra.)

We are told:

$$\text{Area of square} = \frac{1}{5} \times \text{Area of triangle} \qquad \boxed{3}$$

We know that

$$\text{Area of a square} = (\text{side})^2 \qquad \boxed{4}$$

Using the diagram, and substituting into $\boxed{4}$, we get

$$\text{Area of square} = y^2 \qquad \boxed{5}$$

Substituting $\boxed{2}$ and $\boxed{5}$ into $\boxed{3}$, we have

$$y^2 = \frac{1}{5} \times 50$$
$$y^2 = 10 \qquad \boxed{6}$$

Take the square root of both sides of $\boxed{6}$. We get

$$y = \sqrt{10}$$

17. Choice C is correct.

$$\text{Given:} \quad \text{Print rate} = \frac{80 \text{ characters}}{\text{second}} \qquad \boxed{1}$$

$$\frac{\text{Number of characters}}{\text{Page}} = 2400 \qquad \boxed{2}$$

(Use Strategy: Find unknowns by division.)

Dividing $\boxed{2}$ by $\boxed{1}$, we have

$$\frac{2,400 \text{ characters}}{\text{page}} \div \frac{80 \text{ characters}}{\text{second}} =$$

$$\frac{2,400 \text{ characters}}{\text{page}} \times \frac{\text{second}}{80 \text{ characters}} =$$

$$\frac{2,400 \text{ second}}{80 \text{ page}}$$

$$= \frac{30 \text{ seconds}}{\text{page}} \qquad \boxed{3}$$

The time for an *M*-page report will be

$$\frac{30 \text{ seconds}}{\text{page}} \times M \text{ pages} =$$

$$\text{Time for } M\text{-page report} = 30\,M \text{ seconds} \qquad \boxed{4}$$

(Use Strategy: Know how to use units.)

To change time from seconds to minutes we multiply

by $\dfrac{1 \text{ minute}}{60 \text{ seconds}}$. $\boxed{5}$

Applying $\boxed{5}$ to $\boxed{4}$, we get

Time for M-page report, in minutes $= 30M$ seconds $\times \dfrac{1 \text{ minute}}{60 \text{ seconds}}$

$= \dfrac{30\,M \text{ minutes}}{60}$

$= \dfrac{M}{2}$ minutes

18. Choice B is correct.

Given: On Friday, the satellite passed over Washington, D.C., at midnight $\boxed{1}$

Complete orbit = 5 hours $\boxed{2}$

(Use Strategy: Use the given information effectively.)

Using $\boxed{2}$, we see that five complete

orbits $= 5 \times 5 = 25$ hours $= 1$ day $+ 1$ hour $\boxed{3}$

From $\boxed{1}$ and $\boxed{2}$ we know that

DAY	TIME PASSING OVER D.C.	
Friday	7:00 P.M., midnight	$\boxed{4}$

Applying $\boxed{3}$ to $\boxed{4}$, and continuing this chart, we have

Saturday	8:00 P.M., 1:00 A.M.
Sunday	9:00 P.M., 2:00 A.M.
Monday	10:00 P.M., 3:00 A.M.
Tuesday	11:00 P.M., 4:00 A.M.
Wednesday	midnight, 5:00 A.M.

19. Choice D is correct. **(Use Strategy: Know how to find percent of a number.)**

Let x = price of car $\boxed{1}$

Given: 1st reduction = 30% $\boxed{2}$

2nd reduction = 40% $\boxed{3}$

We know amount of discount

$= $ percent $\times$ price $\boxed{4}$

Using $\boxed{1}$, $\boxed{2}$, and $\boxed{4}$, we get

Amount of 1st discount $= 30\% \times x$

$= .30x$ $\boxed{5}$

(Use Strategy: Find unknowns by subtraction.)

Subtracting $\boxed{5}$ from $\boxed{1}$, we have

Reduced price $= x - .30x$

$= .70x$ $\boxed{6}$

Using $\boxed{3}$, $\boxed{6}$, and $\boxed{4}$, we get

Amount of 2nd discount $= 40\% \times .70x$

$= .40 \times .70x$

$= .28x$ $\boxed{7}$

Subtracting $\boxed{7}$ from $\boxed{6}$, we have

Price after 2nd reduction $= .70x - .28x$

$= .42x$ $\boxed{8}$

(Use Strategy: The obvious may be tricky!)

Since $\boxed{8} = .42x$, it is 42% of the original price of x. This is *not* the answer to the question.

Since $\boxed{8}$ is 42% of the original it is the result of a 58% discount.

The answer is 58%.

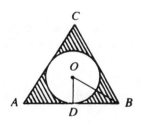

20. Choice A is correct.

Given: Diameter of circle = 2 $\boxed{1}$

(Use Strategy: Draw lines to help find the answer.)

Draw radius OD, with D the point of tangency and OB as shown above. $\boxed{2}$

(Use Strategy: Remember the equilateral triangle.)

Given: Triangle ACB is equilateral $\boxed{3}$

From $\boxed{2}$ we get $OD \perp AB$, since radius $\perp$ tangent at point of tangency. $\boxed{4}$

From $\boxed{4}$, we get $\angle ODB = 90°$ $\boxed{5}$

From $\boxed{3}$, we get $\angle ABC = 60°$ $\boxed{6}$

From the geometry of regular polygons, we know that OB bisects $\angle ABC$. [7]

From [6] and [7] we get $\angle DBO = 30°$ [8]

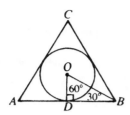

From [5] and [8] we have

$\triangle ODB$ is a 30–60–90 triangle

From [1], we get $OD = 1$ [9]

(Use Strategy: Remember the special right triangles.)

Using [9] and the properties of the 30–60–90 right triangle, we get

$OB = 2, DB = 1\sqrt{3} = \sqrt{3}$ [10]

We know $AB = 2 \times DB$ [11]

Substituting [10] into [11], we have

$$AB = 2\sqrt{3}$$ [12]

We know the Area of an equilateral triangle =

$$\frac{(\text{side})^2 \sqrt{3}}{4}$$ [13]

Substituting [12] into [13], we get

$$\text{Area of } \triangle ABC = \frac{(2\sqrt{3})^2 \sqrt{3}}{4}$$

$$= \frac{12\sqrt{3}}{4}$$

$$= 3\sqrt{3}$$ [14]

We know the Area of a circle $= \pi(\text{radius})^2$ [15]

Substituting [9] into [15], we get

$$\text{Area of circle O} = \pi(1)^2$$
$$= \pi$$ [16]

(Use Strategy: Find unknowns by subtraction.)

Subtracting [16] from [14], we get

Shaded area $= 3\sqrt{3} - \pi$

Section 3: Math

As you read these solutions, do the following if you answered the Math question incorrectly:

When a specific Strategy is referred to in the solution, study that strategy, which you will find in Regular Math Strategies (beginning on page 77).

1. Choice A is correct. **(Use Strategy: Translate from words to algebra.)**
Let x = Amount that Greg had to start.
Then $x + 5$ = Amount that Greg has after receiving $5 from David. ☐1

$$\$25 = \text{Amount David has.} \quad \boxed{2}$$

We are told that Greg now has $\frac{1}{5}$ as much as David does.
This translates to:

$$\text{Greg} = \frac{1}{5}(\text{David}) \quad \boxed{3}$$

Substituting $\boxed{1}$ and $\boxed{2}$ into $\boxed{3}$, we get

$$x + 5 = \frac{1}{5}(25)$$
$$x + 5 = \frac{1}{5} \times 5 \times \cancel{5}$$
$$x + 5 = 5$$
$$x = 0$$

2. Choice C is correct.
The ratio of the perimeter of the larger square to that of the smaller is

$$\frac{6+6+6+6}{2+2+2+2} = \frac{24}{8} = \frac{3}{1} \text{ or } 3:1$$

One can arrive at this result directly if one remembers that the ratio of the perimeters of two squares is the same as the ratio of the lengths of the sides of the two squares.

3. Choice E is correct. **(Use Strategy: Remember the rate, time, and distance relationship.)**
Remember that rate × time = distance

$$\text{or} \quad \text{average rate} = \frac{\text{total distance}}{\text{total time}}$$

$$\text{or} \quad \text{average rate} = \frac{1056 \text{ feet}}{12 \text{ seconds}}$$

$$= 88 \text{ feet/second}$$

4. Choice B is correct.
Given: $2z + 1 + 2 + 2z + 3 + 2z = 3 + 1 + 2$
(Use Strategy: Cancel numbers from both sides of an equation.)
We can immediately cancel the $+1$, $+2$, and $+3$ from each side.

$$\text{We get } 2z + 2z + 2z = 0$$
$$6z = 0$$
$$z = 0$$

Thus, $z + 4 = 0 + 4 = 4$

5. Choice B is correct.

$$2(w)(x)(-y) - 2(-w)(-x)(y) =$$
$$-2wxy - 2wxy =$$
$$-4wxy$$

6. Choice A is correct. **(Use Strategy: Translate from words to algebra.)**
The sum of the square of x and the square of y

$$x^2 \qquad + \qquad y^2$$

So, five times that quantity is

$$5(x^2 + y^2)$$

7. Choice C is correct. **(Use Strategy: Translate from words to algebra.)** We are given

$$p > 0 \qquad \boxed{1}$$
$$q > 0 \qquad \boxed{2}$$
$$x < 0 \qquad \boxed{3}$$
$$y < 0 \qquad \boxed{4}$$

(Use Strategy: Know how to manipulate inequalities.)

$$p > q \text{ or } q < p \qquad \boxed{5}$$
$$x > y \text{ or } y < x \qquad \boxed{6}$$

For I: Add $-p$ to both sides of inequality $\boxed{5}$:

$$q - p < 0$$

Thus, I is less than zero.

For II: From inequalities 2 and 4, $qy < 0$, and II is less than zero.

For III: The value of p and x depends on specific values of p and x:

(Use Strategy: Use numerics to help decide the answer.)

EXAMPLE 1

$$p = 3 \text{ and } x = -5$$

Thus, $\qquad p + x < 0$

EXAMPLE 2

$$p = 5 \text{ and } x = -3$$

Thus, $\qquad p + x > 0$

Thus, II is not always less than zero. Choice C is correct.

8. Choice A is correct.

Given: $\qquad a = 1, b = -2, c = -2 \qquad \boxed{1}$

$$\frac{b^2 c}{(a-c)^2} \qquad \boxed{2}$$

Substitute $\boxed{1}$ into $\boxed{2}$. We get

$$\frac{(-2)^2(-2)}{(1-(-2))^2} =$$

$$\frac{4(-2)}{(3)^2} =$$

$$\frac{-8}{9}$$

9. Choice A is correct.

Given: $\qquad y = 28j \qquad \boxed{1}$

$\qquad\qquad j$ is any integer $\qquad \boxed{2}$

(Use Strategy: Find unknowns by division.)

Divide $\boxed{1}$ by 2. We have

$$\frac{y}{2} = \frac{28j}{2}$$

$$\frac{y}{2} = 14j \qquad \boxed{3}$$

(Use Strategy: Factor.)

Factor the 14 in $\boxed{3}$. We get

$$\frac{y}{2} = (2)(7)(j) \qquad \boxed{4}$$

Using $\boxed{2}$ and $\boxed{4}$ we see that $\frac{y}{2}$ is an integer with a factor of 2.

Thus, $\frac{y}{2}$ is even.

10. Choice B is correct.

Given: $3a + 4b = 4a - 4b = 21 \qquad \boxed{1}$

From $\boxed{1}$, we get

$$3a + 4b = 21 \qquad \boxed{2}$$

$$4a - 4b = 21 \qquad \boxed{3}$$

(Use Strategy: Find unknowns by addition.)

Add $\boxed{2}$ and $\boxed{3}$ together. We get

$$\begin{aligned} 3a + \cancel{4b} &= 21 \\ + \quad 4a - \cancel{4b} &= 21 \\ \hline 7a \qquad\quad &= 42 \\ a \qquad\quad &= 6 \end{aligned}$$

11. Choice D is correct. **(Use Strategy: Translate from words to algebra.)**

$$N + 6N + 9N = 16N$$

Any divisor of 16 or of N will divide $16N$.

(Use Strategy 8: When all choices must be tested, start with Choice E and work backward.) Starting with Choice E, we see that 16 divides $16N$ evenly. Choice D, however, does *not* divide $16N$ evenly. Thus we have found the answer.

12. Choice D is correct.

We are given: $x = 3a - 18 \qquad \boxed{1}$

$\qquad\qquad\qquad\quad 5y = 3a + 7 \qquad \boxed{2}$

We need $5y - x$. $\qquad\qquad\qquad\quad \boxed{3}$

(Use Strategy: Find unknown expressions by subtracting equations.)

Subtracting $\boxed{1}$ from $\boxed{2}$, we get

$$\begin{aligned} 5y - x &= 3a + 7 - (3a - 18) \\ &= 3a + 7 - 3a + 18 \\ 5y - x &= 25 \end{aligned}$$

13. Choice B is correct. **(Use Strategy: Translate from words to algebra.)**

Given:

$$p + pq = 4(p - pq) \qquad \boxed{1}$$

(Use Strategy: Find unknown expressions by division.) Since $pq \neq 0$, divide 1 by p.

$$1 + q = 4(1 - q) \qquad \boxed{2}$$
$$\text{or} \quad 1 + q = 4 - 4q$$
$$\text{or} \quad 5q = 3$$
$$\text{or} \quad q = \frac{3}{5}$$

Thus, q has exactly one value.
Since p cannot be determined from equation $\boxed{1}$, none of the other choices is correct.

14. Choice D is correct. **(Use Strategy: Use the given information effectively.)**

Since $2 + \frac{1}{z} = 0$, we have

$$\frac{1}{z} = -2$$
$$z = -\frac{1}{2} \qquad \boxed{1}$$

We need $9 + 9z$ $\qquad \boxed{2}$

Substituting $\boxed{1}$ into $\boxed{2}$, we get

$$9 + 9\left(-\frac{1}{2}\right) = 9 - 4\frac{1}{2} = 4\frac{1}{2} = \frac{9}{2}$$

15. Choice C is correct. We set $y = x^2 = x$.
$x = 1$ or $x = 0$
Thus they intersect twice.

16. Choice C is correct.

$$\text{We are given: } wx = y \qquad \boxed{1}$$
$$\text{or } w = \frac{y}{x} \qquad \boxed{2}$$

(Use Strategy: Translate from words to algebra.) If x and y are multiplied by 6, in $\boxed{1}$, we have

$$w(6)(x) = (6)(y)$$
$$wx = y$$
$$w = \frac{y}{x} \qquad \boxed{3}$$

$\boxed{2}$ and $\boxed{3}$ are the same.

$$\text{Therefore } \frac{y}{x} = 1\left(\frac{y}{x}\right)$$

The answer is now clear.

17. Choice B is correct. **(Use Strategy: The whole equals the sum of its parts.)** The path is made up of 4 semicircles, three of diameter 4 and one of diameter 8.

[Remember circumference is $2\pi r$. Thus, $\frac{1}{2}$ circumference $= \frac{1}{2}(2\pi r)$.]

Therefore, the length of the path is

$$-\frac{1}{2}(2\pi)\left(\frac{4}{2}\right) + \frac{1}{2}(2\pi)\left(\frac{4}{2}\right) + \frac{1}{2}(2\pi)\left(\frac{4}{2}\right)$$
$$+ \frac{1}{2}(2\pi)\left(\frac{8}{2}\right)$$
$$= 10\pi$$

18. Choice C is correct. **(Use Strategy: Know how to use units.)**

$$\frac{7x}{144} \text{ yards} = \left(\frac{7x}{144} \text{ yards}\right)\left(\frac{36 \text{ inches}}{\text{yards}}\right) =$$

(Use Strategy: Factor and reduce.)

$$= \frac{7x}{12 \times 12} \times 12 \times 3 \text{ inches}$$
$$= \frac{7x}{3 \times 4} \times 3 \text{ inches}$$
$$\frac{7x}{144} \text{ yards} = \frac{7x}{4} \text{ inches} \qquad \boxed{1}$$
$$\frac{5y}{12} \text{ feet} = \left(\frac{5y}{12} \text{ feet}\right)\left(12 \frac{\text{inches}}{\text{foot}}\right) =$$
$$\frac{5y}{12} \text{ feet} = 5y \text{ inches} \qquad \boxed{2}$$

(Use Strategy: Find unknown expressions by addition of equations.) Adding $\boxed{1}$ and $\boxed{2}$, we have

$$\frac{7x}{144} \text{ yards} + \frac{5y}{12} \text{ feet} = \left(\frac{7x}{4} + 5y\right) \text{ inches}$$

19. Choice A is correct.

$$\text{Given: } x < 0 \qquad \boxed{1}$$
$$y < 0 \qquad \boxed{2}$$

(Use Strategy: Know how to manipulate inequalities.)

Multiply $\boxed{1}$ by $\boxed{2}$, we get

$$x \cdot y > 0 \qquad \boxed{3}$$

Thus I is always positive

Adding $\boxed{1}$ and $\boxed{2}$ we get

$$x + y < 0 \qquad \boxed{4}$$

Thus II is not positive
(Use Strategy: Use numerics to help find the answer.)

$$\text{Let } x = -2, y = -3$$
$$\text{III becomes } x - y = -2 - (-3)$$
$$= -2 + 3$$
$$= 1 \qquad \boxed{5}$$

Now let $x = -3$, $y = -2$

III becomes $x - y = -3 - (-2)$

$$= -3 + 2$$
$$= -1 \qquad \boxed{6}$$

From $\boxed{5}$ and $\boxed{6}$ we see that III is not always positive.

Using $\boxed{3}$, $\boxed{4}$ and $\boxed{7}$, we find that only Choice A, I only, is correct.

20. Choice D is correct.

Given: $a + 3b = 11 \qquad \boxed{1}$

a and b are positive integers $\qquad \boxed{2}$

(**Use Strategy: Use the given information effectively.**)

From $\boxed{1}$, we get

$$a = 11 - 3b \qquad \boxed{3}$$

From $\boxed{3}$ we see that a will be largest when b is smallest. Using $\boxed{2}$, we get

$$b = 1 \text{ is its smallest value} \qquad \boxed{4}$$

Substituting $\boxed{4}$ into $\boxed{3}$, we have

$$a = 11 - 3(1)$$
$$a = 11 - 3$$
$$a = 8$$

Section 4: Critical Reading

As you read these Explanatory Answers, refer to Sentence Completion Strategies (p. 21) or Reading Comprehension Strategies (p. 27) whenever a specific Strategy is referred to in the answer.

1. Choice E is correct. See **Sentence Completion Strategy.** Examine the first word of each choice. Choice (A) committees and Choice (B) tribes are incorrect because it is clear that committees and tribes cannot be equated with cities such as Athens. Now consider the other choices. Choice (E) societies . . participated is the only choice which has a word pair that makes sentence sense.

2. Choice C is correct. See **Sentence Completion Strategy.** Examine the first word of each choice. Choice (A) abolished and Choice (E) discounted do not make sense because we cannot say that fossils are abolished or discounted in rock formations. Now consider the other choices. Choice (C) preserved . . hardened is the only choice which has a word pair that makes sentence sense.

3. Choice B is correct. See **Sentence Completion Strategy.** Examine the first word of each choice. We eliminate Choice (A) dominated and Choice (D) cautioned because the trends do *not* dominate or caution affluence. Now consider the other choices. Choice (C) accentuated . . depression and Choice (E) accepted . . revolution do *not* make sentence sense. Choice (B) reflected . . prosperity *does* make sentence sense.

4. Choice A is correct. See **Sentence Completion Strategy.** The word "conserve" (meaning to "protect from loss") completes the sentence so that it makes good sense. The other choices don't do that.

5. Choice B is correct. See **Sentence Completion Strategy.** The word "prevalent" (meaning widely or commonly occurring) completed the sentence so that it makes good sense. The other choices don't do that.

6. Choice B is correct. Since this question has two blank choices, let us use **Sentence Completion Strategy.** Consider *both* words of each choice and the meaning they give to the sentence. When we do so, we find that only Choice (B) control . . foolishly makes good sentence sense.

7. Choice B is correct. See **Sentence Completion Strategy.** "Because" is a *result indicator*. Since the generating system was not functioning efficiently, the use of electricity had to be *diminished* or *curtailed*.

8. Choice B is correct. See **Sentence Completion Strategy.** Something staple, such as bread, is in constant supply and demand. Beer, then, is considered a liquid bread by the Bavarians. Choices A, C, D, and E do not make good sense in the sentence.

9. Choice D is correct. One can see from the gist of the whole passage that the author is warning the reader of the dangers of anarchy and war. See line 4: "It is the age of war" and the need for "the age of civilized man" (line 5). Thus Choice D would be best.

10. Choice A is correct. See lines 8–10 where the author says that "It calls for total awareness, total commitment" indicating limited hope.

11. Choice B is correct. It can be seen that the author contrasts novel reading in the past with novel reading in the present throughout the passage. Although the author does mention a "defect in today's novels" (choice A), that is not the main consideration in the passage.

12. Choice E is correct. See lines 2–6: "there were few diversions . . . not irritated by the digressions and irrelevances. . . ." Do not be lured into Choice B: Although some great novels are long, not all are.

13. Choice B is correct. See paragraph 2: "Most social scientists . . . have assumed that the minimum economic needs of the aged should be lower than those of the younger family."

14. Choice E is correct. Given the context of the sentence and the next sentence, Choice E is the best.

15. Choice A is correct. See paragraph 5: "[The data] disclose sharp income inequalities within every age group . . ."

16. Choice E is correct. For I, see paragraph 6: "Those sixty-five and over are expected to increase 672 percent." For III, see paragraph 4: "For the growing, working-class family, limited in income by the very nature of the breadwinner's occupation . . ."

17. Choice C is correct. See paragraph 2: The sentence after the "functional ethos" sentence refers to "these values."

18. Choice D is correct. See paragraph 6: "With the more rapid expansion of these two low-income groups, the young and the old . . ."

19. Choice D is correct. For I, see paragraph 5: "A spending unit's income-tenth position *within his age category* varies much less, if at all, and is determined primarily by his occupation." For III, see paragraph 4: "For the growing working-class family, limited in income by the very nature of the breadwinner's occupation . . ."

20. Choice A is correct. From the context of the sentence, it can be seen that Choice A is the best.

21. Choice C is correct. See paragraph 3: "Despite his seniority, the older worker is likely to be downgraded to a lower-paying job . . ."

22. Choice C is correct. See paragraph 4: "The early and lower income period of a person's working life, during which he acquires his basic vocational skills . . ."

23. Choice C is correct. See paragraph 5: "A spending unit's income-tenth position is . . . determined primarily by his occupation."

24. Choice D is correct. The phrase "the legendary land of economic opportunity where any man can work his way to the top" (lines 86–88), in contrast to what the author really believes, represents *sarcasm*.

Section 5: Writing

1. **(C)** Choice A is awkward and wordy. Choice B is indirect. Choice C is correct. Choice D is unacceptable idiomatically even though the meaning intended is there. Choice E changes the meaning of the original sentence.

2. **(D)** Choice A has incorrect punctuation. A dash (not a comma) is required after "that's not all." In Choice B, the expression "another thing" is too general. Choice C changes the meaning of the original sentence. Choice D is correct. Choice E is too indirectly expressed.

3. **(E)** Choice A suffers from too many "ands" (and-itis). Choice B and C are incorrect because they lack parallel construction. In Choice D, the correct form of the infinitive meaning "to rest" is "(to) lie"—not "(to) lay." Choice E is correct.

4. **(B)** Choice A is awkward. Choice B is correct. Choice C is ungrammatical—"courses" cannot act as a direct object after the copulative construction "am not certain." Choice D is too wordy. Choice E does not make sense.

5. **(A)** Choice A is correct. Choice B is too indirectly stated. Choice C is verbose—since the people "had no doubt," there is no need to use the expression "it was clear." Choice D is indirect and awkward. Choice E changes the meaning of the original sentence.

6. **(B)** Choice A is too wordy. Choice B is correct. Choice C is indirectly stated. Choices D and E change the meaning of the original sentence.

7. **(D)** Choice A is indirectly stated. Choice B deviates from the original statement. Choice C makes the whole sentence run-on. Choice D is correct. Choice E changes the meaning of the original sentence.

8. **(E)** Choice A is awkward. Choice B has a meaning which differs from that of the original sentence. Choices C and D are unidiomatic. Choice E is correct.

9. **(D)** The clause "that was rotten" is misplaced in Choices A, B, and C. Choice D is correct. Choice E is incorrect because the passive use of the verb is not as effective as the active use, in this context.

10. **(B)** Choice A uses wrong tense sequence. Since the reading of the book took place before the watching of the picture, the reading should be expressed in the past perfect tense, which shows action prior to the simple past tense. Choice B corrects the error with the use of the past perfect tense, "had read," instead of the past tense, "read." Choices C, D, and E do not correct the mistake, and Choice E in addition changes the meaning.

11. **(D)** Choice A is wrong because the word "them," being plural, cannot properly take the singular antecedent, "anyone." Choices B and C do not correct this error. Choice D corrects it by substituting "him" for "them." Choice E, while correcting the error, changes the meaning of the sentence.

12. **(D)** "... between *him* and *me*."
The object of the preposition *between* must be an objective case form (*me*—not *I*).

13. **(E)** All underlined parts are correct.

14. **(A)** "The subject ... was *we* ..."
The predicate nominative form is *we*—not *us*.

15. **(B)** "... the prize would go to him ..."
The object of the preposition *to* must be an objective case form (*him*—not he).

16. **(E)** All underlined parts are correct.

17. **(B)** "... if you *had gone to him* ..."
In the "if clause" of a past contrary-to-fact, condition, one must use the past perfect subjunctive form *had gone*—not the future perfect subjunctive form *would have gone*.

18. **(A)** "The *child's* asking ..."
The subject of a gerund is in the possessive case. We, therefore, say *child's asking*—not *child asking*.

19. **(E)** All underlined parts are correct.

20. **(D)** "... who are younger than *she*."
The nominative case (*she*—not *her*) must be used after the conjunction *than* when the pronoun is the subject of an elliptical clause ("than she is").

21. **(E)** All underlined parts are correct.

22. **(A)** "The novelists *whom* readers choose . . ."
The direct object of the verb (choose) must be the objective case form (*whom*—not *who*).

23. **(C)** "The problem . . . disturbs . . ."
The subject (*problem*) is singular. Therefore the verb (*disturbs*) must be singular.

24. **(B)** ". . . son *could have* gone . . ."
The phrase *could of* is always considered substandard. Do not use *of* for *have*.

25. **(D)** ". . . the horse *which* had fallen . . ."
The pronoun *which* should be used to refer to animals and things; *who* should be used to refer only to people.

26. **(D)** ". . . then *he* should make . . ."
A pronoun must agree with its antecedent (*someone*) in number. Since *someone* is singular, the pronoun must be singular (*he*—not *they*).

27. **(A)** "The man *whom* Mexican authorities believe to be . . ."
The subject of an infinitive must be in the objective case. The pronoun "whom" in the objective case—not "who" in the nominative case—is the subject of the verbal infinitive "to be."

28. **(C)** ". . . the child fell *off* the unscreened porch."
The correct preposition is simply "off"—not "off of"—to introduce a noun or pronoun.

29. **(A)** ". . . ran *more swiftly* . . ."
We must use an adverb—not an adjective—to modify a verb. Therefore, we use the adverbial comparative construction "more swiftly" instead of the comparative adjective "swifter" to modify the verb "ran."

30. **(D)** Choice A is incorrect because ending the sentence after company would destroy the charming contrasting idea which follows. Choice B is incorrect because sentence 3 clearly interrupts the flow of thought between sentences 2 and 4. Choice C is incorrect because sentence 3 relates closely in structure and content to sentence 1, especially in the reference to the caves of France, and should follow sentence 1. Choice D is correct. Choice E is incorrect because the explanation for Lampe-Pigeon which now introduces the passage is the best opening sentence. Sentence 3 clearly needs prior information to explain its references to the lamp and to the caves of France.

31. **(C)** Choices A and D are incorrect because they create a contradictory impression by equating tall with nine and one-half inches, even though Choice D is preferable because it is more concise. Choice B is incorrect because it conveys an unwarranted apologetic note for the height of the lamp by using the conjunction although. Choice C is correct because it concisely and clearly describes the height and type of lamp being described. Choice E is incorrect because it is wordy and therefore awkward.

32. **(A)** Choice A is correct because the simple prepositional phrase is preferable to the more awkward gerund form of the incorrect Choice B. Choice C is incorrect because it is too wordy and awkward. Choice D, in addition to being the above-mentioned more awkward gerund form, is incorrect also because of the inappropriate use of the preposition to after the adjective suitable. Choice E is incorrect because it is overly long and also would create an inappropriate repetition with the word centerpiece which is used in the next phrase.

33. **(B)** Choice A is incorrect because glass globed is an awkward descriptive phrase. Choice B is correct because it is more concise than the repetitive clause which contains within it a glass globe. Choice C is incorrect and completely changes the focus of the sentence from the lamp to the globe. Choice D is incorrect because it is wordy and repetitive, and Choice C is incorrect because it is too verbose.

34. **(B)** Sentence 6 contradicts and is not consistent with the paragraph and should be deleted. It would also make no sense to include that sentence in any other part of the paragraph.

35. **(D)** Since the author of the paragraph wants to show the beauty of the Lampe-Pigeon, he would contrast that lamp with the modern lamps and use the word "but" not "and." For choice A, "manufactured" is appropriate and it is not necessary to change the word to "produced." For Choice B, "Lampe-Pigeon" sounds better than "lamp in question." After all, this is not a legal document! For Choice C, "modernization" would contradict the antiquity of the lamp.

Section 6: Math

As you read these solutions, do the following if you answered the Math question incorrectly:

When a specific Strategy is referred to in the solution, study that strategy, which you will find in Regular Math Strategies (beginning on page 77).

1. Choice E is correct. Subtract 14 from both sides of the equation:

$5\sqrt{x} + 14 = 20$

$5\sqrt{x} = 6$

Divide by 5:

$\sqrt{x} = 6/5$

Square both sides:

$x = 36/25$

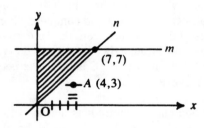

2. Choice A is correct. **(Use Strategy: Use the given information effectively.)** Since n goes through point O, the origin, whose coordinates are $(0,0)$, and through $(7,7)$, all of the points on n have the same x and y coordinates. Choice A, $(4,3)$, is 4 units to the right of O but only 3 units up. It is below n and not in the shaded area.

3. Choice B is correct. **(Use Strategy: Translate from words to algebra.)** This problem tests the concepts of set union and set intersection. We can solve these types of problems with a diagram. Let

c = set of all calculus students
p = set of all physics students

Thus, draw the diagram:

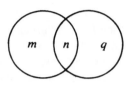

Where

    m = number of students taking *only* calculus
    q = number of students taking *only* physics
    n = number of students taking *both* calculus and physics

Thus,

    $m + n$ = number of students in calculus class
    $n + q$ = number of students in physics class
$m + n + q$ = number of students taking either calculus or physics or both

We are given that

$$m + n + q = 36 \quad \boxed{1}$$
$$n = 10 \quad \boxed{2}$$
$$m + n = 31 \quad \boxed{3}$$

We want to find

$$n + q \quad \boxed{4}$$

(Use Strategy: Find unknowns by subtracting equations.) Subtract equation $\boxed{2}$ from equation $\boxed{3}$ to get

$$m = 21 \quad \boxed{5}$$

Now subtract equation $\boxed{5}$ from equation $\boxed{1}$ to get

$$n + q = 15$$

4. Choice D is correct. In order to show a counterexample to refute Mr. Simmons' argument, we must come up with two numbers a and b such that $a^2 > b^2$ but that a is not greater than b. Choice A is incorrect since it is not true that $a^2 > b^2$ in this case. Choice B is incorrect since it is true that $a^2 > b^2$ and that $a > b$.

Choice C is incorrect because $a^2 > b^2$ and $a > b$. Choice D is correct: a^2 is greater than b^2 since $(-4)^2 > (-2)^2$. But it is not true that $a > b$ since -4 is *not* greater than -2.

5. Choice E is correct. **(Use Strategy: Use specific numerical examples to prove or disprove your guess.)**

$$\sqrt{2+2} \neq \sqrt{2} + \sqrt{2}$$
$$2^2 + 2^2 \neq (2+2)^2$$
$$2^1 + 2^2 \neq 2^{1+2}$$

Therefore, neither (I) nor (II) nor (III) is generally true.

6. Choice B is correct. The only element common to R and S is $x = 1$.

7. Choice A is correct. To find the coordinates of the intersection point, we must first solve the equations $y = x - 1$ and $2x + 5y = 9$. In the equation $2x + 5y = 9$, we substitute $y = x - 1$. We obtain

$$2x + 5(x - 1) = 9$$

Thus

$$2x + 5x - 5 = 9$$

and

$$7x = 14$$
$$x = 2$$

From the first equation, $y = x - 1$ so, $y = 2 - 1 = 1$. Thus $x = 2$ and $y = 1$ so the coordinates of the point are (2,1).

8. Choice D is correct. **(Use Strategy: The whole equals the sum of its parts.)**

Volume of rectangular solid
= Volume of small compartment
+ Volume of larger compartment   ☐1
    Area of rectangular dividing wall
    $= l \times w$
$39\text{cm}^2 = 13\text{cm} \times w$
$3cm = w$

☐2 is the height of the rectangular solid as well.

Volume of rectangular solid $= l \times w \times h$
$= 15\text{cm} \times 12\text{cm} \times h$ ☐3

Substituting ☐2 into ☐3, we get

Volume of rectangular solid =
$15\text{cm} \times 12\text{cm} \times 3\text{cm}$
Volume of rectangular solid $= 540\text{cm}^3$ ☐4

Volume of small compartment
= Area of base × height
$= \dfrac{1}{2} \times 12\text{cm} \times 5\text{cm} \times 3\text{cm}$ ☐5

Volume of small compartment = 90 cm^3

Substitute ☐4 and ☐5 into ☐1. We get

$540\text{cm}^3 = 90\text{cm}^3 +$ Volume of larger compartment
$450\text{cm}^3 =$ Volume of larger compartment

9. $\dfrac{7}{18}$ or .388 or .389

(Use Strategy: Simplify by cancelling.)

$$\left(\frac{1}{2} - \frac{1}{3}\right) + \left(\frac{1}{3} - \frac{1}{4}\right) + \left(\frac{1}{4} - \frac{1}{5}\right) +$$

$$\left(\frac{1}{5} - \frac{1}{6}\right) + \left(\frac{1}{6} - \frac{1}{7}\right) + \left(\frac{1}{7} - \frac{1}{8}\right) +$$

$$\left(\frac{1}{8} - \frac{1}{9}\right) =$$

$$\frac{1}{2} + \left(-\frac{1}{3} + \frac{1}{3}\right) + \left(-\frac{1}{4} + \frac{1}{4}\right) +$$

$$\left(-\frac{1}{5} + \frac{1}{5}\right) + \left(-\frac{1}{6} + \frac{1}{6}\right) + \left(-\frac{1}{7} + \frac{1}{7}\right) +$$

$$\left(-\frac{1}{8} + \frac{1}{8}\right) - \frac{1}{9} =$$

$$\frac{1}{2} + 0 + 0 + 0 + 0 + 0 + 0 - \frac{1}{9} =$$

$$\frac{1}{2} - \frac{1}{9} =$$

$$\frac{9}{18} - \frac{2}{18} =$$

$$\frac{7}{18}$$

10. **8**

(Use Strategy: Use new definitions carefully.)
The first five elements of the series, calculated by the definition, are

$$1, 2, 2, 4, 8$$

11. $\dfrac{2}{3}$ or .667 or .666

(Use Strategy: Translate from words to algebra.)

$$p = \frac{3}{5}m \qquad \boxed{1}$$

$$q = \frac{9}{10}m \qquad \boxed{2}$$

(Use Strategy: Find unknowns by division of equations.)

Thus, $\dfrac{p}{q} = \dfrac{\dfrac{3}{5}\not{m}}{\dfrac{9}{10}\not{m}}$

$= \dfrac{\dfrac{3}{5}}{\dfrac{9}{10}}$

$= \dfrac{3}{5} \times \dfrac{10}{9} = \dfrac{3}{\underset{1}{\not{5}}} \times \dfrac{\overset{2}{\not{10}}}{\underset{3}{\not{9}}}$

$\dfrac{p}{q} = \dfrac{2}{3}$

12. 60

(Use Strategy:

$$\text{Average} = \frac{\text{sum of values}}{\text{total number of values}}\bigg)$$

Given: $\dfrac{40 + 40 + 40 + z}{4} = 45$ $\boxed{1}$

Multiplying $\boxed{1}$ by 4,

$$40 + 40 + 40 + z = 180$$
$$120 + z = 180$$
$$z = 60$$

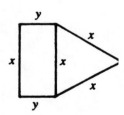

13. 36

(Use Strategy: Translate from words to algebra.) When the given diagram has been labeled as above, then we know

$$3x = 39 \qquad \boxed{1}$$
$$xy = 65 \qquad \boxed{2}$$

From $\boxed{1}$ we have

$$x = 13 \qquad \boxed{3}$$

Substituting $\boxed{3}$ into $\boxed{2}$, we have

$$13y = 65$$
$$\text{or} \quad y = 5 \qquad \boxed{4}$$

The perimeter of the rectangle

$$= 2x + 2y$$
$$= 2(13) + 2(5)$$
$$= 36$$

14. 44

(Use Strategy: Use the given information effectively.)

Game		Darrin	Tom
1		69	43
2		59	60
3		72	55
4		70	68
5		78	73
Totals		348	299

We need the scores at the end of the first four games. We have been given the totals for all five games.

(Use Strategy: Find unknowns by subtraction.)

Darrin's Total = 348 $\boxed{1}$
Darrin's Game 5 = 78 $\boxed{2}$
Tom's Total = 299 $\boxed{3}$
Tom's Game 5 = 73 $\boxed{4}$

Subtract $\boxed{2}$ from $\boxed{1}$. We get

Darrin's Total for 1st four games = 348 − 78
$= 270$ $\boxed{5}$

Subtract $\boxed{4}$ from $\boxed{3}$. We get

Tom's total for 1st four games $= 299 - 73$
$= 226$ $\boxed{6}$

Subtracting $\boxed{6}$ from $\boxed{5}$, we have

Number of points Tom was behind Darrin after the first four games $= 270 - 226$
$= 44$

15. Choice $\dfrac{1}{4}$ or .25

(Use Strategy: Use the given information effectively.)

The 17 slips, numbered from 1 to 17, consist of $\boxed{1}$

8 even numbers (2,4,6, . . . 16) and $\boxed{2}$

9 odd numbers (1,3,5, . . . 17). $\boxed{3}$

Subtracting 5 even-numbered slips from $\boxed{2}$ leaves

$8 - 5 = 3$ even-numbered slips. $\boxed{4}$

Adding $\boxed{3}$ and $\boxed{4}$ we have

$$9 + 3 = 12 \text{ slips remaining} \qquad \boxed{5}$$

We need $\dfrac{\text{even-numbered slips}}{\text{total numbered slips}}$ $\boxed{6}$

Substituting $\boxed{4}$ and $\boxed{5}$ into $\boxed{6}$, we have

$$\frac{3}{12} = \frac{1}{4}$$

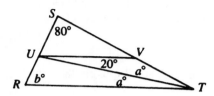

16. 60

Given: $\quad UV \parallel RT$ $\qquad \boxed{1}$

From $\boxed{1}$ we get $a = 20$, since alternate interior

angles are equal $\qquad \boxed{2}$

(Use Strategy: The whole equals the sum of its parts.) From the diagram we see that

$$\angle STR = a + a \qquad \boxed{3}$$

Substituting $\boxed{2}$ into $\boxed{3}$, we have

$$\angle STR = 20 + 20 = 40 \qquad \boxed{4}$$

We know that the sum of the angles in a triangle = 180, thus

$$\angle R + \angle S + \angle STR = 180 \qquad \boxed{5}$$

We are given, in the diagram, that

$$\angle R = b \qquad \boxed{6}$$
$$\angle S = 80$$
$$\boxed{7}$$

Substituting $\boxed{6}$, $\boxed{7}$ and $\boxed{4}$ into $\boxed{5}$, we get

$$b + 80 + 40 = 180$$
$$b + 120 = 180$$
$$b = 60$$

17. 10

(Use Strategy: Translate from words to algebra.)

Given: $\quad$ Rose's earnings = \$44 $\qquad \boxed{1}$
$\qquad\qquad$ Rose's time worked = 8 days $\boxed{2}$

(Use Strategy: Find unknowns by division.)

Dividing $\boxed{1}$ by $\boxed{2}$, we have

$$\text{Rose's daily rate} = \frac{\$44}{8 \text{ days}}$$

$$\text{Rose's daily rate} = \frac{\$11}{2 \text{ days}} \qquad \boxed{3}$$

Given: Total earnings to equal \$99 $\qquad \boxed{4}$

Substituting $\boxed{1}$ from $\boxed{4}$, we get

Amount left to be earned = \$55 $\qquad \boxed{5}$
We know
(daily rate)(days worked) = money earned $\qquad \boxed{6}$

Substituting $\boxed{3}$ and $\boxed{5}$ into $\boxed{6}$, we get

$$\left(\frac{\$11}{2 \text{ days}}\right)(\text{days worked}) = \$55$$

Multiplying $\boxed{7}$ by $\dfrac{2}{11}$ days, we have

$$\frac{2 \cancel{\text{days}}}{\cancel{11}}\left(\frac{\cancel{11}}{2 \cancel{\text{days}}}\right)(\text{days worked}) = (\cancel{55})^{5}\frac{2}{\cancel{11}} \text{ days}$$

$$\text{days worked} = 10 \text{ days}$$

18. 48

Given: $\quad$ Areas of all 12 triangles are the same $\boxed{1}$
$\qquad\qquad$ Area of outlined region = 256 $\qquad \boxed{2}$
$\qquad\qquad$ Area of square $ABCD$ = 128 $\qquad \boxed{3}$

(Use Strategy: The whole equals the sum of the parts.)

By looking at the diagram, we observe

Area of 8 triangles (I, II, ... , VIII) = Area of Outlined Region − Area of Square $ABCD$.
Substituting $\boxed{2}$ and $\boxed{3}$ into the above, we get

Area of 8 triangles (I, ... , VIII)

$$= 256 - 128$$
$$= 128 \qquad \boxed{4}$$

Using $\boxed{1}$, we get

Area of each of the 12 triangles =

$$\frac{\text{Area of 8 triangles}}{8}$$

Substituting $\boxed{4}$ into the above, we get

Area of each of the 12 triangles = $\dfrac{128}{8}$

Area of each of the 12 triangles = 16 $\qquad \boxed{5}$

(Use Strategy: The whole equals the sum of its parts.)

Shaded Area = Area ΔV + Area ΔVI +
Area ΔXI $\qquad \boxed{6}$

Substituting $\boxed{1}$ and $\boxed{5}$ into $\boxed{6}$, we get

Shaded Area = 16 + 16 + 16 = 48

Section 7: Critical Reading

As you read these Explanatory Answers, refer to the sentence completion strategies or Critical Reading Strategies (beginning on page 7) whenever a specific Strategy is referred to in the answer.

Note: All Reading questions use Reading Comprehension Strategies 1, 2, and 3 (pp. 27–32) as well as other strategies indicated.

1. Choice D is correct. See **Sentence Completion Strategy.** The word "extreme" is the most appropriate among the five choices because the forest fire season is in *full swing.* The other choices are, therefore, not appropriate.

2. Choice A is correct. See **Sentence Completion Strategy.** Examine the first words of each choice. We eliminate Choice (C) imagined and Choice (E) intuitive. Reason: The effect of the long war was *not* imagined or intuitive (meaning knowing by a hidden sense). Now we consider Choice (B) immediate . . staring and Choice (D) delayed . . rebuilding. Neither word pair makes sense in the sentence. Choice (A) cumulative . . corrosion *does* make sense in the sentence.

3. Choice E is correct. See **Sentence Completion Strategy.** If you had tried to complete the sentence *before* looking at the five choices, you might have come up with any of the following words meaning "continually" or "regularly": constantly, always, perpetually, persistently, habitually.

   The other choices are, therefore, incorrect.

4. Choice E is correct. See **Sentence Completion Strategy.** Examine the first word of each choice. Choice (D) crushes is eliminated because it is not likely that the bee will crush the nectar from different flowers. Now consider each pair of words in the other choices. We find that Choice (E) extracts . . converts has the only word pair that makes sense in the sentence.

5. Choice D is correct. See **Sentence Completion Strategy.** The plan turned out to be impractical, unable to be logically supported. Note the root "ten" *to hold*, so "untenable" means *not holding.* Also note that the word "since" in the sentence is a *result indicator.*

6. Choice C is correct. In lines 8–11, the author is showing that through the "weedy falsities," truth can be created.

7. Choice C is correct. See the last lines 15–18 . . . "we can feel all the poverty, despair, and unfairness in our world . . ." For choice A, there may be value for the spectator: see lines 14–15 "and perhaps how we should change them."

8. Choice E is correct. See lines 8–11, 13–15, and 15–18. This describes how something positive can come out from something negative. In Choice A, although specific references (lines 4 and 5) are made, there are no specific references in Paragraph 2. In Choice B, there is no indication of both being completely objective, especially in Paragraph 1 line 1 where the author states that the theater is the "most preposterous of all." Choice C is incorrect in that in Paragraph 1, the author certainly does not believe in the accuracy of the time (16th century) whereas in Paragraph 2, the author does believe in the accuracy of the time. Choice D is incorrect in that it appears that the intensity and passion of the author's arguments in Paragraph 1 is far greater than that of the author's in Paragraph 2.

9. Choice D is correct. In lines 8, 9 note the words "lily" (a flower) and "jungle" (a place), which are used as analogies. We do not see such analogies in Paragraph 2. In Choice A, both authors would disagree as the author in Paragraph 1 states that theater is fiction, not reality, and the author in Paragraph 2 states that the theater is real. In Choice B, see line 5: "the much admired Miss Huckaby." In Choice C, in lines 7–8, the author is sarcastic when he says that "people were ever so marvelously articulate." In Choice E, see lines 13–14: the author believes the contrary, that the theater is quite realistic.

10. Choice A is correct. See lines 42–44: "The fundamental fact . . . in their environment." Choices B, D, and E are incorrect because the passage does not indicate that these statements are true. Choice C is incorrect because it is only partially true. The passage does not state that *all* animals and plants are successful in adjusting themselves to changes in their environments.

11. Choice E is correct. See lines 4–7: "Originally the term *acclimatization* . . . altered temperature." Also see lines 9–12: "But aside from temperature . . . originally accustomed to." Choices A, B, C, and D are incorrect because one *cannot* infer from the passage what any of these choices state.

12. Choice A is correct. Acclimatization and adaptation are both forms of adjustment. Accordingly, these two processes are similar. The difference between the two terms, however, is brought out in lines 32–36: "By and large . . . as 'adaptation.'" Choice D is incorrect because the passage does not indicate what is expressed in Choice D. See lines 29–32: "Let us define acclimatization . . . lethal for it." Choices B, C, and E are incorrect because the passage does not indicate that any of these choices are true.

13. Choice D is correct. A person going from daylight into a darkened room is an example of adaptation—not acclimatization. See lines 32–36: "By and large . . . as 'adaptation.'" Choices A, B, C, and E all require the process of acclimatization. Therefore, they are incorrect choices. An ocean fish placed in a lake (Choice A) is a chemical change. Choices B, C, and E are all pressure changes. Acclimatization, by definition, deals with chemical and pressure changes.

14. Choice B is correct. Given the context in the sentence, Choice B is the best.

15. Choice B is correct. See lines 33–36: "The term [acclimatization] should not be taken . . . as 'adaptation.'" Choices A, D, and E are incorrect because the passage does not indicate that these choices are true. Choice C is partially correct in that acclimatization does apply to adjustments, but

the choice is incorrect because adaptation also applies to adjustments. See lines 35–36: "This type of adjustment . . . as 'adaptation.'"

16. Choice E is correct. See paragraph 2 (beginning): "The tie which bound this world-embracing empire together . . . was as much cultural as political."

17. Choice A is correct. See paragraph 1 (end): "Centuries of training had bred in them the conviction that all other rulers should be tributary to the Son of Heaven."

18. Choice B is correct. See the last paragraph about the close relationship between "ethical standards" and "Confucian patterns."

19. Choice C is correct. The reader should infer from paragraphs 3 and 4 that Han and T'ang were dynasties—just as there was a Manchu dynasty.

20. Choice D is correct. The passage points out that since more emphasis was placed on being members of the same culture, rather than on being members of the same race, there was a "comparative contentment of Chinese under alien rulers" (paragraph 4: beginning).

21. Choice B is correct. See paragraph 5 (middle): "In contrast with India, where caste and religion have tended to keep apart the racial strata, in China assimilation made great progress."

22. Choice B is correct. Paragraph 4 (end) points out that the Manchus never gave up some of their ancestral ways, and this disturbed segments of the population.

23. Choice A is correct. The passage states that assimilation made great progress in China. (See the answer to question 21.)

24. Choice C is correct. From the context of the sentence and the sentence before and after it, it can be seen that "restiveness" must mean impatience or restlessness.

Section 8: Math

As you read these solutions, do the following if you answered the Math question incorrectly:

When a specific Strategy is referred to in the solution, study that strategy, which you will find in Regular Math Strategies (beginning on page 77).

1. Choice C is correct. **(Use Strategy: Translate from words to algebra.)** The key is to be able to translate English sentences into mathematical equations.
Let p = price of one frying pan
m = price of one coffee mug
We are given

$$p + 2m = \$27 \qquad \boxed{1}$$
$$p + m = \$23 \qquad \boxed{2}$$

Subtract equation $\boxed{2}$ from equation $\boxed{1}$ to get

$$m = \$4 \qquad \boxed{3}$$

Substitute equation $\boxed{3}$ into equation $\boxed{2}$

$$p + \$4 = \$23$$

Subtract $4 from both sides of the above equation

$$p = \$19$$

2. Choice E is correct. **(Use Strategy: Translate from words to algebra.)**

Each tile is a square with perimeter = 2 feet
Each side of the tile is $\frac{1}{4}$ (2 feet) = $\frac{1}{2}$ foot
$$\boxed{1}$$

The area of each tile is $(Side)^2$.
Using $\boxed{1}$, we get area of each tile

$$= \left(\frac{1}{2}\right)^2 = \frac{1}{4} \text{ square foot} \qquad \boxed{2}$$

The area of the floor is $b \times h =$
8 feet $\times$ 6 feet =
48 square feet $\qquad \boxed{3}$

(Use Strategy: Use the given information effectively.)

The number of tiles necessary, at minimum, to cover the floor

$$= \frac{\text{Area of floor}}{\text{Area of 1 tile}} \qquad \boxed{4}$$

Substituting $\boxed{2}$ and $\boxed{3}$ into $\boxed{4}$ we get:

The number of tiles necessary, at minimum, to cover the floor

$$= \frac{48}{\frac{1}{4}} = \$48 \times \frac{4}{1}$$

The number of tiles necessary, at minimum, to cover the floor

$$= 192$$

3. Choice E is correct.
The only restriction is that 9 and 12 must each divide Q without a remainder. $\qquad \boxed{1}$

(Use Strategy: Use numerics to help find the answer.)

Choose specific values for Q that satisfy $\boxed{1}$.

EXAMPLE 1

$$Q = 36$$

Then, Q will divide 36 and 72.

EXAMPLE 2

$$Q = 108$$

Then, Q will divide neither 36 nor 72. Clearly, the answer to this question depends on the specific value of Q.

4. Choice B is correct. Since $DC \perp AC$, $\angle DCB$ is a right angle and has a measure of 90°. **(Use Strategy: The whole equals the sum of its parts.)** Since the sum of the angles of a $\triangle$ is 180°, we have

$$\angle DBC + 90 + 20 = 180$$
$$\angle DBC = 70 \qquad \boxed{1}$$

Since $EB \perp BD$, $\angle DBE$ is a right angle and has a measure of 90° $\qquad \boxed{2}$

(Use Strategy: The whole equals the sum of its parts.) The whole straight $\angle ABC$ is = to the sum of its parts. Thus

$$\angle DBC + \angle DBE + x = 180 \qquad \boxed{3}$$

Substituting $\boxed{1}$ and $\boxed{2}$ into $\boxed{3}$ we have

$$70 + 90 + x = 180$$
$$x = 20$$

5. Choice E is correct. (Use Strategy: Use the given information effectively.)

Given: x $\qquad \boxed{1}$

$11 - x$ $\qquad \boxed{2}$

$x - 4$ $\qquad \boxed{3}$

as the lengths of the three sides of a triangle.

We know that the sum of any two sides of a triangle is greater than the third $\qquad \boxed{4}$

First, we use $\boxed{1} + \boxed{2} > \boxed{3}$. We have

$$x + 11 - x > x - 4$$
$$11 > x - 4$$
$$15 > x \qquad \boxed{5}$$

Next, we use $\boxed{2} + \boxed{3} > \boxed{1}$. We have

$$11 - x + x - 4 > x$$
$$7 > x \qquad \boxed{6}$$

To satisfy $\boxed{6}$ and $\boxed{5}$, we choose $\boxed{6}$.

$$7 > x, \text{ or } x < 7 \text{ satisfies both} \qquad \boxed{7}$$

Finally, we use $\boxed{1} + \boxed{3} > \boxed{2}$. We have

$$x + x - 4 > 11 - x$$
$$2x - 4 > 11 - x$$
$$3x > 15$$
$$x > 5, \text{ or, } 5 < x \qquad \boxed{8}$$

(Use Strategy: Know how to manipulate inequalities.) Combining $\boxed{7}$ and $\boxed{8}$, we get

$$5 < x < 7$$

6. Choice B is correct.

Given: a, b are integers

Average of a, b and 4 is 6

$$\left(\text{Use Strategy:}\right.$$
$$\left. \text{Average} = \frac{\text{Sum of values}}{\text{Total number of values}}\right)$$

Using $\boxed{2}$, we have

$$\frac{a + b + 4}{3} = 6 \qquad \boxed{3}$$

(Use Strategy: Find unknowns by multiplication.)

Multiply $\boxed{3}$ by 3. We get

$$3\left(\frac{a + b + 4}{3}\right) = (6)3$$
$$a + b + 4 = 18$$
$$a + b = 14 \qquad \boxed{4}$$

Using $\boxed{1}$ and $\boxed{4}$, the possibilities are:

$a + b$	ab	
$1 + 13$	13	Choice A
$2 + 12$	24	
$3 + 11$	33	
$4 + 10$	40	Choice C
$5 + 9$	45	
$6 + 8$	48	Choice D
$7 + 7$	49	Choice E

Checking all the choices, we find that only Choice B, 14, is not a possible value of ab.

7. Choice D is correct. (Use Strategy: Use the given information effectively.)

$$\frac{1}{n^2}\left(\frac{m^5 n^3}{m^3}\right)^2 = \frac{1}{n^2} = (m^2 n^3)^2 = \frac{m^4 n^6}{n^2} = m^4 n^4$$

8. Choice A is correct. The total number of ways is $2 \times 2 \times 2 = 8$. The favorable number of ways is represented as MMF, MFM, and FMM, which is a total of 3. Thus, the probability is $\frac{3}{8}$

9. Choice E is correct. (Use Strategy: Use new definitions carefully.)
Since $W, X, Y,$ and Z are distinct digits from 0 to 9, the largest possible sum of $W + X + Y = 7 + 8 + 9 = 24$. $\qquad \boxed{1}$

By definition, $W + X + Y = 5Z$ $\qquad \boxed{2}$
Substituting $\boxed{1}$ into $\boxed{2}$, we get

$$\text{largest value of } 5Z = 24$$

(Use Strategy: When all choices must be tested, start with Choice E and work backward.)
Look at the choices, starting with Choice E.
If $Z = 5$, then $5Z = 25$, which is larger than 24. Thus, Choice E is correct.

10. Choice C is correct. (Use Strategy: The whole equals the sum of its parts.) From the diagram, we see that each straight angle is equal to the sum of two smaller angles. Thus,

$$m = 180 - x \qquad \boxed{1}$$
$$n = 180 - z \qquad \boxed{2}$$

(Use Strategy: Find unknown expressions by addition of equations.) Adding $\boxed{1}$ and $\boxed{2}$ we have

$$m + n = 180 + 180 - x - z \qquad \boxed{3}$$

We know that the sum of the angles of a triangle = 180

Therefore, $y + x + z = 180$

or $y = 180 - x - z \qquad \boxed{4}$

Substituting $\boxed{4}$ into $\boxed{3}$, we have

$$m + n = 180 + y$$

Accordingly, Choice C is the correct choice.

11. Choice C is correct. **(Use Strategy: Translate from words to algebra.)**
We know that the volume of a cube = e^3
We are told that $e^3 < 25$

(Use Strategy: Use the given information effectively.)

Since e is a positive integer (which was given),

$$e \text{ can be: } 1 \to 1^3 = 1$$
$$2 \to 2^3 = 8$$
$$3 \to 3^3 = 27$$
$$\text{etc.}$$

For $e = 2$, the volume is 8, which is < 25
Any larger e, will have a volume > 25
Thus, area of one face = $e^2 = 2^2 = 4$
Total area = 6(4) = 24

12. Choice E is correct. **(Use Strategy: Translate from words to algebra.)**
Let s = number of smokers
n = number of nonsmokers
Then $s + n$ = Total number of passengers.

We are given: $\dfrac{s}{n} = \dfrac{2}{3}$ or $s = \dfrac{2}{3}n \qquad \boxed{1}$

and: $s = \dfrac{1}{3}(s + n) + 5 \qquad \boxed{2}$

Substituting $\boxed{1}$ into $\boxed{2}$, we have

$$\frac{2}{3}n = \frac{1}{3}\left(\frac{2}{3}n + n\right) + 5$$

$$\frac{2}{3}n = \frac{1}{3}\left(\frac{2}{3}n + \frac{3}{3}n\right) + 5$$

$$\frac{2}{3}n = \frac{1}{3}\left(\frac{5}{3}n\right) + 5$$

$$\frac{2}{3}n = \frac{5}{9}n + 5 \qquad \boxed{3}$$

Multiplying both sides of $\boxed{3}$ by 9, we get

$$9\left(\frac{2}{3}n\right) = 9\left(\frac{5}{9}n + 5\right)$$

$$\frac{18}{3}n = 5n + 45$$

$$6n = 5n + 45$$

$$n = 45$$

$$s = \frac{2}{3}(45) = 30$$

$$s + n = 75$$

```
A   B   C   D   E   F   G
|_a_|_a_|_a_|_a_|_a_|_a_|
```

13. Choice C is correct.

Given:
AG is divided into 6 equal segments $\qquad \boxed{1}$

Radius of circle, centered at $F = \dfrac{1}{5}AG \qquad \boxed{2}$

(Use Strategy: Label unknown quantities.)

Label segments with "a" as shown in above diagram.

Using $\boxed{2}$, radius of circle centered at $F = \dfrac{1}{5}(AG)$

$$= \frac{1}{5}(6a)$$

$$= 1\frac{1}{5}a$$

This means from the center at F, the left tip of the radius of the circle is $1\dfrac{1}{5}a$ from point F. Thus the circumference hits the line between D and E.

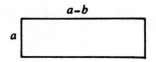

14. Choice B is correct. **(Use Strategy: Translate from words to algebra.)**

Perimeter of a rectangle
$$= 2(\text{length}) + 2(\text{width}) \; \boxed{1}$$

Substituting from the diagram into $\boxed{1}$, we have

$$\text{Perimeter} = 2(a - b) + 2(a)$$
$$= 2a - 2b + 2a$$
$$\text{Perimeter} = 4a - 2b$$

15. Choice E is correct.

$$\begin{array}{r} AB \\ +\ \ BA \\ \hline CDC \end{array}$$

Given: A, B, C, and D are different digits. $\boxed{1}$

The largest possible AB is 98. Thus,

$$\begin{array}{r} 98 \\ +\ \ 89 \\ \hline 187 \end{array}$$

Thus, the only possible value for C is 1 $\boxed{2}$

(It cannot be greater than 1 since we used the largest value of AB.)

Using $\boxed{2}$, the problem becomes

$$\begin{array}{r} AB \\ BA \\ \hline 1D1 \end{array} \qquad \boxed{3}$$

We know that the sum of $B + A$ must end in a 1. $\boxed{4}$
Using $\boxed{4}$ and $\boxed{1}$ we know $B + A = 11$
$\boxed{5}$

16. Choice A is correct. $g(-1) = 1$,
$f[g(-1)] = f(1) = 1^2 + 1 = 2$.

Section 9: Critical Reading

As you read these Explanatory Answers, refer to Sentence Completion Strategies (p. 21) or Reading Comprehension Strategies (p. 27) whenever a specific Strategy is referred to in the answer.

1. Choice C is correct. See **Sentence Completion Strategy.** Examine the first word of each choice. Choice (E) a futile does *not* make good sense because we do not refer to momentum as futile. Now consider the other choices. Choice (C) an increasing . . athletics is the only choice which has a word pair that makes sentence sense.

2. Choice E is correct. See **Sentence Completion Strategy.** The word "effective" (meaning "serving the purpose" or "producing a result") makes good sense in the sentence. The other choices don't do that.

3. Choice D is correct. See **Sentence Completion Strategy.** The word "despite" is an opposition indicator. A strange and inevitable or *ineluctable* fate seemed to keep him helpless and unhappy, despite occasional interludes of *serenity*.

4. Choice B is correct. See **Sentence Completion Strategy.** Try each choice, being aware that "result" is, of course, a result indicator: Samuel Clemens chose the pen name Mark Twain.

5. Choice A is correct. See **Sentence Completion Strategy.** The word "versatile" means capable of turning competently from one task or occupation to another. Clearly, Choice (A) versatile is the only correct choice.

6. Choice B is correct. See **Sentence Completion Strategy.** Examine the first words of each choice. We eliminate Choice (C) avoided and Choice (D) realized because it does not make sense to say that Leonardo realized or avoided the law of gravity. Now we consider Choice (A) examined . . colorful and Choice (E) suspected . . mural, neither of which makes sentence sense. Choice (B) anticipated . . anatomical is the only choice that makes sentence sense.

7. Choice E is correct. The author is stressing the point that the true artist—the person with rare creative ability and keen perception, or high intelligence—fails to communicate well with those about him—"differs from the rest of us" (line 4). He is likely to be considered a "nut" by many whom he comes in contact with. "Great wits" in the Choice E quotation refers to the true artist. The quotation states, in effect, that there is a thin line between the true artist and the "nut." Choices A, B, C, and D are incorrect because they have little, if anything, to do with the main idea of the passage.

[Note: Choices C and E were composed by John Dryden (1631–1700), and Choices A, B, and D by Alexander Pope (1688–1744).]

8. Choice C is correct. See lines 8–10. The artist creates because he is "less fitted to prosper and enjoy himself under the conditions of life which he and we must face alike." Choices A and E are incorrect. Although they may be true, they are never mentioned in the passage. Choice B is incorrect because, although the artist may be a threat to the social order, he is by no means an unnecessary one. The author, throughout the passage, is siding with the artist against the social order. Choice D is incorrect. See lines 10–11: "Therefore he takes . . . attempt to escape from life." A person who is attempting to escape from life hardly knows how to enjoy life.

9. Choice B is correct. The author ridicules Samuel Johnson, saying that he is as much a true artist as a kazoo player is a musician. He then says that if Johnson were alive today, he would be a senator or a university president. The author thus implies that these positions do not merit high respect. Choice A is the opposite of Choice B. Therefore, Choice A is incorrect. Choice C is incorrect because, although the statement may be true, the author neither states

nor implies that senators and university presidents are generally appreciative of the great literary classics. Choice D is incorrect. The fact that the author lumps Johnson, senators, and university presidents together as non-artistic people indicates that senators and university presidents do not have native writing ability. Choice E is incorrect for this reason: The author believes that Johnson lacked the qualities of an artist. Johnson, if alive today, would be a senator or a university president. We may conclude, then, that senators and university presidents lack the qualities of an artist.

10. Choice C is correct. Although a love of beauty is a quality we usually associate with artists, that idea about artists is never mentioned in the passage. All of the other characteristics are expressly mentioned in the first two paragraphs of the passage.

11. Choice B is correct. The author's sincere sympathy is shown toward artists in lines 17–24: "From Dante to Tolstoy . . . actually fugitives from range and reprisal." There is no evidence in the passage to indicate that the author's attitude toward artists is Choice A, C, D, or E. Therefore, these choices are incorrect.

12. Choice C is correct. See the sentence in the second paragraph of Passage 2: "He and only he knows the world."

13. Choice B is correct. See the first paragraph in Passage 2.

14. Choice C is correct. From the context in Passage 2, we see that "world's eye" and "world's heart" refer to culture and wisdom, respectively. See lines 56–60, ". . . public and illustrious thoughts . . . resist the vulgar prosperity . . . by preserving and communicating. . . . noble biographies . . . melodious verse . . ." This is all about *culture* and *wisdom*.

15. Choice E is correct. See the first sentence in Passage 2: ". . . the self-accusation, the faint heart, the frequent uncertainty and loss of time, which are the nettles and tangling vines. . . ." Here "nettles and tangling vines" refers to "self-accusation" and "uncertainty." Nettles are plants covered with stinging hairs. Tangling vines give the impression of weaving all around in no particular or certain direction. So nettles can be thought of as "self-accusation"—something "stinging." And "tangling vines" can be thought of as "uncertainty."

16. Choice C is correct. See Passage 2: The most appropriate groups are the hardships of the scholar, the scholar's functions, and the scholar's justifications for disregarding the world's business, as can be seen from the structure and content of the passage.

17. Choice C is correct. Given the context of the rest of the sentence, the author uses the phrase "seems to stand" as "giving the false impression of being."

18. Choice A is correct. See lines 91–98 and 54–56 in Passage 2 and lines 13–17 and 25–34 in Passage 1.

19. Choice E is correct. The statements in I can be seen to be associated with the artist in Passage 2 from lines 85–86 and 57–58 respectively. The statements in II can be seen to be associated with the artist in Passage 1 from lines 27–33 and 5, respectively. The statements in III can be seen to be associated with the artist in Passage 2 from lines 53–54 and 45–52 respectively.

Section 10: Writing

1. **(E)** Choice A contains a "false series," meaning that the word "and" connects the three words in the series—bread, butter, cheese—with a wholly different clause, instead of with a similar fourth word. The series, therefore, needs its own "and" to complete it. Only Choice E furnishes this additional "and."

2. **(D)** Choice A violates the principle of parallel structure. If the first thing the children liked was "swimming" (a gerund), then the second thing they liked should be, not "to watch" (an infinitive), but "watching" (the gerund). Choice B does not improve the sentence. Choice C repeats the beginning of the sentence with the repetitious words "that they liked." Choice D is correct. Choice E simply reverses the gerund and the infinitive without correcting the error.

3. **(D)** Choice A is incorrect because the pronoun must be singular ("he"—not "they") since the antecedent ("individual") is singular. Choice C is incorrect for the same reason. Moreover, this choice is roundabout. Choice B is incorrect because it is roundabout. Choice D is correct for the reason that Choice A is incorrect. Choice C is incorrect because its subject is "you" (understood). A third person subject is required to coincide with the third person of the antecedent "individual."

4. **(E)** Choices A, B, C, and D are incorrect because these choices do not make it clear whether the dog or the food ought to be put through the meat grinder. Moreover, "it's" in Choice B is wrong. Choice 5 is correct because it makes clear that the food—not the dog—is to be put through the meat grinder.

5. **(B)** Choices A, C, and D are incorrect because the word "money" is incorrectly the antecedent in these three choices. Choice B is correct because "a decision" correctly refers to the whole idea— "The bank agreed to lend Garcia the money." Choice E is incorrect because it does not retain the complete meaning of the original sentence.

6. **(C)** Choices A and D are incorrect because the expression "that in" is required to complete the comparison. Choice C is correct because it includes the required expression "that in." Choice B is incorrect because "then" is incorrect here for "than." Choice E is incorrect because it changes the meaning of the original sentence.

7. **(D)** Choices A, C, and E are incorrect because they do not fulfill the requirement of contributing to the composition of a complete sentence. Choice D is correct because it does complete that requirement. Choice B is incorrect because it is awkward.

8. **(E)** Choices A, B, and D are incorrect because they lack balance of grammatical structure. Choice C is incorrect because the "and-and" construction is frowned upon by grammarians. Choice E is correct because the grammatical structure is balanced. This choice consists of three well-formed prepositional phrases.

9. **(A)** Choice A is correct. The words which make up the choice act as the subject of the sentence. Choice B is incorrect because it is awkward. Choice C is incorrect because one should never begin a sentence with "Being that." Choice D is incorrect as it stands. If "Charles" were changed to the possessive "Charles'" or "Charles's" the choice would be correct. Choice E is incorrect because it, in itself, is a complete sentence which, as it stands, cannot act as the grammatical subject of the verb "disappointed."

10. **(C)** Choice A is incorrect because the pronoun *which* has an indefinite antecedent. Choices B and E are incorrect because they are too wordy. Choice C is correct. Choice D is incorrect because *damaging* is an inappropriate word choice.

11. **(E)** In this sentence we are looking for correct parallel structure in the last of a series of nouns. Choices A, B, C, and D are incorrect because they destroy the noun balance. Choice E is correct.

12. **(A)** Choice A is correct. Choices B and D are incorrect because the word *most* is unnecessary and incorrect here. Choice C is incorrect because it is wordy. Choice E is incorrect because *premium* is not the correct word for the meaning intended.

13. **(A)** Choice A is correct. Choice B is incorrect because the phrase *for facial lacerations* is mis-

placed. Choices C and D are incorrect because they are wordy. Choice C also contains the pronoun *it* which has an indefinite antecedent. Choice E is incorrect because of the awkward use of *facial lacerations* as an adjective modifying treatment.

14. **(C)** In this sentence we must have an adjective to balance with *tough* and *single-minded*. Choices A, B, D, and E are incorrect because they do not maintain the required parallel structure. Choice C is correct.

What You Must Do Now to Raise Your SAT Score

1) a) Follow the directions on pages 265–267 to determine your scaled score for the SAT Test you've just taken. These results will give you a good idea about whether or not you ought to study hard in order to achieve a certain score on the actual SAT.

   b) Using your test correct answer count as a basis, indicate for yourself your areas of strength and weakness as revealed by the "Self-Appraisal Chart" on page 268.

2) Eliminate your weaknesses in each of the SAT test areas (as revealed in the "Self-Appraisal Chart") by taking the following Giant Steps toward SAT success:

Critical Reading Part

Giant Step 1

Take advantage of the Critical Reading Strategies that begin on page 7. Read again the Explanatory Answer for each of the Critical Reading questions that you got wrong. Refer to the Critical Reading Strategy that applies to each of your incorrect answers. Learn each of these Critical Reading Strategies thoroughly. These strategies are crucial if you want to raise your SAT Verbal score substantially.

Giant Step 2

You can improve your vocabulary by doing the following:

1) Learn all three Vocabulary Strategies begining on p. 7.

2) Read as widely as possible—not only novels. Non-fiction is important too . . . and don't forget to read newspapers and magazines.

3) Listen to people who speak well. Tune in to worthwhile TV programs also.

4) Use the dictionary frequently and extensively—at home, on the bus, at work, etc.

5) Play word games—for example, crossword puzzles, anagrams, and Scrabble. Another game is to compose your own Sentence Completion questions. Try them on your friends.

Math Part

Giant Step 3

Make good use of the Regular Math Strategies that begin on page 77. Read again the solutions for each Math question that you answered incorrectly. Refer to the Math Strategy that applies to each of your incorrect answers. Learn each of these Math Strategies thoroughly. These strategies are crucial if you want to raise your SAT Math score substantially.

Giant Step 4

You may want to take the test in the Test Yourself section on page 60, and make sure you understand the answers in the Correct Yourself section. Also make sure you know everything in Arm Yourself on page 72.

Writing Part

Giant Step 5

Take a look at the SAT Writing test which describes the various item types in the Writing Section and sample questions with answers and explanations.

Giant Step 6

For the math, critical reading, and writing parts, make sure you know the General Strategies (page 1).

If you do the job *right* and follow the steps listed above, you are likely to raise your SAT score on each of the Verbal, Math, and Writing parts of the test 150 points—maybe 200 points—and even more—toward the 2400 SAT score. Maybe you'll even get a 2400!

> I am the master of my fate;
> I am the captain of my soul.
>
> —From the poem "Invictus"
> by William Ernest Henley